GW00702717

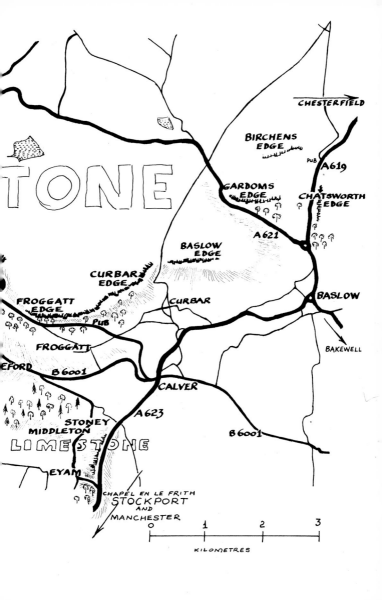

PEAK ROCK CLIMBS – FIFTH SERIES

Volume 3

Eastern Gritstone

Froggatt

Series Editor: Geoff Milburn

Volume Compiler & Sub-Editor: Keith Sharples

Guidebook Team	**Guidebook Committee**	
Steve Bancroft	Malc Baxter	
Jon Barton	Carl Dawson	(Secretary)
Malc Baxter	Dave Farrant	(Computing Co-ordinator)
Bill Gregory	Neil Foster	
Dave Gregory	Dave Gregory	(Chairman)
Graham Hoey	Brian Griffiths	(Treasurer)
Hilary Lawrenson	Chris Hardy	
Jon Lawton	Graham Hoey	(Business Manager)
Keith Sharples	Hilary Lawrenson	
William Taylor	Geoff Milburn	
	Geoff Radcliffe	
	Keith Sharples	(Artwork Co-ordinator)
	Malc Taylor	
	Bill Wright	(B.M.C. Officer)
	Chris Wright	

Produced on a voluntary basis by the BMC
Guidebook Committee for the British
Mountaineering Council.

1923 Recent Developments on Gritstone. Edited by Fergus Graham.

1951 Climbs on Gritstone. Vol. 2. Sheffield Area. Edited by Eric Byne.

1956 Climbs on Gritstone. Vol. 2 Revised Edition. Sheffield Area. Edited by Eric Byne.

1957 Climbs on Gritstone. Vol. 4. Edited by Eric Byne and Wilfred White.

1965 The Sheffield-Froggatt Area (Rock Climbs in the Peak. Vol. 3). Edited by Eric Byne.

1978 The Froggatt Area (Rock Climbs in the Peak. Vol. 3). Edited by Dave Gregory.

1983 Stanage Millstone (Peak District Climbs. Fourth Series). Edited by Geoff Milburn

First Edition: 1991
Second Edition: 1999   Reprint: 2002

IBSN 0 903908 86 7

Prepared by the BMC Guidebook Committee in 8/9 Rockwell (rock on) using Ventura Publisher.

Output by Saxon Ltd., Heritage Gate, Derby, DE1 1DD.

Produced by Hi-Tec Print, North Anston Trading Estate, Dinnington, South Yorkshire.

Distributed by Cordee, 3a De Montfort Street, Leicester, LE1 7HD.

BMC Peak District Guidebooks are produced on a wholly voluntary basis and any surpluses raised are re-invested for future productions. In addition a 5% levy is included in the price which is contributed to the BMC's Access and Conservation Fund. This is used to campaign for access to and conservation of crags and mountains throughout Britain and is a vital contribution to climbing.

CONTENTS

CONTENTS

4

PHOTOGRAPHS

Front Cover: Mike Lea on Elder Crack, Curbar Edge.
Photo: Chris Wright.

First Colour Photo: Johnny Dawes on the first ascent of Offspring,
Burbage South.
Photo: Neil Foster.

Frontispiece: Pete O'Donovan on Boulevard, Lawrencefield.
Photo: Ian Smith.

Inside Rear Cover: Dave Hoyle on Route 1, Baslow Edge.
Photo: Andrew Milne.

Rear Cover: Johnny Dawes during the first ascent of White Lines,
Curbar Edge.
Photo: Ian Smith.

COLOUR PHOTOGRAPHS

PHOTOGRAPHS

BLACK AND WHITE PHOTOGRAPHS

INTRODUCTION

*'It was Wilf White who introduced us to Froggatt Edge near
Sheffield. He went into raptures about fantastic walls and
slabs of rough gritstone. "All blank they are, and nobody
has touched them." We were disinclined to believe him but
it was true. There were only a few routes on the crag; we
worked along the edge making dozens of new routes. Some
of them were extremely hard, such as Brown's Eliminate.
The rock was friable and I top-roped the face three times
before leading it. The holds were microscopic and the climb
was only possible in nails, which could be hooked perfectly
on to tapering flakes that were uniformly about one-eighth
of an inch wide. These flakes broke off in time, leaving a
larger gripping edge and the route has gradually become
easier.'*

Joe Brown in 'The Hard Years', 1967.

Tradition has it that the Eagle Stone on the moor near Baslow
Edge was used to test the young men, from local villages, who
were contemplating marriage. (Those who were successful were
undoubtedly let off the hook while those who failed to surmount
the rock were forced into marriage.) It is not on record however
whether or not those who proved to have an aptitude for
climbing on gritstone ever pursued the sport for the sheer
enjoyment of soloing at will.

If one discounts the above rather dubious example of local rock-
climbing the remaining history of the Eastern Edges south of
Stanage is relatively recent. For a long time several of the crags
such as Burbage were merely overlooked while others such as
Millstone Edge at first sight were deemed to be too difficult. As
far as the Froggatt-Curbar escarpment was concerned it was a
case of strict gamekeeping which kept many climbers at bay.
In addition some of the quarries were still being worked to
provide stone for local use. Tegness North Quarry, for example,
yielded kerbstones for the city of Sheffield.

In the latter years of the nineteenth century J.W. Puttrell began to
explore the Peak District from his Sheffield base. In 1890, after
ascending *Solomon's Crack*, the first route on Froggatt Edge, he
topped the pinnacles of both Froggatt Edge and Tegness
Quarry. Puttrell continued to work his way along the Eastern

Edges finding routes such as *Gun Chimney* and *Capstone Chimney* on Baslow Edge, but none of these routes appeared in John Laycock's first gritstone guidebook of 1913.

After the First World War the *'only Peakland climber comparable to Kelly was Henry Bishop who was still baiting the gamekeepers on Stanage and Froggatt'*, yet in the 1924 Recent Developments on Gritstone there was only one passing reference to Bishop having pioneered many routes on Froggatt Edge. Perhaps after George Bower inspected Millstone's sweeping blank walls in the 1920s he directed people's attention to more amenable places such as Stanage.

For those wishing to prospect for new routes in the 1930s there were several obstacles to be negotiated. The many notice-boards proclaiming 'Keep Out' and 'Private Land' led first to barbed-wire entanglements, then to the enemy – teams of gamekeepers who were heavily armed not only with cudgels but also guns. Although a few climbers got through the defences to sneak the odd route, prudence usually dictated that climbing activities were concentrated on the less-well defended edges. On Burbage Edge, for example, a very strong team soon emerged in the shape of Harry Dover and Gilbert Ellis. Of their routes *Dover's Progress* and *The Knight's Move* were both hard leads for their day but the *Dover and Ellis Chimney* in 1932 was to be one of the hardest routes on gritstone for some years. Although not appreciated at the time it was one of the first Extremes to be done on gritstone.

Soon the Sheffield Climbing Club descended on Burbage in force and by 1934 over sixty routes had been climbed which Eric Byne recorded in The Mountaineering Journal. Byne, accompanied by Clifford Moyer, was to discover Yarncliffe Edge where they did several minor routes. However, it was during the Second World War that Byne realised the potential of Froggatt Edge and subsequently he directed other Sheffield climbers to the wealth of virgin rock. It was the Polaris Mountaineering Club members however who, in 1948, recorded *P.M.C. 1* – the first climb on Curbar Edge. This was a line on which Puttrell had failed many years previously. Things were about to change as a generation of tough post-War climbers began to emerge from the big cities:

'During the early months of 1948 the Valkyrie climbers visited Froggatt and Curbar, where they met Thomsett and

*Chapman of the Polaris. The latter showed them their own
route and those of the Sheffield University climbers Davies
and R.A. Brown. From that time on these two crags became
the Valkyrie's particular hunting ground.'*

One teenager in particular showed a natural talent and it wasn't
long before Joe Brown was notching up a long list of new climbs
on Froggatt, such as *Tody's Wall*, *Three Pebble Slab* and *Valkyrie*.
It was clear that he had the ability to go beyond existing
climbing standards and, after peeling off carpets of grass,
Brown's Eliminate (E2 5b) was a clear step forward. This was
surpassed by even harder routes in the early 1950s. Several of
Brown's early routes were graded Extremely Severe and later
two of his new routes, *The Great Slab* on Froggatt and Curbar's
Right Eliminate were given a grade of E3. Both were led on sight.

Brown's companion on many routes, Don Whillans, was a
veritable powerhouse although he did not match Brown's new
route output in the Froggatt area. *Dead Bay Crack* on Curbar was
however a typical Whillans creation.

Lawrencefield was first opened up in 1952 by Reg Pillinger and
Bert Shutt, but that year one disturbing trend was heralded by
Piton Route on Froggatt which yielded to Nat Allen with the aid of
four pegs. *'It has nothing to commend it except possibly the
perverse pleasure of swinging on loose pitons.'* It was another four
years however before the full piton arsenal was unleashed
against Millstone Edge. Three teams spearheaded the attack:
Sheffield University Mountaineering Club members, George
Leaver and Kit Twyford, hammered their way up *Petticoat Lane*
and *Lyons Corner House* while Dave Johnson pegged *The Great
West Road*, *Twikker* and *Pinstone Street*. The third team of Peter
Biven and Trevor Peck was even more persistent and in addition
to pegging *Great North Road*, *Regent Street*, *Coventry Street* and
Oxford Street spent over four hours with extra-thin pegs to start
opening up the hairline crack of *London Wall*.

The 1957 guidebook 'Further Developments in the Peak District'
both inspired and intimidated an emerging generation of
enthusiastic climbers. In retrospect it was something of a
contradiction in that it not only highlighted the hardest new free
routes but also glorified the 'bang and dangle' artificial climbs.
When opinion had hitherto been firmly against pitons, the
reasons for such a reversal of attitude need to be understood to

11

avoid drawing the wrong conclusions. Eric Byne made things quite clear when introducing the 1957 guidebook:

'This is the first Gritstone Guide to a piton climbing ground. It thus marks a new phase in Peakland climbing. Previously artificial aids have been frowned upon when used on the older traditional Gritstone Edges, but Millstone has no tradition, its magnificent walls are not for the free-climbing purist, and so it has awaited the generation whose ambitions are to tackle the big artificial continental routes.'

Despite the fact that some climbers felt the call of the great alpine faces, the ethos of the 'free-climbing purist' was still firmly backed up by the attacks on 'the impossibles' by the climbing machine Joe Brown and Don Whillans. Loy and Clarke summed up the situation in 1965:

'However, by late 1957 it was realised that many of the peg routes could have been led free and possibilities of great routes existed for the climbers who might be prepared to look at the crag as other than a "whack and dangle" playground.'

It was thus largely the exploits of Brown and Whillans which thankfully prevented the spread of pegs to the gritstone edges. Although a few routes were done with pegs by lesser climbers, the Valkyrie climbers usually demonstrated that they could equally well be done without. It is of interest to note that in the year of the siege of Millstone, Brown and Whillans completed *The Rasp* on Higgar Tor with only one rest from a sling. The Rasp description read:

'Extremely Severe. One of the hardest climbs on Gritstone. So called from the damage to the hands from the rough pebbles in the cracks......the route overhangs 14 feet in its own length.'

Eric Byne had, on the whole, a very acute awareness of what was going on in the climbing world which was far more insular in those early days. It is quite interesting to note his comments on the hardest new routes of the day:

'Perhaps Gritstone climbing has now reached its peak in the standard of difficulty that has been attained – a standard that fifteen years ago would have seemed fantastic.'

The Leaning Block

Don Whillans was to disprove this statement in 1958 when he produced two outstanding routes: *Cave Wall* (E3 5c) on Froggatt off which he amazingly jumped from the lip of the overhang; and the outrageously fierce Burbage crack of *Goliath* (E5 6a) which was merely given the bland grade of Extremely Severe at the time (about as useful to others as traditional Scottish VS!). One other route from the late-Fifties was to intimidate leaders for some years – the 'appallingly delicate' *Millwheel Wall* on Burbage by Len Millsom.

The Sixties was a time of consolidation when other climbers began to tackle some of the harder routes and much time was spent in producing primitive protection devices from drilled-out nuts and stray bits of plumbing equipment. With adequate protection from home-made nuts, some of the old aid routes were freed during this period and certainly Regent Street, by Terry King, was well ahead of its time. Undoubtedly the big route of this era was Tom Proctor's *Green Death* (E5 6b) at Millstone. The crowds frequently rolled up to stare at it in disbelief but few were prepared to follow in Proctor's footsteps. (Proctor originally used boulders to overcome the start.)

During the mid-1970s there was a period of intense activity unparalleled so far in the history of Peak District climbing. Not only the gritstone but the limestone too saw a race to fill the gaps between existing lines, as well as to free as many of the aid routes as possible. At Lawrencefield it was a time which saw Jim Reading freeing *High Street* (E4 6a) and Geoff Birtles on *Billy Whiz* (E2 5c), while slightly later at Yarncliffe Quarry Ron Fawcett tamed the arete of *Crème de la Crème* (E5 6b). Most of the credit however, either together or singly, must go to John Allen and Steve Bancroft who were one of the strongest teams ever to set foot on British rock. Early in 1974 they followed Alan McHardy up a bold Millstone arete which had been screaming out for attention for some time, *Edge Lane* (E5 5c). The hunt was then on!

On the Burbage Edges alone, Allen climbed *The Knock* (E5 6a), *Above and Beyond...* (E4 6b) and *Pebble Mill* (E5 6b) as well as sharing *Silent Spring* (E4 5c,5c) with Bancroft. One could also point to *Hairless Heart* (E5 5c) or *Strapadictomy* (E5 6a) on Froggatt or even Curbar's *Moon Crack* (E5 6b) – which Gabe Regan was later to solo. Nearly all of Allen's hard routes were hallmarked with the stamp of quality and two of his very best were the stunning *London Wall* (E5 6a) on Millstone and Curbar's own *Profit of Doom* (E4 6b) which was pronounced as a great advance at the time.

Although John Allen gets much of the glory, his partner Steve Bancroft had a major role to play in his own right with routes such as *White Wall* free (E5 6b) at Millstone and his audacious solo of *Narcissus* (E6 6b) on the Froggatt Pinnacle – an achievement which must be a contender for the hardest lead of its era. And then of course there was Mick Fowler's free ascent of *Linden* (E6 6b) on Curbar. Golden years indeed.

Another Froggatt guidebook was published in 1978 to herald the imminent arrival of the 1980s. During the Eighties half of the crags in the guidebook were to amalgamate with those in the Stanage guidebook in 1983, while the rest of the crags went in with the Chatsworth area to become the Derwent Gritstone guidebook which was published in 1985.

Of the mega-routes of the Eighties, one of the best was by Jonny Woodward. He stunned the climbing world by his success on the mind-bending line of *Beau Geste* (E6 6c). Froggatt had been protecting its best remaining routes for many years and the superlatives soon flowed freely. This clearly was a contender for the major new route in the post-Allen/Bancroft era or even THE route of the early 1980s. However it was only 1982 and much more was to come.

The Master's Edge (E7 6b) was one of Millstone's prime targets and it was firmly on the hit list of several top climbers. Ron Fawcett couldn't leave it much longer and finally made his push in less than ideal conditions at Christmas 1983.

The decade had started quietly with few new routes on Burbage South but *Nosferatu* (E6 6b), by Andy Barker, was followed in earnest in 1984 when Johnny Dawes embarked on his *Braille Trail*. The route was protected by two hand-placed pegs, but it was nevertheless an outstanding achievement. Later, after some pebbles snapped off, the route became even harder and currently it is graded E7 6c. Not far away is Jerry Moffatt's *Messiah* (E6 6c), a desperate arete which sees few repeats owing to the bad landing as much as to the hard climbing.

1985 saw the first named 7a pitch on Peak gritstone with Burbage's *West Side Story* by John Allen. It was becoming emminently clear that 'the numbers' were starting to creep up. By 1986 we reached E7 7a with Britain's hardest micro-route,

INTRODUCTION

Mark Leach's *The Screaming Dream* on Froggatt. Supposedly *The End of the Affair* might equally have been when Johnny Dawes stared death in the face on the arete of Moon Buttress but he survived and produced an E8 6c. This route was repeated within the month by Dawes's second – Nick Dixon.

And so by the late-Eighties, forty years after Curbar's first route, we reached the dizzy height of E9 which is the current state of the art. And for E9 you've got to be prepared to die! Andy Pollitt, who has several times gone to the known limit of what is humanly possible, took a deep breath, controversially pre-placed a peg and climbed the rather optimistically named *Knockin' on Heaven's Door* (E9 6c). The only other ascent to date was by Ron Fawcett who down-graded it to E8 6c – but Fawcett also felt it necessary to pre-place the peg.

As part of a television programme the nation gazed in amazement while watching Johnny Dawes dynoing acrobatically up some of the hard routes of the day and there were gasps as he hurtled down through space while attempting to top-rope a desperate new line on Burbage. Life at the top nowadays is very competitive however and despite the fact that Dawes could not envisage himself completing the route in the near future other eager aspirants were waiting in the wings. It was left to John Dunne to claim the *Parthian Shot* (E9 7a).

And finally we have a new Froggatt guidebook. It represents almost as much effort, stress, and heartache as is needed for a whole cluster of E9s. It is sufficient to say that we have come through the storm clouds and the rock is drying fast as the sun climbs high to flood the Eastern Edges and start a new day. The choice is yours. The 1990s are already calling and the rock is waiting...... so who will accept the challenge?

Geoff Milburn, Series Editor, June 1991

NOTE: Grades given in brackets after route names are those which have been assessed for this guidebook. The climbs were not necessarily first ascended at these particular grades. It must be remembered that aid points were sometimes used and the climbs when later freed became much harder. In other cases after frequent traffic the climbs became cleaner and therefore easier – until excessive use wore down the holds and polished them. Holds may have broken off and previously inserted chockstones in cracks – as for example in Right Eliminate – may now be missing.

16

ACKNOWLEDGEMENTS

So much of what has been accomplished in this volume is based on the efforts of our predecessors, and in particular Eric Byne the first Series Editor who laid the foundations for many of the features that are included in this guidebook. Eric was followed first by Paul Nunn, and then Dave Gregory whose contributions to the Peak's guidebooks stretch back to the 1957 Further Developments volume. Dave is still very active today, as is another stalwart Nat Allen who also began contributing in 1957 with Yarncliffe Quarry. After editing nearly all of the Third Series of guidebooks, Dave Gregory was succeeded by Geoff Milburn who is currently presiding over the Fifth Series.

The Guidebook Committee steers each volume through to production and these hard working voluntary activists willingly and tirelessly offer their services. Specific thanks are due to: Geoff Milburn for his error-seeking keen eye; Dave Gregory for being Dave Gregory; Dave Farrant for his computer knowledge for 'he has got inside the PC and is looking out'; Graham Hoey for his ever-questioning approach; and to Carl Dawson for new ideas to keep us on our toes.

The crag writers are credited at the front of the book but Dave Gregory in particular did sterling work with those 'nasty little bits and pieces' while Graham Hoey stepped, or rather was pushed, into the breach for Froggatt. In the autumn of 1989 he was to be seen pacing the distances between routes (and checking descriptions) while conversing with Dave Farrant's dictaphone; "Three hundred dictaphones to the right is......" – Nice one Graham.

Lists of first ascents rely heavily on sources such as: Climber and Rambler, Crags, High, Mountain, Mountain Life, On the Edge, and Rocksport; journals of the Climbers' Club, Midland Association of Mountaineers and Rucksack Club; previous guidebooks and supplements; the somewhat unreliable 'Stoney' new routes books; and lastly the individuals who did respond to requests for information. Andy Barker photographed the Burbage Valley down to Froggatt, but then broke his collar-bone in a biking accident. Steve Yates was drafted in as a replacement until work commitments took him. At the eleventh hour, Geoff Radcliffe and Brian Griffiths completed the work. Our seasoned campaigner, Malc Baxter, then burnt the midnight oil to produce a brilliant set of diagrams. The action photographers provided an excellent portfolio of shots from which to choose.

Various people worked on the draft scripts and proofs. The groundwork for the first ascent lists was done by the Volume Compiler, but he received valuable assistance from Nat Allen, Dave Gregory, Chris Hardy, John Loy and Geoff Milburn in unravelling the vagaries of the past. The following climbers provided details of their own routes: John Allen, Andy Barker, Geoff Birtles, Bob Bradley, Phil Burke, John Codling, Chris Craggs, Johnny Dawes, Graham Desroy, Gary Gibson, Paul Deardon, Al Evans, Mick Fowler, John Hart, Mark Leach, Dominic Lee, Bill McKee, Jerry Moffatt, Pete Oxley, Chris Plant, Mark Pretty, Jim Reading, Nigel Slater and Martin Veale.

The painstaking task of converting a rough script through to camera-ready artwork involves hour upon hour of work. Carolyn Lee and Carolyn Matthews both helped with typing corrections while Chris Craggs, Dave Gregory, Graham Hoey, Rosie Slater and Richard Watkinson helped the Volume Compiler to prepare the diagrams for printing. Dave Farrant, who has more bytes than most, not only worked extensively on corrections but also 'fed' the script through Ventura Publisher as he is our resident computer boffin (his byte's worse than his bark!). Graham Hoey was the go-between with the printer.

As is now usual, we dedicate this guidebook to a climber whose contribution to the area has been outstanding. Over the last few years one climber has consistently produced new routes of the highest calibre and so this volume is dedicated to Johnny Dawes.

Nor can the opportunity be passed without mentioning the people with whom I have shared so many happy days both on and off the crags: Chris Holden, Steve Clegg and Dave Rawcliffe, with whom I began regular climbing in 1974; Mick Anderson with whom I began to realise what might be possible; Pete (Pod) O'Donovan with whom I started serious training in an attempt to achieve what might be possible; Graham Hoey who showed me what was possible on gritstone; Nigel Slater with whom I began to achieve that which I knew was possible and to Chris Wright, Chris Hardy and many other friends with whom I continue to climb. Finally I must thank my wife Liz, and our daughters Kathy and our new arrival Victoria, — without whom nothing would be worthwhile.

Keith Sharples, Volume Compiler, (June 1991)

THE CRAG ENVIRONMENT
and ACCESS

INTRODUCTION

The crags documented within this guidebook are some of the most accessible to large centres of population found in Britain, if not Europe as a whole. Within 20-30 minutes one can escape the congestion and urban stress of Sheffield's city centre to reach these jewels of gritstone edges, surrounded by their crowning heather moors. The great conurbations of Manchester, Stockport, Leeds, Bradford, and Nottingham are all within an hour's 'swift' drive.

As a consequence of their accessibility, and also the exceptional quality of climbing found on them, they are also under some of the most severe pressures found on any crags. As well as climbers they attract naturalists, walkers, picnickers, ornithologists, lovers, school parties and just about anyone else you can think of who is in search of their own idea of nirvana in the outdoors.

Fortunately the crags in this guidebook area all lie within the boundary of the Peak District National Park and the authority has done much to resolve the conflicting pressures on access to and conservation of this area. The increasing erosion found at the top and bottom of many of these crags acts as a testament to their enjoyment by many thousands of people in the past, but serves as a warning for the future for all of us to be increasingly vigilant about these places where we climb.

Because of this concern the BMC and its Guidebook Committee feel it is increasingly important that climbers observe the best possible practice when visiting our climbing grounds. The notes set out below, and the introduction to each crag, outline a few simple steps that you can take in order to protect access to and conservation of these crags, and also briefly explains their natural value and why they should be protected. PLEASE READ, THINK ABOUT and HEED THEM.

THE ROCK

The rock on which we climb in this area, millstone grit, was formed about 300 million years ago and it is the visible result of a bedding process which, to put it very simply, laid down alternate layers of hard (gritstone) and soft strata (shale). Also layers of coal are found where other Carboniferous deposits approach the surface in the adjacent Lancashire and Yorkshire coalfields.

This layering process occurred as a result of erosion of the mountains to the north, probably in Scotland; movement of the materials by river southwards, then their deposition at river mouths or deltas which were later to become the Peak District and Pennines. Vegetation grew on top of these deposits, which when not washed away was buried underneath accumulations of marine shale as the sea level rose then fell again. A new river delta would then spread across the area to start the process all over again.

All the crags in this area were formed from one band of gritstone, the same band as nearby Stanage and Chatsworth. Throughout much of the area the bed dips eastward and, therefore, where it comes to the surface the outcrops face west.

Although all these crags are from the same band of rock, they vary in character depending on the degree of weathering to which they have been subjected.

Where there are natural outcrops, such as Burbage North and parts of Froggatt and Curbar, holds can be rather rounded due to prolonged weathering along bedding places and joints, but they can also have good friction. Where the rock was quarried a long time ago, such as Burbage South, other parts of Froggatt and Curbar, the rock has more squared holds and sharper-edged cracks and smoother walls. Where the rock has been more recently quarried, e.g. Millstone, the walls are smoother still and holds are even sharper but occasionally loose, while weathering may not yet have eroded clay or minerals deposited in cracks which formed the joints in the bedding planes.

THE ECOLOGY

Much of the area surrounding the Froggatt edges is covered by heather moorland fringed by scrub and little of it is unaffected by people. Over the years it has been subjected to: management for the purposes of grouse shooting and sheep rearing; acid rain; timber felling; and the passage of millions of pairs of feet.

Nevertheless there is an abundance of wildlife in the area of these crags and much of the climbing is within Sites of Special Scientific Interest – The Eastern Moors behind Froggatt and Curbar being of particular interest as the habitat of a variety of ground nesting birds. In summer they provide an important habitat for birds such as the Curlew and the much rarer Dunlin and, where the sweep of the moor is broken by rocks or cloughs, the Ring Ouzel. This is a type of mountain blackbird with a white bib and a distinctive piercing call. Hen Harriers overwinter in the area and can sometimes be seen flapping low over the moor, quartering the grassland for prey.

Below the crags, and in nearby valleys such as at Grindleford, mixed woods of Oak, Birch and Rowan support the secretive Hawfinch and rare summer visitors such as the Pied Flycatcher and the Redstart. They provide a rich, relatively undisturbed habitat for much bird, mammal, insect and plant life. In some of them, fenced enclosures to keep out grazing animals have allowed the natural woodland plants to reach their full size. It may be a surprise to see just how big a Bilberry bush can be!

Another well-known denizen of the Lawrencefield birch woods is the Wood Ant. Its large mound-shaped nests and their many, large aggressive occupants are unmistakable. (They are famous for their ability to squirt methanoic (formic) acid from their tail ends, so beware).

On the rocks of the less-frequented edges there are some rare lichen communities. The main crags may sport the occasional hardy bilberry bush or clump of heather, the persistent pigeon or bold stoat amongst the boulders, but a century of climbing has taken its toll.

This area is an important one for wildlife, and bird and animal populations are changing all the time. For example, it was once famous for Nightjars, but they are now very much in decline. Climbers are often fortunate to be about at times when no-one else is (though you may not think so if you visit Froggatt on a busy Sunday). If you see or hear any unusual wildlife please report it to the BMC which will pass on the information to the appropriate organisations.

MANAGEMENT and OWNERSHIP

While climbing is an important use of these edges, other uses such as sheep rearing and grouse shooting, which provide income and jobs and which are still key parts of the local culture and economy, can claim as much right to these areas as climbers. Other recreations including 'abseiling' use these places as well and we, as climbers, should question whether we really have a greater right to these crags.

The costs to landowners in terms of time and money, of damage to fences, livestock and paths can be considerable, due to the heavy use of their land by a variety of interests, and we cannot, as climbers, avoid our responsibilities as users of the countryside if further restriction on our activities is not to be enforced.

Fortunately all of the crags in this area fall within the boundary of the Peak District National Park and Froggatt and Curbar are actually within the National Park Board's ownership. The wardening service of the Board has done much to resolve the conflicts that can arise both on the land the Board itself owns and land that is owned by other authorities or private interests.

The crags other than Froggatt and Curbar have different owners. Millstone and Burbage are owned by Sheffield City Council which has a policy of unrestricted access to these crags. Others are owned by the National Trust which has a varying attitude to access depending on which crag is concerned.

Whoever is the owner of each crag, all climbers have a responsibility to ensure that their actions do not give owners reason to effect restrictions or bans which would apply to all climbers and the climbing world as a whole. The following considerations should be borne in mind.

PARKING

Can be problematic, especially at Burbage South and at the white gate at Froggatt. The important issue at any crag is not to block access for other vehicles or users such as the owner's landrover or the emergency vehicle which is coming to pick you up after you've decked out from those 'oh so near' finishing holds.

DOGS

There is much evidence to suggest that Man's best friend is not the best friend of livestock or wildlife, no matter how cuddly they may be. PLEASE ALWAYS KEEP DOGS UNDER VERY STRICT CONTROL. During the lambing and nesting seasons it is probably best to leave them at home.

EROSION

Erosion is a growing problem on the footpaths running up to and adjacent to crags. Climbers can only do so much to help fight this problem other than volunteer to give a few hours of their time for path restoration work carried out by bodies which control the National Park. They can however, wherever possible, walk on the more hardwearing sections (e.g. where a path has been restored) and use the lightest possible footwear in which it is safe to approach the crags.

DROUGHT

When there have been prolonged periods with less than average rainfall there is, of course, considerably greater possibility of dead surface vegetation, or even the underlying peat, catching fire. WHERE SUCH FIRES OCCUR THEIR EFFECTS ARE DISASTROUS FOR ANYONE – INCLUDING CLIMBERS – WHO IS CONCERNED ABOUT THE POSSIBILITY OF CAUSING SUCH A FIRE.

As a result THE BMC ADVISES ALL CLIMBERS TO BE VERY CAREFUL WITH THE USE OF COMBUSTIBLES, i.e. MATCHES, CIGARETTES AND STOVES, BUT PARTICULARLY DURING PERIODS OF DROUGHT WHEN THEY SHOULD PREFERABLY LEAVE SUCH MATERIALS BEHIND IN THE CAR OR AT HOME.

During high risk periods it is also advisable to be vigilant for any signs of smoke or actions which may cause fire to start and report any such signs immediately.

LITTER

Letters will be gratefully received from anyone who actually likes litter on our crags and moors, along with a letter from their doctor saying that they are of sound mind and judgement. Our crags continue to be bedevilled by this problem. All climbers are urged to CARRY A PLASTIC BAG and to TAKE HOME NOT ONLY THEIR OWN LITTER but also ANY OTHER LITTER THAT THEY FIND.

Litter is not only visually intrusive but it also can affect the ecological balance of an area. Predators which may not previously have been found there can be attracted by apple cores and other foods which might be considered to be biodegradable. The key is to take it all home with you.

Human excrement – no we're not necessarily saying that you should stick it in a plastic bag as well, but please be as discreet as possible should the need to leave it on the moors occur.

CHIPPING, BOLTING and DRILLING

Once a piece of rock has been chipped or drilled it can never be restored to its completely natural state. Chipping in particular leaves an ugly scar on an otherwise well-weathered cliff face. The answer simply is PLEASE DO NOT CHIP, DRILL or BOLT ANY OF THE CRAGS DOCUMENTED IN THIS GUIDEBOOK.

PEGGING

While it is recognised that this practice may, in the past, have left some very fine rock-climbs that are now climbed free (at Millstone and Lawrencefield in particular), climbers are asked to refrain from any further such action as the regular placement and removal of pitons leaves scars at least as intrusive as chipped holds.

The practice of gardening can be even more damaging and nowadays should be no longer necessary. Large flakes which are dislodged can present the ugliest scars of all.

MODERN 'NATURAL' PROTECTION

Please take care when placing nuts or camming devices behind dubious flakes as the consequences can be the same as that of gardening outlined above, as well as, needless to say, resulting in a trip to the casualty ward in The Royal Hallamshire.

CHALK

Please always remember to pull the drawcord on chalkbags to close them between routes.

ACCESS DIFFICULTIES

Even if you have parked considerately, left Bonzo at home, left the crag as you have found it, apart from those bits of litter which you've found and taken away with you, access problems can still arise.

On most of the crags described, there is a general right of access as they are owned by the National Park Board, National Trust, or are subject to an official access agreement negotiated by the National Park Board on behalf of the public. In each of these cases bye-laws normally apply which are common sense rules about the use of the land by the public. These bye-laws and consequent rights of access may, however, be suspended by the National Park Authority during period of drought.

If difficulties are encountered when visiting any of the crags described please telephone the BMC which will pursue the problem with either the Peak District National Park Board or the Landowner concerned. Please also maintain a courteous and diplomatic response to such approaches as tact and diplomacy have virtually always reaped more benefits than indignantly lecturing an already agitated landowner or gamekeeper what are the moral rights of the situation.

Following the practices explained above will help considerably in avoiding access problems.

Whatever our wishes are for maintaining or improving access in the future please remember

"THE INCLUSION OF A CRAG, OR THE ROUTES UPON IT, IN THIS GUIDEBOOK, DOES NOT MEAN THAT ANY MEMBER OF THE PUBLIC HAS THE RIGHT OF ACCESS TO THE CRAG OR THE RIGHT TO CLIMB UPON IT."

The following addresses may be useful:

BMC
177-179 Burton Road
Manchester
M20 2BB
Tel: 0161 445 4747
Fax: 0161 445 4500
e-mail: office@thebmc.co.uk

Peak National Park Authority
Aldern House
Baslow Road
BAKEWELL
Derbyshire
DE4 1AE

Tel: 01629 81 4321

Bill Wright
BMC Access & Conservation Officer
16th April 1991

TECHNICAL NOTES

Grading Classifications

'Scottish VS or E5 6b?'

What are grades and why do we use them?

Simple enough questions but climbers have been wrestling with them since the early days of our sport. Cannot a grade be defined as the objective classification based on a subjective assessment of the difficulty of a move or pitch of a climb? Furthermore, do we not use grades to classify the difficulty so that other climbers may assess their interest or otherwise in a route?

Clearly these matters are open to considerable debate. For example, do we grade for the hardest move on a pitch or for cumulative difficulty? And once we have understood the 'system', how do we cope with the under/overgrading variations that still seem to occur these days?

Grades in this guidebook

Boulder problems are usually only given a technical grade whereas pitches and/or routes are given both adjectival and technical grades.

Adjectival grades on gritstone

Adjectival grading is open-ended. It starts at Moderate and currently disappears somewhere off the horizon at about E9. In between are: Difficult (D), Hard Difficult (HD), Very Difficult (VD), Hard Very Difficult (HVD), Severe (S), Hard Severe (HS), Very Severe (VS), Hard Very Severe (HVS) and Extremely Severe. Extremely Severe is split into E1, E2, E3.... etc. Adjectival grading considers seriousness, including both quantity and quality of protection, rock quality, the exposed nature of the route and the cumulative difficulty of doing the route. It has long been thought that the adjectival grade implicitly gives a measure of how many climbers can do that route. Whilst this is true in a broad sense, what it is really measuring is the number of climbers who want to do the route as well as the number of climbers who can do the route. Pedantic, well maybe, but true.

Technical grades on grit

Technical grades are meant to be an assessment of the hardest move on a pitch without regard for the position of that move, the sustained nature of the climbing up to that move, or the seriousness of the move. Crux moves on gritstone climbs are usually easy to identify and are therefore easier to grade technically than limestone routes. It has long been thought that the technical grade is best assessed on a top-rope. Current technical grades include; 4a, 4b, 4c, 5a, 5b, 5c, 6a, 6b, 6c, 7a and 7b. Again this is an open-ended system which only talent, strength, ability and dishonesty restrain.

Combined grades

The complexity of the British grading system becomes extreme, if you pardon the pun, when the adjectival and the technical grades are combined. A pitch might be well-protected and technically difficult and as such it would get an adjectival grade which reflected the effort involved; a so-called 'E-for-effort' grade if the route were an Extreme. Alternatively, another pitch might be less well-protected but technically easier. Now its high adjectival grade reflects the route's serious nature. The combination of the adjectival and the technical grades will indicate in which of these categories a pitch lies. It is also very likely that a route description will contain further qualification such as 'well-protected but desperate', London Wall for example, or 'serious and bold', as in the case of say Edge Lane.

ETHICS AND STYLE

> *'Man's ability to perform skilled tasks is strongly affected by the degree to which he is motivated'.*

> Fitts and Posner, Human Performance.

Guidebook writers since the year dot have always included a section on ethics. Many climbers, whose eyes inadvertently stray on to such sections, pass on quickly as soon as they realise their mistake. Before you too pass on, can it simply be stated that there are no misguided hopes that these few words are going to alter your ethics or your life-style. Telling grandma how to suck eggs has never been a good idea:

> *'frankly my dear, I don't give a ....'*

Although it may be enjoyable, if you top-rope every route before you lead it, or solo it; lead it on pre-placed gear; or rest on every piece, you are kidding no one but yourself. Climbers have, and always will, climb routes according to their own ethics and abilities. Simply, you get out what you put in.

However, the two fundamental provisos are that you shall not damage the rock and, if the route concerned is a first ascent, then you should honestly record your style of ascent.

By far and away the most ethically pure and stylish ascent is an on-sight, ground up flash. Top-roping, yo-yoing and dogging are all popular methods of 'frigging' which are widely used today and lead to tainted ascents. However, some of the routes in this guidebook have not been done without top-roped practice. The grades given are however, meant to reflect an on-sight ascent.

PROTECTION

Pegs
With the exception of a few pegs in the Burbage, Millstone, Lawrencefield and Yarncliffe quarries, all protection on these crags is natural. This reflects the time-honoured tradition that no pegs should be permanently fixed on natural grit. Regrettably hand-placed pegs are used on a few routes but these are mentioned in the text.

Bolts
There are a number of old and rotting bolts in the aforementioned quarries. Some of these bolts offer crucial protection on their respective routes. Almost without exception these bolts are museum pieces and the protection that they realistically offer must be questioned. It is undeniable that with the passage of time their condition worsens. Current consensus is that no new bolts should be placed in these quarries.

ROUTE QUALITY
The usual system of stars is used to denote the quality of routes. One star indicates that the route is worthwhile and better than average on that particular edge, while two stars indicate a quality route for the region. Three stars indicate a nationally important route and one which should be on anybody's hit list if they climb at that grade.

Readers of Treasure Island will be fully aware of the significance of the dreaded black spot.

The presence of the ominous dagger is merely a gentle warning. Daggers were originally used to indicate suspicious routes where the first ascent details were 'suspect' for some reason or other. Later, daggers were used for routes where there had been no second ascent. With suspicions about first ascent claims now running rife you may notice the odd double dagger here and there. Routes with three daggers are no longer in the text.

NEW ROUTES

Claims, together with details, of new routes on crags in this guidebook should be sent to the Series Editor, Geoff Milburn, 25 Cliffe Road, Whitfield, GLOSSOP, Derbyshire, SK13 8NY, as well as written-up in the new-route books which proliferate in the shops and cafes throughout the length and breadth of the Peak District. Claims should give the date of the ascent as well as details of the first ascent party and any mitigating pleas. Please also feel free to quote reliable witnesses!

RETROSPECTIVE CLAIMS

A number of well-known routes 'appear' to have changed names in this guidebook. This is often the result of old information coming to light. It would not appear that retrospective claimants are acting maliciously, but that information often disappears or just disseminates slowly. Climbers are therefore urged to report their activities to the Guidebook Committee as soon as possible.

FALSE CLAIMS

There is, sadly, nothing new about false claims, it has been big business in the past. The climbing world usually gives the individual the benefit of the doubt and, even when a fraud is finally exposed, conclusive proof is hard to procure.

During the preparation of this guidebook the Committee has been given the 'low down' on a number of new routes claimed by climbers who have been 'active' in the Froggatt area (as well as elsewhere!). It would seem that a large number of the routes claimed by these climbers were not, in fact, climbed. As a result, certain routes have not therefore been included in this guidebook. However, where these 'routes' are known to have had a 'second ascent', that route has been included, with an appropriate name, and credited as a first ascent. This guidebook is now all the better because of these disclosures and we as climbers should make every effort to 'rout', route frauds.

Climbers in general take a dim view of fraudulent claims and we will be looking in considerable detail at doubtful claims in all of our volumes. If any climbers know of any such fraudulent claims, they are urged to come forward. We are not obliged to describe all routes, nor will we if there appears to be reasonable certainty that routes have not been climbed by claimants.

LISTS OF FIRST ASCENTS

To compile the first ascent lists as many different sources of information and climbers as possible have been consulted. However mistakes are bound to occur and we apologise in advance. Please send all counter-claims, as well as your comments (if reasonably polite!), to the Series Editor, Geoff Milburn, 25 Cliffe Road, Whitfield, GLOSSOP, Derbyshire, SK13 8NY.

MOUNTAIN RESCUE and FIRST AID

Dial 999 or Ripley (0773) 43551 and ask for POLICE OPERATIONS ROOM.

Rescue equipment is kept at;

1. The Mountain Rescue Post at Hollin Bank below Stanage (O.S. ref. SK 238836), close to the middle (Plantation) car park;

2. The Ranger Briefing Centre at Brunts Barn, Nether Padley (O.S. ref. SK 247789). This is open from 09.00 to 17.30 hours and can be telephoned on (0433) 31405.

Telephone Kiosks (originally not vandalised) are located at the following positions;

Map reference	Location	Nearest crags
O.S. ref. SK 235833	North Lees Campsite	Burbage North, Higgar Tor
O.S. ref. SK 291837	Norfolk Arms Pub	Burbage North
O.S. ref. SK 241807	Hathersage	Higgar Tor, Millstone and Lawrencefield
O.S. ref. SK 267803	Fox House	Burbage South and Quarries and Carl Wark
O.S. ref. SK 245778	Grindleford Bridge	Yarncliffe crags, Padley Quarry and Tegness Quarry
O.S. ref. SK 252745	Curbar Bridge	Froggatt, Curbar and Baslow

FIRST AID (For all except those found chipping holds)

1. IF SPINAL INJURIES or HEAD INJURIES are suspected, DO NOT MOVE THE PATIENT without skilled help, except to maintain breathing.

2. IF BREATHING HAS STOPPED, clear airways and commence artificial respiration. DO NOT STOP UNTIL EXPERT OPINION DIAGNOSES DEATH.

3. STOP BLEEDING BY APPLYING DIRECT PRESSURE AND NOT A TOURNIQUET.

4. KEEP THE PATIENT WARM.

5. SUMMON HELP.

Reports of accidents should be sent to the Secretary of the Mountain Rescue Committee, R. J. Davies, 18 Tarnside Fold, Simmondley, GLOSSOP, Derbyshire.

BRITISH MOUNTAINEERING COUNCIL
(Your friendly national body)
The British Mountaineering Council, Crawford House, Precinct Centre, Booth Street East, MANCHESTER, M13 9RZ, is the official body representing climbers in Britain. Clubs and/or individuals may, on application, become members.

The BMC is not the nebulous, nefarious body that it is sometimes considered to be. The Guidebook Committee has, as one of its members, the Access and Conservation Officer of the BMC. The present incumbent is Bill Wright, to whom you should make representation on all matters concerning access and conservation. The Committee supports the Access and Conservation Fund of the BMC by collecting a levy, currently five per cent, on the sale of every Peak District Guidebook. This fund, which is thus heavily supported by donations from the sale of these guidebooks, is our last means of defence when access to our crags is threatened. Where problems arise, for whatever reason, get the BMC involved.

COUNCIL FOR THE PRESERVATION OF RURAL ENGLAND
The Sheffield and Peak District branch has a fine record of defending the Peak District from various threats. Contact Lt. Col. G Haythornthwaite, 22 Endcliffe Crescent, SHEFFIELD, S10 3ED.

TECHNICAL NOTES

PUBLIC TRANSPORT

Rail

British Rail's trans-Pennine, Sheffield – New Mills, service stops at both Hathersage and Grindleford. From there it is possible to catch a local bus to most crags. For information on train services ring either local stations or BR's Derby Travel Centre on Derby (0332) 32051.

Bus

Although many of the most important Eastern Gritstone crags are in this guidebook, the area which is covered is geographically compact. Nevertheless the crags are served by a plethora of buses emanating from Sheffield, Chesterfield, Buxton and New Mills. Anybody travelling from farther afield should travel to one of these centres first and then catch a 'local' bus. Derbyshire County Council publishes a comprehensive guide to the bus, coach and rail services in the Peak District. In 1991 it cost 50p. It can be obtained, by post, from Derbyshire County Council, Public Transport Unit, Chatsworth Hall, Chesterfield Road, Matlock, Derbyshire, DE4 3FW, or from most transport information offices, or Tourist Information Offices.

A summary of the companies operating services in the Peak District is given below. Details of bus services, regardless of the operators, can be obtained by ringing Busline on Buxton (0298) 23098 between 07.00-20.00 daily.

To travel by bus to the crags in this guidebook you need services to either the Norfolk Arms on the Ringinglow Road (for Burbage North and Higgar Tor), the Fox House (for Burbage South and Carl Wark), the Surprise View (for Millstone and Lawrencefield), Grindleford (for Yarncliffe, Padley and Tegness), the Grouse/White Gate/Chequers (for Froggatt), or Calver Sough (for Froggatt, Curbar and Baslow). Below is a summary of the buses, where they stop, and the operators.

Steve Earnshaw on Irrepressible Urge, Burbage North Edge.
Photo: Richie Brooks.
Overleaf: Shaun Hutson on The Knock, Burbage South.
Photo: Ian Smith.

From	To	Service
Sheffield	Baslow	X23
Sheffield	Calver	X65
Sheffield	Fox House	X65
Sheffield	Grindleford	X65
Sheffield	Hathersage	272
Sheffield	Ringinglow	SYT 81-82
Chesterfield	Baslow	X66
Chesterfield	Baslow	170
Chesterfield	Calver	X66
New Mills	Baslow	X67
Buxton	Baslow	X23
Buxton	Calver	X65
Bakewell	Baslow	X23
Bakewell	Calver	SYT 240
Bakewell	Fox House	SYT 240
Bakewell	Grindleford	SYT 240

Currently the services below are run by the following operators.

Operator	Services
SYT No's. 81, 82, 240 and 272	South Yorkshire Transport
PMT No. X23	Potter Motor Transport
No. 170	Hulleys Transport
No. X65	Whites Transport
No. X66	Whites Transport/ East Midlands

TECHNICAL NOTES

Thumb

Stand beside road (preferably one going in the direction of the nearest crag) with rope over shoulder and stick out a thumb whenever a fast car goes by. Don't forget to smile. When a car stops, establish where it is going before diving in.

The ensuing conversations and events will set you up for life with a wealth of tall (but probably true) stories and even if you don't reach a crag you'll have lots of fun.

CAFES

There are three 'local' cafes which are used by climbers in the area. The following is a summary of the services which they offer.

Lover's Leap, Stoney Middleton, Tue.-Fri. 9.00-15.00 Sat.-Sun. 8.30-17.30 (cafe closes 1 hour earlier in winter), Traditional climbers' food at average prices in utilitarian surroundings. Popular with climbers, bikers and truckers.

Grindleford Station Cafe, 7 days 8.30-18.30, (cafe closes at 17.00 during winter). Traditional climbers' food at average prices in basic cafe. Popular with climbers and walkers alike.

Longlands, Outside, Hathersage, Tue.-Fri. 11.00-17.30, Sat.-Sun. 9.00-17.30 (cafe closes at 17.00 during winter months), Fri.-Sat. 18.45-21.00. A comprehensive range of meals and drinks at 'affordable' prices in attractive and trendy/progressive surroundings. Popular with climbers, walkers, and shoppers. Recommended in the Vegetarian Good Food Guide.

PUBS

There are several good pubs in the area.

The Norfolk Arms, Ringinglow Road. Suitably placed for a quick pint after a summer evening on Burbage North. Popular with Sheffield's yuppies, dinkies and posers alike; get down there and check it out!

The Fox House, Hathersage Road, A625. Well placed irrespective of your destination. Popular with anybody and everybody.

The Grouse Inn, B6054. Suitably placed for that well-earned pint after a strenuous day on Froggatt. Popular with the 'well-heeled' but with a bar at the back for climbers and walkers.

The Chequers, B6054, As above but even better placed for that après-Froggatt pint.

The Moon, Stoney Middleton, A623. The 'climbers' pub, well tried and tested with a good atmosphere.

CLIMBING SHOPS

Sheffield, Nottingham, Glossop and Manchester are all well-served by climbing shops. Within the Peak District itself, there is a limited number of shops selling equipment.

Outside, Hathersage, (0433) 51936. 7-day opening. Extensive outdoor, sporting and climbing equipment and clothing. End-of-season sales and discount are worth waiting for.

Hitch and Hike, Park Garden Centre, Hope, (0433) 51013. 7-day opening. Comprehensive range of selected manufacturers outdoor/climbing equipment and clothing at competitive prices.

Lover's Leap Cafe, Stoney Middleton, (0433) 30334. Opening as for cafe. Limited range of climbing hardware only, though bargains are rare. They also hire caving lamps and belts.

ACCOMMODATION

CAMP SITES

Camping sauvage, as the French say, is illegal on private land and is frowned upon everywhere else. Good bivouacs do exist in this area but it would be irresponsible to be seen to promote such activities. Anyway, you'll have fun finding them! Remember to pack out all you pack in.

There are only four official camp sites in the area.

Fox Hagg Farm, Lodge Lane, Rivelin, Sheffield, O.S.ref. SK 292861 (0742) 305589. Water, toilets and showers.

North Lees Camp Site, Hathersage, O.S.ref. SK 235833, (0433) 50838. Hot and cold water, showers, toilets, wash basins and drying facilities.

Stocking Farm, Calver, O.S.ref. SK 247746, (0433) 30516. Water, toilets, showers, shaving points, wash basins and laundry.

Eric Byne Camp Site, Moorside Farm, Birchen Edge, Baslow, O.S.ref. SK 277726, (024688) 2277. Water, wash basins, flush toilets and telephone.

HOSTELS AND BARNS

There are Youth Hostels in Eyam and Hathersage; there are no bunk barns offering accommodation in the area. However, various bed and breakfast places can be found. Various clubs have huts in the area, such as the Climbers' Club hut below Froggatt, but in general the use of these is restricted to members only. Arrangements can however often be made with the clubs for group bookings.

CLIMBING WALLS

Of the surrounding cities and towns, Sheffield, Barnsley, Leeds, Nottingham, Glossop and Manchester have good indoor climbing walls. The British Mountaineering Council publishes details of the opening hours and costs, but the following gives an indication of the 'local' walls.

Sheffield City Polytechnic, Collegiate Crescent, Sheffield, (0742) 532449. Open 7 days: 9.00-21.00 (term time only) Mon. – Fri. 10.00–15.00 (holiday periods), Britain's only **FREE** wall. Traditional DR wall which is good for power problems and sustained traversing on edges. High density of holds makes it good for beginners and the ageing.

YMCA, Broomhall Road, Sheffield, (0742) 684807. The climbing wall, a traditional brick-built wall with concrete features, is, at the time of writing, closed pending a feasibility study on a new purpose-built wall. Phone the YMCA for the current position.

Glossop Leisure Centre, High St. East, Glossop, Derbyshire, (0457) 873223. Open 7 days: Mon. – Fri. 9.00 – 22.30, Sat. – Sun. 9.00 – 21.00, £1.00/session. Bendcrete overhanging panels.

Metro Dome, Barnsley (0226) 730060, Mon. – Fri. 7.30–22.30, Sat. – Sun. 9.00–22.30, £1.85/session. Traditional DR wall with overhanging DR concrete wall and outrageous roof. The traditional walls are suitable for relative beginners, whilst the overhanging wall gives good power bouldering and stamina traversing.

The Foundry, Mowbray Street, Sheffield. Sheffield's soon to be open mega climbers' centre, featuring a cafe, outdoor retailer and competition-standard on-sight leading wall, capable of giving routes of up to 15m. Other walls will cater for technical bouldering of all standards and a cellar roof is planned for cellar-dwellers. 2 sessions per day, £2.00-3.00 per session. Due to open in late 1991.

Remember: A day on the climbing wall will help to cut down the erosion and pollution on the natural crags. Better still, go train in the cellar and become a troglodyte.

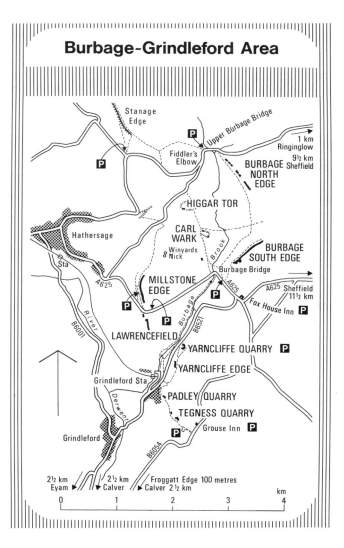

Burbage-Grindleford Area

Stanage Edge

Upper Burbage Bridge

Fiddler's Elbow

1 km Ringinglow

9½ km Sheffield

BURBAGE NORTH EDGE

HIGGAR TOR

Hathersage

CARL WARK

Winyards Nick

BURBAGE SOUTH EDGE

Burbage Bridge

Sta

A625

MILLSTONE EDGE

A625 Sheffield 11½ km

Fox House Inn

LAWRENCEFIELD

B6521

River

B6001

YARNCLIFFE QUARRY

YARNCLIFFE EDGE

Grindleford Sta

PADLEY QUARRY

TEGNESS QUARRY

Grouse Inn

Grindleford

Derwent

B6054

2½ km Eyam

2½ km Calver

Froggatt Edge 100 metres

Calver 2½ km

km

0   1   2   3   4

THE BURBAGE VALLEY

The Burbage Valley is some 11km west of Sheffield, just inside the Peak District. The valley, which lies roughly north to south, is both wide and open, unlike the confined limestone valleys just to the south-west. The Burbage Brook runs southward down the valley from the Upper Burbage Bridge, (O.S. ref. SK 262830) to the Burbage Bridge near the Toad's Mouth Rock (O.S. ref. SK 262807). The Upper Burbage Bridge is on Ringinglow Road (the Sheffield/Ringinglow to Hathersage road), whilst the Toad's Mouth is on Hathersage Road, the A625, which is the main Sheffield to Hathersage road.

Running through the valley, and forming the main access path, is a broad crescent-shaped track known as the Green Drive. It follows a roughly parallel route to the brook and is used by climbers, walkers and runners alike. Recently, mountain-bikers have also begun to exact their toll.

The crags are attractively laid out around the rim of the valley and effectively form a horseshoe. Burbage North, South and the quarries lie on Burbage Moor to the east and south-east respectively, whilst Higgar Tor and Carl Wark lie on Hathersage Moor to the west of the valley. Higgar Tor and the North Edge face south-west and therefore get the sun most of the day. The South Edge and the Quarries face north-west and only come into the sun on summer evenings. Carl Wark faces north-east and so gets the sun only in the mornings.

Typically, the rock in the valley is very rough Rivelin Grit. The climbs are therefore invariably on sound rock, although the overall stability of some areas in the quarries is a little doubtful. All types of climbing are well represented. The diversity of styles ranges from horrendous, off-width cracks to desperate slabs and walls which are climbed on sloping holds, pebbles, or worst of all, faith and friction. The valley also has a tremendous amount of quality bouldering, with perhaps the South Edge being the home of the hardest problems.

All the climbs are readily accessible (usually only 5 to 10 minutes) and the longest approach is unlikely to take more than thirty minutes. Notes on individual approaches are given later, but the North Edge and Higgar Tor are most easily reached from Ringinglow Road, whereas the quarries, the South Edge and Carl

Wark are usually approached from Fox House along the Green Drive.

The Burbage Valley is owned by Sheffield City Council and access is freely given.

HISTORY

The crags in the Burbage Valley, and Burbage North in particular, have one of the longest climbing histories in the area. Along with Froggatt and Curbar Edges, Burbage North attracted the attentions of James W. Puttrell, W.J. Watson and Ernest Baker. Although these intrepid explorers wandered extensively over the hills of The Peak, and no doubt climbed many easy lines, records of exactly what they did are both limited and vague.

The Burbage Valley had to wait until the early Thirties until routes were climbed and recorded to any significant degree. Activity on Burbage North pre-dates that on Froggatt and Curbar by some ten to fifteen years. *Dover and Ellis Chimney*, climbed by Frank Dover and Gilbert Ellis, was *the* route at that time. Today it is graded E1, and deservedly so. The same pair added *The Knight's Move* which, though less difficult, is much finer. Rupert Brooks, Eric Byne and Jack Macleod produced routes of their own at that time, as did Frank Burgess, Byron Connelly and Eric Byrom.

Members of the Rock and Ice Club began new route activity towards the end of the Forties and at the beginning of the Fifties. Their dominance of new route activity on these crags was total. The Joe Brown 'new route machine', ably assisted by Merrick (Slim) Sorrell and J.R. (Nat) Allen amongst others, slowly wound itself up. In November of 1956 Brown, climbing with Don Whillans, forced his hardest route up to that time; *The Rasp*. Unfortunately they used a sling to rest, but nevertheless the route was a significant breakthrough.

Local climbers, usually from Sheffield, started their campaigns and in 1958 Len Millsom balanced his way up the delicate *Millwheel Wall*. This route took a steep slab and as such was not perhaps quite the flavour of the time. In 1958 Whillans surpassed himself and produced what is still today a fearful route; *Goliath*. Brutal, imposing and revered, Goliath is seldom climbed even today. Its thirty or so feet represent all that history records about Whillans himself!

Dave Gregory, Andrew Brodie, George Kitchin, Gerry Rogan and Alan Clarke all climbed new routes in the years up to the publication of the 1965 Sheffield Froggatt guidebook. Clarke produced perhaps the hardest routes in *Long Tall Sally* and *The Boggart*, though on the latter route he used some aid to surmount the initial difficult section.

1971 saw the arrival of Ed Ward-Drummond, as he was calling himself at that time. He only produced two significant routes in the Burbage Valley, one of which was long on words and the other long, for gritstone anyway, on action! Both were noteworthy and both controversial. *Banana Finger* was effectively a boulder problem, yet Ward-Drummond saw fit to give it a full description.

> '**Banana Finger**   *20ft   XS*
> *Left of Overhanging Buttress is a small face protected underneath by a long narrow overhang. Where the overhang fades out to the right use a poor edge to reach a small, poor finger hold way to the left. Change hands on this (hard) and fidget slightly left. Up with some difficulty to reach better hand holds and then up to a good resting place. Straight up easily now'. – Ed Drummond, 1971.*

Flute of Hope, by comparison, was a much sterner test and one which required two aid points. Interestingly enough, Geoff Birtles had been trying it the day before but, preferring not to use aid, had failed. As usual though, Ward-Drummond challenged the establishment.

In the early Seventies the self-proclaimed 'angry young men' of Sheffield well and truly grasped the nettle and set about new-routing on an hitherto unsurpassed scale. John Allen and Neil Stokes began quietly enough, although in 1975 Allen alternated leads with Steve Bancroft on *Silent Spring*. This route represented, perhaps more than any other, their ability to seek out and climb impressive, challenging, and not altogether, well-protected rock. Proctor, of course had been active on nearby Millstone, but here we had young climbers producing hard routes. Their activities continued. Bancroft added, amongst others, *Rasp Direct*, *Boggart Left-hand* and *Remergence*, but it was Allen's routes, *The Knock*, *Above and Beyond the Kinaesthetic Barrier* and *Pebble Mill* that were really impressive. They continued the trend of bold and technically difficult routes that for so long has been the hallmark of gritstone climbing.

A plethora of relatively unimpressive routes was added during the late Seventies by other climbers; a free ascent of *Flute of Hope* by Ron Fawcett perhaps being the only noteworthy addition. Nearby, Paul Bolger added *Bat out of Hell*. This was a natural continuation to *Flute of Hope*, not only in a developmental sense, but in a physical sense as well. Rather than representing an increase in standard, it highlighted the fact that an increasing number of climbers were capable of adding hard routes. This trend was forcibly emphasised in 1980, when Andy Barker added the hard and serious *Nosferatu*, and Andy Woodward the desperate *Pulsar*.

The partnership of Andy Barker and Paul Mitchell developed and some impressive, though all too often obscure, routes were added. *Simpering Savage* however was hardly obscure and it proved to be as hard as it was obvious. It was everybody's 'secret' line, but it fell to determined efforts from Barker and Mitchell, with Mitchell finally getting the first ascent. Mitchell also added *Big Bad Wolf* in 1982. This route, despite being tucked away on the extreme left-hand end of Burbage South, is well worth seeking out. Barker soloed the innocuous-looking *Renobulous Bongetl*, but not without considerable difficulty.

Other climbers were also actively new-routing in the early Eighties, but they added little of real note. In the autumn of 1984 however, Al Rouse finally completed his *piece de resistance*, *Blind Date*. A desperate boulder problem start led to more reasonable climbing through the finishing roofs. No sooner had Rouse reported the route than a boulder, which was used to start the route, 'migrated', first towards the crag, making the start easier, and then 'disappeared' altogether, thereby making the start utterly desperate. John Allen, having returned from an extended leave of absence abroad, added some short but testing little pieces; *Blind Date* and *Ai No Corrida*.

It was however newcomers to the valley who added the most impressive new routes at that time. In 1984 Jerry Moffatt added *Messiah* and Johnny Dawes *The Braille Trail*. Both routes had been blatantly obvious to the devotees of the valley and some activists had even cleaned and tried them with the assistance of a top-rope. None of these attempts however came to anything. At the time of writing, *Messiah* has only had three ascents and its grade has risen a notch each time! *The Braille Trail* lost some 'crucial' pebbles after Dawes's first ascent and it was some time before it was re-climbed.

John Allen, back from New Zealand and other foreign climes and with his crown well and truly threatened, hit back with the 'first true 7a on grit', *West Side Story*, though perhaps some of Al Manson's problems in Yorkshire might rival that honour. He then went on to produce other short, but desperate, routes; *The Sphinx* and *Small is Beautiful*. Allen's old partner in-crime, Steve Bancroft, even climbed a few new routes at that time but, as if to restate his ability, Allen added *Lost World* to the hidden ramparts of Carl Wark.

Visiting Yorkshireman, John Dunne, felt as though *Life Assurance* was needed, and another expatriate from the northern climes, Ron Fawcett, added his second route to the valley, up the wall to the right of *Byne's Crack*. Fawcett's route went un-noticed, a fact probably helped by Ron having failed to name it! The quarries attracted some attention towards the end of the Eighties, with Andy Pollitt leading *Masters of the Universe* up the arête of The Cioch.

In 1989 John Dunne claimed what is probably one of the most serious routes anywhere on gritstone; *Parthian Shot*. This line had previously been the subject of a video featuring a top-roped ascent by Johnny Dawes. Dawes himself felt at the time that he was a number of years away from climbing it. The obvious, previously aided, line on the front of The Cioch has attracted the attention of Sheffield's finest climbers. An ascent, by Sean Myles, of *Captain Invincible* at the eleventh hour, was the culmination of considerable effort. Burbage Valley has, on its ramparts, once again some of the most serious and technically difficult routes in the country. And then of course there are the boulders!

BURBAGE WEST and NORTH EDGES

SITUATION and CHARACTER

by Keith Sharples

> *'Definitely a low class edge; they lack style; they look as if hens had been over them.'*

> On Foot in the Peak, Patrick Monkhouse, 1932.

The North Edge is the most continuous of all the edges in the valley. It starts from a point some 100m south of Ringinglow Road and extends roughly halfway down the valley. Without exception, the rock is sound. The climbs are fairly short, even for gritstone, and consequently the edge is a popular venue for beginners or those out soloing and bouldering. So popular is the edge that the usually rough rock has been worn smooth on the much frequented northern buttresses.

Routes follow walls and cracks in roughly equal proportions. Overhangs and roofs are numerous, though arêtes are somewhat under-represented. For regular visitors the numerous low-level traverses on the northern buttresses provide a means of testing their fitness, and for the newcomer they are to be savoured.

Facing south-west, the North Edge gets any afternoon sun going, though its outlook and elevation does mean that it is exposed to westerly winds. In summer it is a popular evening venue, although in very hot weather the routes become appreciably harder.

Burbage West is basically a collection of boulders (big ones though) and small outcrops. It faces south-east and gets the sun in the early part of the day.

APPROACHES and ACCESS

These edges are easily approached from Ringinglow Road where cars can be left in either of the two parks adjacent to the upper Burbage Bridge. From there, the first routes on Burbage North can be reached in a matter of seconds.

For those without cars, the edge can be approached on foot from the Fox House in less than thirty minutes, (see the South Edge approaches). For those looking for even more adventure, catch the very occasional SYT No. 81-82 bus to its terminus at the Norfolk Arms on Ringinglow Road. The road then snakes off uphill towards the upper Burbage Bridge and Stanage Edge beyond.

BURBAGE WEST   O.S. ref SK 261828

This collection of mini-buttresses and boulders facing the start of Burbage North has long been popular among devotees of bouldering. Countless problems exist and only a few of the

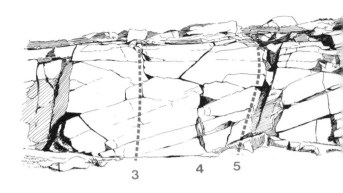

longer ones are described here; the rest are left in order to preserve some sense of enjoyment and discovery. The largest buttress is situated to the left-hand end of the crag and sports a steep wall with the brilliant **West Side Story**, E4 7a, (1985) up its centre. **Rumblefish**, HVS 5b, (1979) takes the right arête of the buttress and the arête of the buttress down and left is followed on either side by **Crow Man Meets the Psychotic Pheasant**, E1 6a, (1979).

BURBAGE NORTH   O.S. ref. SK 263829 to SK 269820

The first recorded climbs on the North Edge are on **LITTLE WALL** which consists of two small buttresses. Over thirty 'routes' and problems have been climbed here by obsessive devotees who rarely progress any farther down the edge. Only the traditional lines of ascent are recorded here but every pebble and crease has been well used!

THE CLIMBS are described from LEFT to RIGHT.

1   Route 1   6m   S   (1934-1951)
Climb neatly up the left-hand arête.

A short HVS 5c problem takes the wall left of the arête, starting at the obvious carved initials.

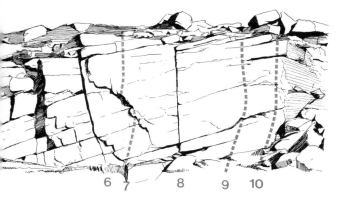

Little Wall

2 Route 1.5 6m VS 5b (1978-1983)
The wall just left of Route 2.

3 Route 2 6m S (pre-1934)
Climb the wall three metres right of the arête. *'Half-way, a hole allows the right hand and elbow to be jammed palm upwards – this is necessary for succeeding movement.' – 1951.*

Route 2.5, VS 5a,(1991), takes the wall just to the right.

4 Route 3 6m VD (pre-1934)
Ascend the obvious zig-zag cracks three metres right again.

Route 3.5, E1 6a, (1982), is the wall one metre right of the cracks – with no deviation!

5 Route 4 5m VS 5b (1978-1983)
Climb just left of the right-hand arête of the wall.

Two HVS lines have also been squeezed in on this wall.

A low-level traverse from right to left is possible at 6a-ish, whilst the right arête is a juggy 4b.

The right-hand wall is split by two cracks.

6 Cranberry Crack 6m D (1951)
Climb the wider left-hand crack.

The wall to the left of The Chant is E2 6a.

* **7 The Chant** 6m HVS 5a   (1958-1959)
The wall between the cracks has a leftward-curving overlap.
Follow this to the top break, then step right on to the face. A
couple of hard moves, the crux, prove entertaining. Mantras are
not considered essential, but may nevertheless help.

It is possible under normal climatic conditions to climb the wall
just right at HVS 5b. Under hot humid conditions you can name
your own grade!

8 Twenty-Foot Crack 20ft S 4b   (pre-1934)
An interesting exercise in crack technique. *'The holds are small
and the finish poor during or after wet weather owing to loose soil.'*
– 1956. Traditionalists should feel at home on this, the only
imperial route on the Eastern Edges!

The wall just right can be climbed at VS 5b.

9 The Curse 6m VS 5b   (1977-1978)
A choice of starts gives access to the centre of the wall on the
right: well-named.

10 Lost in France 5m VS 5b   (1978-1983)
Climb the face one metre left of the right-hand arête.

The low-level traverse rightwards from Twenty-Foot Crack to the
arête is a nasty little 6b number. Try it first mid-week and then
show off your prowess at the weekend. Failure, especially at
busy times, is unlikely to impress.

Eight metres along the drive is the somewhat obscurely-named
TRIANGLE BUTTRESS, *the centre of which is split by the deep
cleft of Triangle Crack.*

11 Little Plumb 6m D   (1957-1965)
Climb the cracked groove three metres left of the obvious
straight crack.

Base over Apex, VS 4c, (1991),takes the face to the right with a
long reach and a finish up the hanging corner.

12 Baseless 8m VD   (1957-1965)
The straight crack just left of the blunt arête is undercut at its
base.

13 Triangle Buttress Arête   9m   VD   (1932)
Gain the sloping ledge on the blunt arête from either side then
follow it direct.

14 Triangle Buttress Direct   9m   S   (pre-1934)
Just right again, go direct up the face. A difficult direct start, 5b,
is (sometimes) possible, one metre right.

15 Triangle Crack   8m   VD   (1934-1951)
The wide corner crack is awkward.

16 Leaning Wall   9m   S   (pre-1934)
Gain the wide crack of Leaning Wall Direct by a traverse from
two metres up Triangle Crack or a traverse left from Steptoe, HS.

17 Leaning Wall Direct   8m   VS   5a   (1957)
Strenuously climb the right-hand wall of the cleft to the base of a
prominent wide crack. Finish up this. For a harder variant, step
left and attack the upper wall using the left arête of the crack at
will. Award yourself at least an E1 tick for an ascent without
touching the arête.

* **18 Little White Jug**   9m   VS   4c   (1977)
Start one metre right of the previous route and head direct for
the prominent overhanging nose. Pull over direct to an awkward
mantelshelf finish.

Big Black 'Un, HVS 5a, follows the overhanging wall just right
again on surprisingly good holds to a difficult mantelshelf above
the finishing roof.

Yet another low-level traverse is possible from Triangle Crack to
Steptoe at about 6a.

Steptoe, M, (1957-1965) is the easy crack/staircase on the right
and **Triangle Buttress Girdle**, S, (1934-1951) is the obvious
traverse line from left to right.

*30m right, and across a chaos of jumbled boulders, is an undercut
face,* **MONKEY WALL.** *Just before this buttress, and a few metres
below the edge, is a low triangular tent-like cave which faces the
South Edge.*
A crack splits the apex of the cave as though some ancient
Herculean boulderer had dealt a mighty blow. Burrow deep into
the back of the cave, difficult, and then finger-jam out towards
the light and glory; very difficult. The lip provides the crux and is
down-right cruel. Tick **Definitive 5.12**, 6b for a successful ascent.

Returning back to the main edge a 'cave' is tucked away to the left of Monkey Wall.
The writer feels a compulsion to share the 'delights' of a little crack which is tucked away in the side-wall. It is possible to finger-jam this crack at about 6a, but reaching between the breaks on jams is much harder and better.

* **19 Monkey Corner** 8m VD   (pre-1934)
From the undercut groove in the left arête, swing right onto the upper slab.
The arête itself can be climbed direct at 6a.

The stepped, overlapping slab on the right contains possibly the most celebrated route on the buttress:

* **20 Banana Finger** 7m E1 6a   (1971)
Nine times out of ten it would suffice to say 'follow the chalk'. However, start about five metres right of the arête, then 'work' leftwards until a difficult move up which enables easier ground to be reached. A **Direct Start**, joining the 'original' at the end of the traverse is possible at 6b. The route is about two grades easier in polar gear, but a real swine in shorts!

21 Monkey Wall 6m M   (1951-1957)
The slab six metres right of the left arête gives a pleasant route. The ledge at half-height is big enough for a picnic.

22 Monk On 6m HVS 5b   (1982)
The overhang on the right-hand arête is quite formidable if tackled direct but it yields more easily on the right.

Next is the appropriately named **OVERHANG BUTTRESS**.

23 Little Brown Thug 7m HVS 6a   (1980s)
Struggle around the overhang left of Wednesday Climb to an easy finish.

* **24 Wednesday Climb** 8m HVS 5b   (1960-1965)
The obvious central crack yields to a determined approach. A classic struggle with a no-hands rest at the crux.

25 Life in a Radioactive Dustbin 8m E4 6c   (1984)
Use a collection of poor holds to climb the overhang and arête right of Wednesday Climb. Those well over 180cm, sorry 6-footers, are in for an infinitely easier time than the rest of us.

26 The Disposable Bubble 8m E4 6b (1984)
Climb easily to the roof two metres right of the hanging arête
and cross it just left of an obvious slot in the break below the
roof. Hard and with an exceedingly unpleasant landing. Said to
be easier for climbers with short legs and long arms!

* **27 Overhang Buttress Direct** 9m S (pre-1934)
Follow a very blunt arête until beneath the right-hand side of the
bulge. *'This is surmounted direct to a couple of cracks filled with
bilberry.'* – 1951. Continue in a direct line to the top.

* **28 Overhang Buttress Arête** 8m M (pre-1934)
Climb the right-hand arête of the buttress.

Ad Infinitum, 14m, S, (1934-1951). Start on the left wall of the
buttress, then traverse to a ledge above the overhang. Continue
traversing delicately right and finish up the right arête.

Across a gully **Burgess Buttress**, M, (pre-1934) is the obvious
arête. For **Burgess Face**, VS 4c, (pre-1934), climb direct one
metre left of the arête. **Burgess St.**, D, (1957-1965), is the small
corner two metres right again.

50m right is a green wall split by a wide crack:

* **29 All Quiet on the Eastern Front** 7m E1 6a (1978)
The left arête of the wall gained from the left is a popular
problem. A direct start is rumoured at 6c.

30 The Busker 7m VS 4c (1982)
Climb the steep slab just right.

The left arête of the crack is VS 4c.

31 Bracken Crack 7m HVD (1951-1957)
The wide crack.

32 Green Slab 7m VS 4c (pre-1934)
The wall right of Bracken Crack has a steep start.

20m right again is a more continuous and impressive area of rock.

* **33 The Grogan** 8m HVS 5b (1964)
The thin slanting crack at the left-hand edge of the wall is fierce
but can be well-protected. A finger-knackerer if ever there was
one.

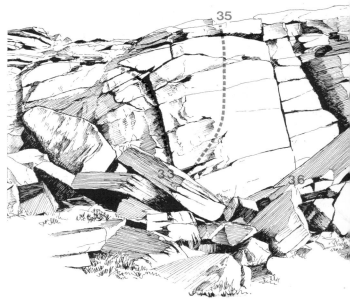

34 Groat 8m E1 6b   (1982-1983)
The enigmatic arête just right of The Grogan. Being tall and
having tunnel vision helps. A side-runner is placed in The
Grogan *en route*.

* **35 Wollock** 9m HVS 4c   (1964)
Starting two metres right of The Grogan, trend right, then go
direct or leftwards up the impressive wall. Quite spacy. Escaping
into Pulcherrime reduces the grade to VS 4b.
The wall immediately right is a scary 5c.

* **36 Pulcherrime** 8m VS 4b   (1951-1956)
The obvious narrowing crack just to the right gives excellent
jamming.

Mutiny Crack Area

37 Slanting Crack 8m VD   (pre-1934)
The crack two metres to the right again.

† **38 Small is Beautiful** 7m E3 6c   (1985)
An infuriatingly desperate route up the centre of the slightly
overhanging wall just right. In this case small is definitely hard
work. The original line trended left after the start and finished up
the centre. Subsequent ascensionists have kept to the right at a
more amenable, protectable and escapable 6b.

39 Slanting Gully 7m M   (pre-1934)
This small gully is in the angle on the right.

40 Chockstone Climb 7m M   (pre-1934)
Keep well inside the chimney in the right-hand wall.

The next three routes share the same start.

* **41 Stomach Traverse** 14m VS 4c (1932)
Gain the left-hand arête of the main face from the gully then
move up until beneath the roof. Hand-traverse the break
rightwards to finish up Mutiny Crack. Completely ungradeable,
and unclimbable, as a stomach traverse.

* **42 Tiptoe** 16m VS 4c (1972)
Having gained the arête from the left, make a delicate traverse
rightwards, parallel to, but at a lower level than the previous
route, to gain Mutiny Crack. Continue rightwards to finish up
Diversion.

† **43 Gymnipodies** 10m E4 6b (1988)
Gain the left arête then climb easily up to the roof. (A **Direct
Start** at 6a is possible just left of the next route.) Gain the lip,
swing right, (Friend 2) and pull over, crux; sounds easy doesn't it!

* **44 Remergence** 12m E4 6b (1977)
Start roughly three metres right of the arête. Using good holds
beneath the roof, gain holds above the roof. Crank these out and
rock-over to gain the traverse of Tiptoe. Note: no stepping stones
are allowed, but water-wings might come in handy at certain
times of the year. Amble up to the top roof then, moving
leftwards, attack it with conviction. A good Friend in the break
above the lip of the overhang protects the final moves.

† **45 Blind Date** 12m E5 7a (1984)
Boulder desperately through the roof right of Remergence then,
with a final committing move, get established above the lip. Take
the middle bulge one metre left of a thin crack to join
Remergence under the final roof. Stretch up and right for a
crease and rock-over boldly to finish. Unrepeated without a
boulder to start off. It is possible to do the upper section by
starting up the next route, but E4 6b is a more realistic grade if it
is climbed this way.

* **46 Mutiny Crack** 11m VS 4b (1934)
The superb crack on the right of the face is followed steeply on
excellent holds and jams.
*'The crack leans over to the left and one's balance is severely tried.
The first two moves are not hard. In 18 feet an overhang on the
right proves a stubborn obstacle. A further two succeeding
overhangs on the left wall prove almost the limit of possibility.
There is a good ledge above, and the remainder is easy'* – 1951.

† **47 Manatee Man** 11m E4 6a   (1985)
A poor eliminate taking an absolutely direct line through the roof right of Mutiny Crack.

48 Meddle 10m HVS 5a   (1976)
The right-hand side of the slabby rib is followed direct before sneaking around the right-hand side of the overhang close to Detour.

49 Detour 11m HVD   (1957)
Go up the next corner to the capping roof then escape left to the arête. Continue left to finish.

50 Diversion 10m HVS 5a   (1964)
From the roof on Detour, swing fiercely round the corner on the right to finish up a short crack.

20m right is an isolated buttress with a wizened dead stump at its base.

51 Dead Tree Crack 7m S   (1957-1965)
Climb the crack just right of the stump.

52 Side Face 6m HVD   (1957-1965)
Round the corner to the right is a slabby wall which eases quickly after a tricky start. It is possible to hand-traverse from Dead Tree Crack.

Immediately to the right is a small slab which gives four great little problems.
Left to right, these are; 5b, 5c, 6a and 6b. Of course numerous combinations can be made to suit all moods.

A quick 150m dash right, (best to take your rock boots off if it is summer), leads to a larger buttress of rock, **ASH TREE WALL**. *Left of the main buttress, and set back above a small oak tree, is a small wall which is split by a crack.*

† **53 Sunlight Caller** 6m HVS 5b   (1985)
Climb the wall one metre left of the next route.

54 Oak Face 6m HS   (1977)
Go up the crack to a tricky finish up a scoop.

55 Boggle Boothroyd 6m VS 4b   (1985)
Climb the scoop two metres right of Oak Face to a break and bulge. Finish direct.

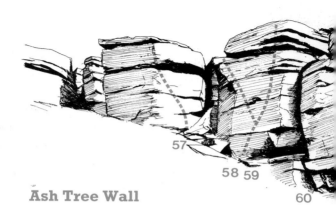

Ash Tree Wall

† **56 Beach Tea One** 7m HVS 6a (1988)
Start left of Ivy Tree at the arête and move left to a break.
Continue direct to finish.

57 Ivy Tree 7m HVS 5b (1977)
Start at the right-hand side of the next buttress. Go up leftwards
to the break from which a longish reach might allow a little
something just left of the arête to be gained. Pull up easily to the
top.

Over to the right and slightly lower down is a large buttress:

58 All Stars' Goal 7m E1 6a (1978)
Start in the centre of the wall but trend left to good jams in a
horizontal break. Now the fun starts. Finish direct. Fortunately it
is possible to jump off leftwards; in which case all that is likely to
be damaged is your ego.

59 Evening Wall 8m E1 5b (1964)
Start as for the previous route then move rightwards into the
middle of the face. Finish, with care, left of the right-hand arête.

60 Wall Chimney 9m HVD (pre-1934)
The chimney. Finish either inside or outside the chockstone.

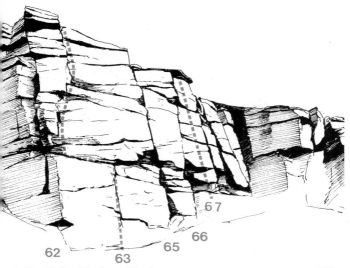

† **61 Nefertiti** 8m E5 6c (1989)

From two metres up Wall Chimney move right to climb the scoop via distant breaks. A runner in a small pocket in the right wall of Wall Chimney and another at the same level in the crack to the right of the scoop (Wall Corner) protect the route.

62 Wall Corner 12m VD (pre-1934)

The next break to the right is followed direct, finishing to the right of the big nose.

* **63 Ash Tree Wall** 14m HVD (pre-1934)

Start up the crack three metres right of the arête then traverse left to gain the prominent 'staircase' which leads to a ledge. Finish up the open groove.

64 Ash Tree Variations 12m VS 5b (1965-1978)

A gymnastic problem below the 'staircase' and the pleasant slab on its right lead to the ledge of Ash Tree Wall. Various finishes are possible.

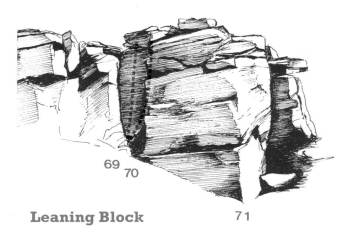

69 70

Leaning Block

71

65 Ash Tree Crack 12m D (pre-1934)
The crack now contains little of the tree that gave this wall its
name.

66 Bilberry Crack 12m VD (pre-1934)
The next crack right, long devoid of its bilberry bush, leads to a
finish up the slab on the left.

67 Bilberry Face 12m VD (pre-1934)
The face right again is climbed direct.

Ash Tree Girdle, S, (pre-1934), is done from left to right, if at all.

68 A Phenomenological Problem 5m HVS 5b (1977)
Climb a small blunt prow about ten metres right in the gully,
starting on the left.

*On the right is a large block which resembles a miniature Higgar
Tor.*
Splitting the crag-facing rear wall of the block is a thin break at
about shoulder height. This provides a good traverse in either
direction, as well as a number of wild, upward dynos for the top.

69 Early Morning Performance 6m HVS 5c   (1978)
Round to the right the green side wall is problematical and
reachy. It is usually started by swinging in from the next route.

70 Leaning Block Crack 6m VD   (1934-1951)
Just to the right is a thin slanting crack.

*† **71 Living in Oxford** 10m E7 6c   (1989)
The bald arête right again is climbed direct. It gives hard and
serious climbing. An RP 0 in a thin seam/crack is said to give
some protection.

This route is perhaps the first of several desperate routes that
might just be possible on the walls hereabouts; only the talented
need apply.

72 Green Chimney 9m VD   (1934-1951)
The cleft which bounds the leaning block on its right has an
awkward start.

75m right is a narrow tower.

73 Jetty Buttress 8m VD   (1934-1951)
Climb direct up the front face of the buttress.

*Just before Jetty Buttress, and at a lower level, is a prominent jutting
boulder which has a thin seam on its left-hand side:*

† **74 The Sphinx** 6m E4 6c   (1985)
Follow the rising traverse line to finish up the front arête. Utterly
desperate climbing along the thinnest of breaks imaginable.

*Down to the right is a fine 5c arête, while through the arch is a roof
at head height.*
Roof Goofe, 6a. Gain the obvious jug on the lip and mantel like
you've never done before. A once-a-night move! A similar
problem exists just to the right.

Up and right is a small but clean wall.
Safe Bet, E1 6a, (1985), takes the left arête and short slab above;
Yabadabadoo, HVS 6b, (1985), the steep wall to the right; and
Answer the Phone, VS 5b, (1985), takes the groove right again.
All are excellent problems.

*About halfway between Ash Tree Wall and The Sentinel Area is an
isolated buttress.*
Shark's Fin Soup, HS 4c, (1986), takes this buttress.

Farther along is a prominent isolated buttress with a square top.

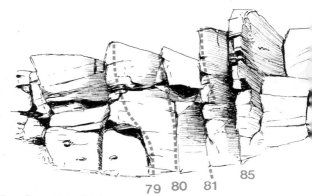

The Sentinel Area

75 The Gargoyle 8m E3 5c (1985)
The left arête of the buttress provides a worthwhile route.

76 Phillipa Buttress 8m VS 4b (1934-1951)
Go easily up to the disconcerting off-width crack which gives the substance of the route.

*The **SENTINEL AREA** is a trio of prominent arêtes 30m to the right.*

77 Stepped Crack 8m M (1957-1965)
This is the crack on the right of the slab at the left-hand end.

78 Black Slab Arête 9m HVD (1934-1951)
From halfway up Stepped Crack traverse rightwards round the arête to finish up a scoop.

* **79 Black Slab** 9m VS 4b (1934-1951)
Go thinly up the slab on the right to finish up the arête.

80 Black Slab Variation 9m D (1934-1951)
To the right climb the vague crack-line and scoop.

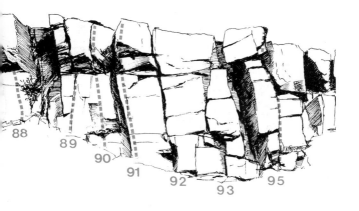

** **81 Now or Never** 12m E1 5b (1971)
Start up the layback flake on the left flank of the second arête.
When it runs out, swing round the corner to a ledge on the front
of the upper arête which is still a little tricky.

82 Too Good to be Forgotten 10m E1 6a (1987)
Take the obvious arête on the right direct to the ledge on the
previous route. Finish as you like.

† **83 Crystal Tips** 10m E4 6b (1989)
Climb the slab/block direct right of the arête. Finish on crystals.

84 Sentinel Chimney 9m D (1934-1951)
The obvious cleft left of the third and most imposing arête.

** **85 The Sentinel** 10m E2 5b (1977)
Follow the fine arête of the prow direct to a finish on good jugs.
One of the best routes in this area.

86 Sentinel Indirect 10m HVS 5a (1971)
Gain the arête via the obvious traverse line from Sentinel Crack.

87 Sentinel Crack 9m D (1934-1951)
Follow the obvious crack-line on the right of the prow past a
ledge.

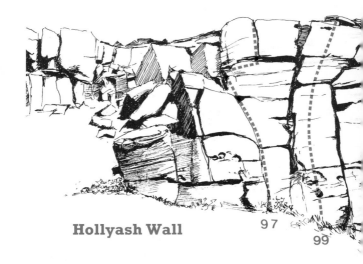

Hollyash Wall

97

99

* **88 High Flyer** 8m E3 5b (1978)
The unprotected bulge right of Sentinel Crack is climbed
trending diagonally leftwards. A confident approach is needed.
Frequently claimed over the last few years and, therefore,
hitherto known by a multiplicity of names. This however is the
definitive name, or is it?

* **89 The Grazer** 7m VS 4c (1957-1965)
A few metres right is an obvious jamming crack which splits a
steep little buttress. Well-named.

90 Lie Back 7m HS 4a (1957-1965)
'Layback and enjoy it' as they say. A vague crack leads to a
layback above the overhang.

91 Ring my Bell 8m E4 6b (1985)
Climb the left edge of the next buttress. The bulge above is
exciting.

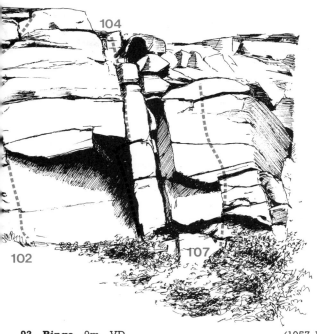

92 Ringo 9m VD (1957-1965)
Just right are two cracks; this, the left-hand one, is undercut at its base.

† **92a Ring Piece** 9m HVS 6a (1991)
The narrow face to the right leads with a hard move, and a side runner, to an easy finish.

93 Ring Climb 9m VD (1934-1951)
The second crack leads to a platform then the face above.

94 Ring Chimney 9m VD (1934-1951)
Ascend the next obvious cleft.

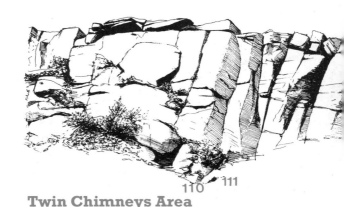

Twin Chimneys Area

95 Agnostic's Arête 8m VS 5a (1977)
The right-hand rib of the buttress is climbed on its right.

96 Pickpocket 8m VS 4c (1978-1983)
Climb the slab just to the right then go over a capping boulder.

HOLLYASH WALL *is the next large buttress; it has a prominent roof.*

97 Still Orange 14m S (1956)
Climb the corner at the left-hand end of the wall, then move right to finish up a stiff little crack.

The Keffer, HVS 5a, (1986), follows the blunt arête left of Still Orange to finish up the arête. **Rise 'n Shine**, HVS 5a, (1979), is a non- line to the right of Still Orange.

* **98 Green Crack** 12m VD (1934-1951)
Climb the obvious vertical break starting as for Still Orange.

99 Dover's Progress 12m HVS 5a (1932)
Go delicately up the slabby wall between Green Crack and Hollyash Crack. *'It is climbed direct up the centre, by minute holds. A rubbers climb.' – 1956.*

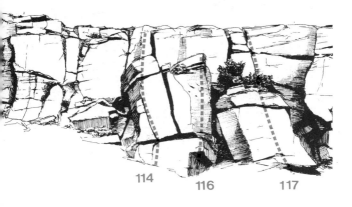

* **100 Hollyash Crack** 13m VS 4b   (1932)
Gain the crack and *'layback for a few feet, then the right arm and knee are jammed until the crack narrows, when the knee is withdrawn and jammed higher. Below the top the crack curves, and it is followed direct.'* – 1956. ... in other words, a right thrutch.

† **101 En Passant** 12m E2 6a   (1990)
The narrow face between the previous route and the next route. Holds in either route are barred.

*** **102 The Knight's Move** 15m HVS 5a   (1933)
One of the best routes hereabouts. Using 'holes' climb up to the left-hand end of the roof. Pull over this then follow the flake-line above. Move slightly rightwards to finish. An airy alternative traverses horizontally right to Great Crack; **Peter's Progress**, VS 4c, (1953).

103ₜ Arme Blanche 14m E5 6a   (1980/1981)
Climb the wall and roof right of The Knight's Move (as far right as your span allows) with a telescopic reach to gain the break. Step right at the lip and climb the slab past a bulge. A side-runner on the left offers some protection.

* **104 Great Crack** 12m VS 5a (1932)
Go up the right-hand end of the roof, which is by-passed by a hard traverse right and a fierce pull to gain the upper crack.

105 The Big Chimney 10m HVD (pre-1934)
Climb direct until progress is blocked by the capstone. This is normally avoided by stepping right to finish up a slab, but it can also be passed on the left at Severe.

106 Windjammer 10m E1 5b (1980)
Start at a cutaway in the middle of the buttress. Climb directly up and pull out to gain a traverse line leading to the left arête up which the route finishes. Needs a direct start really; any takers?

* **107 The Rainmaker** 10m HVS 5a (1977)
Start as for Windjammer but continue directly up the face trending ever-so-slightly leftwards to finish. A poor man's Wuthering?

* **108 Big Chimney Arête** 10m HS 4b (1934-1951)
Climb the arête on the right-hand side.

About 20m farther right is an isolated large nose:

109 Barry Manilow 7m VS 5a (1985)
Climb the occasionally greasy slab to surmount the nose via a pair of nostrils. What can one say?

30m or so right again is a large indefinite bay with a vegetated buttress.
Two poor routes are possible to the left; **Snow Flakes**, D, (1957-1965), and **December Climb**, VD, (1957-1965), respectively.

110 Survivor's Syndrome 7m E2 5b (1984)
Climb the left-hand arête of Twin Chimney's Layback with a final committing move. The name is apposite.

* **111 Twin Chimneys Layback** 7m HVD (1932)
This well-named left-hand corner is very pleasant.

There are two chimneys in the back wall of the recess; they are:

Ian Riddington and Geoff Radcliffe on Silent Spring, Burbage South.
Photo: Keith Sharples.

119 123

Bilberry Wall

112 Left Twin Chimney 7m D   (pre-1934)

113 Right Twin Chimney 7m VD   (pre-1934)

114 Split Slab Crack 12m S   (1957-1965)
Start on the left-hand side of the front face of the next buttress
and climb a thin crack, crux, to a ledge. Finish direct.

115 Split Slab 12m VD   (pre-1934)
Climb the buttress just to the right. Finish up the wide crack.

116 Slide-away 12m E1 5a   (1978)
The unprotected arête right of Split Slab is gained direct.

* 117 Grotto Slab 9m M   (1957-1965)
An excellent route for beginners which takes the easy-angled
slab with a holly at the top. An exciting continuation is to step
airily onto the hanging arête on the right; VD.

118 Grotto Crack 8m VS 4b   (1957-1965)
This route lurks in the angle behind the holly. Grotto indeed!

119 Falstaff's Chimney 9m HD   (pre-1934)
The chimney splits the tower just to the right.

Roy Small on Zeus, Burbage South.
Photo: Ian Smith.

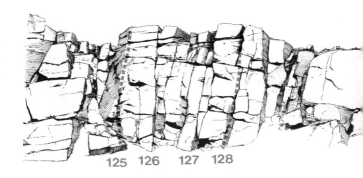

125 126 127 128

Scarred Buttress Area

120 Submission 9m HVS 5b (1978)
Start as for Falstaff's Chimney but step left and continue up the arête.

121 Falstaff's Innominate 8m S (pre-1934)
The crack just right again. *'A sinuous and indefinite crack for rubbers only.' – 1951.*

122 Falstaff's Crack 8m M (pre-1934)
The crack just right again!

Ten metres right is a wall below a small tower.

123 Bilberry Wall 10m HD (pre-1934)
Start below the tower and climb via a short crack to finish up the tower.

124 Bilberry Arête 8m S (1965-1978)
Climb the right-hand arête of the buttress.

Six metres to the right is **SCARRED BUTTRESS**.

125 The Edging Machine 6m VS 5a (1978)
The left-hand arête of the wall is distinctly problematical.

126 Alpha Crack 6m VS 4c (1934-1951)
The first crack is difficult to start.

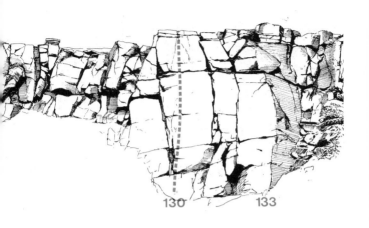

127 Omega Crack 6m VD   (1934-1951)
Two metres right is an ill-defined groove line.

128 Scarred Buttress Climb 6m HD   (1934-1951)
Two metres farther on; climb direct to the final flake.

The next buttress is split by three cracks.

* **129 First Crack** 9m S   (1957-1965)
The left-hand crack slants to the left and is awkward.

* **130 Tharf Cake** 9m HVS 5a   (1977)
The unlikely-looking slabby wall right of the crack yields more
easily than might be expected by virtue of hidden pockets.

On the right are twin cracks:

131 Left Twin Crack 9m HVD   (pre-1934)

132 Right Twin Crack 9m S   (pre-1934)

133 Farcical Arête 8m HVD   (1957-1965)
Start from the right to gain the right-hand arête of the buttress.

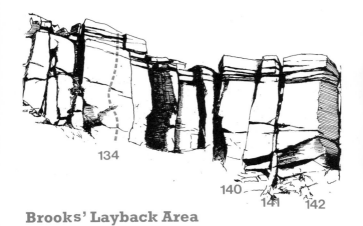

134

140

141   142

Brooks' Layback Area

The next climbs are 30m right near a small recess at the left-hand end of the longest continuous section of rock on the edge.

134   The Irrepressible Urge   6m   E1   5b   (1978)
The steep wall to the left of the recessed cracks bearing right to finish.

* **135   Small Arctic Mammal**   6m   E1   6a   (1978-1983)
Climb the arête right of Irrepressible Urge on its right-hand side without recourse to Left Recess Crack. Unfortunately close to the next route, but nevertheless a little gem which is well worth seeking out.

Immediately right again in the recess are two cracks:

136   Left Recess Crack   6m   S   (1957-1965)

137   Right Recess Crack   6m   HS   4a   (1957-1965)

138   Ace   6m   HS   4a   (1965-1978)
The rather odd-looking arête just to the right.

The crack and chimney just to the right give routes of VD and D and the sharp arête in the back of the recess proves to be a weird problem. Award yourself a 6a tick providing that your bum doesn't touch the back wall.

139 Thrall's Thrutch 7m S (1957-1965)
Right again, climb the wide crack.

** **140 Brooks' Layback** 8m VS 4b (1932)
This fine corner crack is usually jammed, but can, as the name suggests, be laybacked. The arête on its right has also been climbed at HVS 5a, but it is very contrived.

* **141 Wobblestone Crack** 8m VD (pre-1934)
The prominent fissure splitting the front face of the buttress eases towards the top.

142 Red Shift 9m E3 5c (1978)
Follow the left arête of Hollybush Gully; gaining it from the right. A somewhat bold route requiring confidence as the landing is definitely not inviting.

143 Hollybush Gully 8m HD (pre-1934)
The next feature is this square-cut gully.

* **144 The Screamer** 9m E1 5c (1978)
A steep route which follows the sinuous cracks in the right-hand wall of Hollybush Gully.

*** **145 Obscenity** 11m VS 4c (1948)
The impressive crack on the right. *'The first few feet are delicate until the crack can be entered – then 20 feet of very strenuous jamming until the crack narrows to a overhang. This is very hard to overcome as the feet tend to leave the rock, but once a standing position above the overhang is attained the remainder is easy.' –
1956.*

** **146 Amazon Crack** 11m HS 4a (1932)
To the right again is another fine jamming crack. A little easier than Obscenity but not quite so fine.

147 Amazon Gully 9m M (1934-1951)

148 Boney Moroney 9m E1 5c (1969)
The imposing-looking thin crack in the flat arête to the right is mostly avoided by using holds around to the left. Sadly somewhat disappointing after the start.

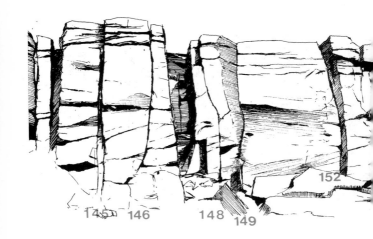

* **149 Long Tall Sally** 10m E1 5b (1960-1965)
The superb shallow corner, which bounds the next bay on its left
gives a delectable little climb at the lower limit of its grade. This
North Burbage classic is very often many climbers' first Extreme
and as such it is a cherished memory. Becoming polished and 5c.

Rockers, E1 5c, (1985), starts up the previous route but once
over the bulge swings out left on to the arête which it then
follows to the top.

Right again is a fine slab which is taken by the next route.

† **150 Short Fat Bar Star** 10m E4 6a (1988)
Climb the gully on the right of the slab until it is possible to move
left and go over the bulge onto the slab proper. Tiptoe left and
climb the centre of the slab. Serious climbing, poorly protected
by very small nuts.

* **151 Greeny Crack** 10m VS 4b (1934-1951)
The right-hand corner crack has good holds and is worthwhile
despite its name and colour.

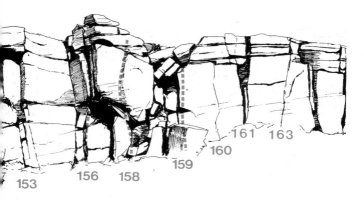

153   156   158   159   160   161   163

Obscenity Area

About 50m below this area is a cave formed by large boulders.
The left-hand crack proves to be 6a, as does the right-hand
crack. Both have good landings.

Returning back to the main edge is:

152   Rhapsody in Green   10m   VS   5a   (1978)
The prow right of Greeny Crack is gained by a delicate start.

153   Left Studio Climb   8m   VD   (pre-1934)
Follow a thin crack three metres right to a ledge. Climb the arête
on the right and a crack above to finish. A slightly harder
alternative exits left to finish up an open crack.

154   Right Studio Climb   8m   VD   (pre-1934)
Start just left of the recess below the very prominent fin. Go up
the crack to a ledge then finish up the corner.

* **155   Rose Flake**   8m   VS   4b   (1958)
From the ledge on the previous route step right to the left-hand
of two impressive cracks on the wall left of the fin.

* **156 The Fin** 8m E1 5b (1970/1971)
The ferocious hanging crack is difficult to enter but relents a little higher up.

* **157 Ai No Corrida** 8m E5 6b (1984)
The undercut arête right of The Fin is climbed using holds on its right-hand side. Utterly desperate and quite serious despite side-runners in the next route.

* **158 Right Fin** 8m HVS 5a (1957-1965)
The flake on the right-hand side of the fin becomes increasingly difficult until a long reach brings good finishing holds. A fine short route.

Just past **THE FIN** *is a slabby wall with several cracks, some of which are more definite than others.*

159 The Enthusiast 6m HVS 6a (1978-1987)
Climb the left-hand edge of the wall using the arête and a thin crack; usually very frustrating, a fact borne out by the heavily used landing.

* **160 Nicotine Stain** 6m E1 6b (1983)
A good problem up the thin crack left of April Fool. Again desperately frustrating unless you hit the right sequence straight off. This is more likely to feel like E2 6c, but then that's life!

161 April Fool 6m HD (1957-1965)
The first real crack on the wall! Its left arête provides a fine 5b layback problem.

162 Approach 6m HVS 5c (1978)
Some good moves on pockets, pebbles, and rugosities provide a way up the wall on the right.

* **163 Spider Crack** 6m VS 5b (1957-1965)
The thin crack two metres right proves to be both technical and fingery.

The next two cracks are both VD. Between them is a tricky problem, **Pest Control**, 6b, (1985).

30m beyond these is the final buttress of note on the North Edge.

164 End Buttress 9m M (1957-1965)
Start up the wide crack and finish up the slab left of the arête.

165 The Penultimate 9m E1 5b   (1977)
The wall to the right of, and avoiding, the aforementioned arête
has a tricky start.

End Slab, M, (1957-1965), is the obvious easy slab on the right.

*20m right of End Slab are two buttresses separated by a wide
chimney.*

166 Ender 8m D   (1965-1978)
This is the left-hand buttress starting up an awkward wide crack.

167 Endste 8m D   (1965-1978)
Climb the right-hand buttress.

*The edge now deteriorates, although some good sport may be had
on the boulders farther to the right. The next crags to be described
are South Burbage and the quarries. If you have 'climbed down'
Burbage North you may be tempted to continue on to South
Burbage, just to irritate you, the climbs there are described from
right to left. Either; read backwards, run down to the far end and
work your way towards Burbage North, or better still call it a day
and have a well-earned pint in the Norfolk Arms!*

BURBAGE QUARRIES and SOUTH EDGE

O.S. ref. SK 265808 to SK 269813

by Keith Sharples

SITUATIONS and CHARACTER

Compared to the North Edge, the quarries and the South Edge are sombre, imposing and altogether more majestic. Their north-western outlook means that the sun doesn't strike the rocks until late in the day; they can be a wonderful place to spend a summer evening. Rarely are they as crowded as their northern neighbour, consequently an hour or two after work spent soloing in solitude is an experience to be savoured.

The quarries, perhaps more so than most others, are confined slits in the hillside. As the quarry tops are at the same level as the surrounding moor, there is no great depth of overlying earth and only a few of the routes suffer from seepage. In the middle of summer they are a cool and pleasant sanctuary, although after rain they can become midge-infested pits especially if there is no breeze. During the winter and early spring they are dank, gloomy and foreboding places (such lavish praise!). Almost without exception the routes are impressive and don't give much away without a fight. Some, especially those on the edge, are amongst the most brutal, technically demanding and serious on gritstone anywhere. As often as not, even the easy routes are hard. The hard ones remain downright impossible for all but a few!

APPROACHES and ACCESS

The quarries and the South Edge are most easily approached from Hathersage Road, the A625 main Sheffield to Hathersage Road. Cars can be left at the obvious park several hundred metres down from the Fox House Inn. The SYT bus routes 240, 272, and the Trent 244 all stop at the Fox House.

From the car park, pass through the gate at the southern end of the Green Drive and either follow this for several hundred metres and then strike up the hillside to the crags, or take an indistinct path leading off rightwards up the hillside once through the gate. Follow this up to a better path which then contours round into the quarries.

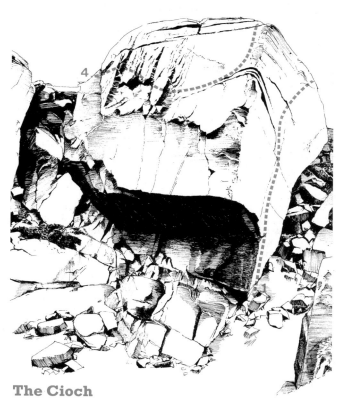

The Cioch

THE CLIMBS are described from RIGHT to LEFT. The first major feature, **THE CIOCH**, is a huge overhanging block, riddled with old bolts and other memorabilia from the bygone age of gritstone aid climbing. The Cioch marks the entrance to the South Quarry.

SOUTHERN QUARRY

† **1 Captain Invincible** 15m E8 6c (1991)
Start at the lowest point on the valley side of the block. Climb the
arête to the base of an obvious hanging groove and two poor
pegs. Climb up the groove, past good pegs, until it is possible to
pull on to the front face, past another peg, to gain a partial rest
and small wires. Move leftwards along the break/crack-line to an
undercut, then go up to Offspring and finish up this.

* **1a Offspring** 11m E5 6b (1985)
A fine route offering powerful climbing in a superb position. It is
usually approached by abseiling down the impressive hanging
arête of The Cioch, fixing nuts on the arête and being belayed
from the ground. From the arête traverse rightwards to climb a
small hanging groove with some considerable effort. It has been
used as a continuation pitch for Silent Spring.

† **2 Masters of the Universe** 12m E7 6c (1988)
This route follows the actual hanging arête of The Cioch itself.
Abseil down the route to start (as for Offspring). Begin beside a
cluster of old bolts (for bolts read rust!) just above the lip of the
roof and get established on the rock at a prominent foothold
1.5m left of the arête. Traverse right with hands on a sloping
shelf, then move around the arête and then up and on to the
shelf. Continue up and rightwards into a little scoop and finish
easily. Friends useful in the final break.

† **3 Grooveamarionation** 12m E4 6b (1988)
Free-climbs the upper half of the old aid route nine metres left of
Masters… Abseil to the lip of the roof and follow the line of old
bolts (a wire is needed on each bolt) directly through the
traverse of Silent Spring. Falling is strictly inadvisable. Definitely
not a sport climb in any sense of the expression!

* **4 Silent Spring** 27m E4 5c,5c (1975)
An excellent, exposed route which girdles The Cioch, starting
high up the gully on the left of the block. The second pitch is
riddled with old bolts but most are unlikely to offer any 'real'
protection.
1. 8m. Follow the thin break to the arête and continue on to the
face to belay on a ledge. It is best to belay on a hanging rope.
2. 19m. Climb rightwards and gain a standing position on a
spike; reverse mantelshelf. It is worth just having a look at this

'spike' and trying to imagine just what is holding it on! If it scares you to death then lower-off and head straight to the limestone dales or down-town to the gym. Still interested?... then finger-traverse right with better protection to finish just left of the arête.

5 Quarry Gully 14m M   (1934-1951)
The dirty gully in the back right-hand corner of the quarry.

* **6 The Dover and Ellis Chimney** 15m E1 5b   (1932)
'This cleft is in the very centre of the quarry and gives a magnificent climb, steep and very exposed.' – Exceptionally Severe, 1956. Climb the prominent corner left of Quarry Gully to a sandy ledge. *'The crack and chimney then curve out to the right and upwards and proves awkward to start, after 8 feet it eases a little although the tension remains to the end.' – 1956.* Often very sandy, especially after rain.

7 Noble Rot 15m E2 5c   (1972)
Climb the acute corner and thin crack just left to a bay. Wander off up easy ground to finish.

8 Creaking Flakes 18m VS 4c   (1964)
Climb the large flake three metres left of Noble Rot and continue to a bay. Finish as for Noble Rot.

9 Gardener's Wall 11m HVS 5a,5b   (1964)
1. 5m. Climb a slanting crack two metres left to a terrace.
2. 6m. Finish up a thin crack in the back wall.

10 The Ramp 11m HVS 5a,4c   (1964)
1. 5m. Left again is another slanting crack; climb this to the terrace.
2. 6m. Finish up a wide crack above.

* **11 Poisoned Dwarf** 8m HVS 5c   (1965-1978)
The peg-scarred crack just left of the quarry entrance.

12 Shattered Cracks 11m D   (1934-1951)
Ascend just left of the previous route.

13 Bracken Crack 11m VD   (1957-1965)
Two metres left again.

** **14 The Simpering Savage** 18m E5 6b,5a   (1981)
1. 10m. Climb up Bracken Crack for 3m, then hand-traverse the thin break leftwards with some difficulty, peg, into The Old Bailey. Those with fingers like sausages are in for a tough time!

2. 8m. From the loose blocks, move up until a traverse left can be made to finish up The Verdict.

15 The Old Bailey 14m HVS 5b (1950-1956)
Climb loose blocks in the corner and the overhanging crack above. Awkward.

11 10 9 8 7 6

Eastern Wall: Southern Quarry

* **16 The Verdict** 11m E2 6a (1972)
Climb the all-too-obvious V-shaped groove left of the previous route, with the initial few metres providing the crux. Follow the awkward continuation crack to the top.

17 G.B.H. 8m E3 6a (1981)
Three metres left climb a thin flake crack in the slightly overhanging wall.

50m left is the:

NORTHERN QUARRY

On the right of the quarry entrance is a small rib with a small right-angled bay on its left.
Right of the rib is a short crack, S, and up the front of the rib are two short cracks, VD. The rib is taken on its left-hand side by **R9**, HVS 5b, (1982).

* **18 Burssola** 8m HVS 5b (1975)
The thin crack in the right wall of the right-angled bay, three metres left of the arête.

19 Spyhole Crack 8m VD (1957-1965)
Climb an easy gully to a ledge and continue up an overhanging wall on more than adequate holds.

20 Giant's Staircase 11m VD (1934-1951)
A ramp lower down on the same wall and sloping leftwards leads to a crack in the right-angled corner, then reach a ledge on the right and finish up easy rock.

21 Scoop Crack 12m VS 4b (1951)
Climb the crack in the corner of the bay to a large ledge. Move well left and climb another corner to a swing right into a scoop which is followed to the top.

22 Cardinal's Backbone 14m HVS 5a (1973-1979)
Climb the steep jamming crack just left of Scoop Crack then step right to Giant's Staircase, and follow it until an awkward ramp leads out left to the scoop. The imposing final tower on the right has excellent holds. For the second pitch first traverse several kilometres south to Curbar Edge!

† **Middle-aged Mutant Ninja Birtles**, E3 6a, (1991), is a poor girdle across Millwheel Wall going from right to left.

·* **23 Millwheel Wall** 12m E1 5b (1958)
Climb the awkward arête on the left to a large ledge. Ascend the wall above starting in the centre and trending rightwards on

---

Right: Bill Dark on Long Tall Sally, North Burbage.
Photo: Ian Smith.
Overleaf: Shaun Hutson on Pebble Mill, South Burbage.
Photo: Ian Smith.

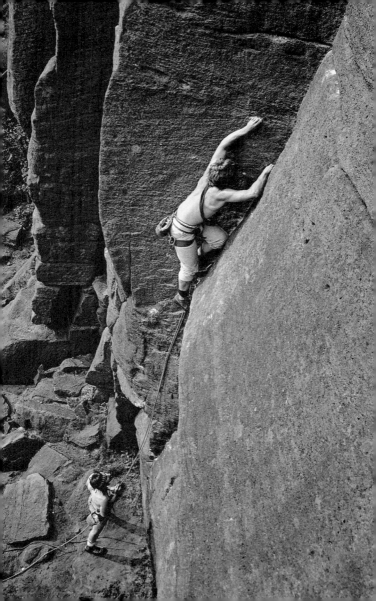

improving holds. A classic route of the quarries but unprotected so a steady approach is advocated. The crux is at mid-height.

† **24 Hell for Leather** 12m E4 6c (1984)
An adventurous climb. As for Millwheel Wall to the ledge then, starting on the right of that route, climb up the precarious scoop which leads to the finish of Millwheel Wall itself. Catching team advisable!

* **25 Pretzel Logic** 12m E3 6a (1979)
If you succeeded on Millwheel Wall, but still need more adrenaline?... try this. Follow Millwheel Wall to the ledge. Start in the centre of the wall then trend slightly leftwards to finish just right of the arête.

Cartwheel Wall, E2 5c, (1985), starts as for Pretzel Logic but continues directly up the centre of the face left of Millwheel Wall. Hardly independent.

* **26 Dunkley's Eliminate** 11m VS 4c (1957-1965)
Step off the millwheel onto the centre of the big ledge. Make a rising traverse leftwards to the arête and follow this first on its right and then on its left. Quite exposed, the VS equivalent of Millstone's Edge Lane.

27 Flaked Out 11m E4 5c (1980)
On the left of the arête, and just inside the quarry proper, climb a thin crack to a break. Go up left to a hollow flake, using holds on the left wall to get established on the flake, and go straight up to finish.

28 Broken Crack 9m S (1934-1951)
Climb the double cracks left of the previous route to a ledge, and finish up the wide crack facing right.

* **29 Twin Cracks** 9m VS 4c (1957-1965)
Two metres left is a ramp; climb this to a ledge, move slightly left to the cracks and follow these to a difficult finish.

30 Broken Wall 12m VD (1957-1965)
Climb the ramp as for Twin Cracks and move left to a grassy ledge. From the left-hand end of this follow a short crack to finish.

Previous Page: Shaun Hutson soloing The Boggart, South Burbage.
Photo Ian Smith.
Left: Joe Brown on the 'epoch-making' first ascent of The Rasp, Higgar Tor.

31 Connoisseur's Crack 9m HVS 5b   (1976)
Ascend the thin crack left of Twin Cracks. Well-named; seen any
connoisseurs lately?

32 Prince Tarquin 9m E2 5b   (1978)
Start two metres left and climb up the centre of the large flake to
its top. Go up the wall above to an atrocious finish. Belay well
back. Often greasy, has some suspect holds, and is becoming
overgrown thank God!

The next two obvious lines to the left are **Shale**, D, (1957-1965),
an unpleasant crack, and **Corner Chimney**, E, (1957-1965),
which gives an easy way down. Don't panic, this isn't E for
Extreme, rather a good old-fashioned Easy.

33 Longest Day 7m HVS 5a   (1984)
The wall right of Corner Chimney.

34 Nice and Tasty 7m HVS 5b   (1984)
The wall left of Corner Chimney, finishing up a short crack.

35 Valk Corner 8m S   (1951)
The groove which cuts off the arête on the left.

Passing a thin, searing, unclimbed crack-line (form an orderly
queue please) *the next route is:*

36 Sand Chimney 11m VD   (1957-1965)
The chimney to the left.

37 Bashed Crab meets Dr Barnard 14m E4 6a (1982)
Climb large ledges to a thin crack in a corner, just right of
Coldest Crack. Bridge to the crack and finish as for Coldest
Crack. Runners in Coldest Crack are frowned upon. Serious and
seldom climbed, and when you see it you'll know why.

* **38 Coldest Crack** 14m E2 5c   (1976)
Follow the thin crack, five metres left of the chimney, to a hard
move leading to a ledge. A worthwhile climb in good conditions.

39 Curving Chimney 12m VD   (1934-1951)
The right-hand corner chimney in the back wall of the quarry.

40 Odin's Piles 12m HVS 4c   (1980-1983)
The loose corner leads to a 'weetabix' finish. No belay. This
route replaces Valhalla which now lies in a heap at the bottom of
the crag. It was said of Valhalla that *'The whole route is strenuous*

and its upper section is on rock of doubtful stability.' – 1965. One can only marvel that Odin's Piles is still standing!

Left again is a long, and often wet, overhanging wall which may, or may not, have some in-situ pegs in it.

† **41 Stockbroker in the Woodpile** 10m E5 6b   (1987)
Towards the left-hand end of the wall is a short thin crack protected by two pegs. Starting up this climb right from the top peg, then move back left on undercut flakes. The pegs are not in place at the time of writing...yes they are... no they aren't!

Beyond this are two small corners on either side of an arête, one of which has a small perched block.

42 Perched Block Route 12m HVS 4c   (1934-1951)
This aptly named route follows the right-hand corner past a perched block to a ledge. Gain a sloping ledge on the right, then go right again to the arête. Climb this on loose holds. It is possible to finish above the sloping ledge at 5a.

43 The Cock 12m VS 4c   (1960-1965)
Ascend the left-hand corner and its easier continuation crack.

Disbeliever, E1 5b, (1982), follows the wall left of The Cock then goes left to finish up the wall right of Hades.

** **44 Fox House Flake** 14m VS 4b   (1934)
Climb the obvious slanting crack, running across the slab on the left, and finish as for The Cock.

** **45 Hades** 11m HVS 5b   (1960-1965)
An awkward route up the crack in the slanting corner on the left.

*** **46 Zeus** 11m E2 5b   (1969)
The slanting crack left of Hades proves a good test of stamina and determination, and is one of the best routes hereabouts. Belay well back; behind the bar at the Fox House is a good place!

47 The Great Flake Route 23m D   (1934-1951)
Left of Zeus is a blocky corner and beyond that, just outside the quarry, is an obvious chimney. Climb this to a large ledge and traverse along it to block belays. Continue to a sloping groove then follow this to the top. A start can also be made up the blocky corner.

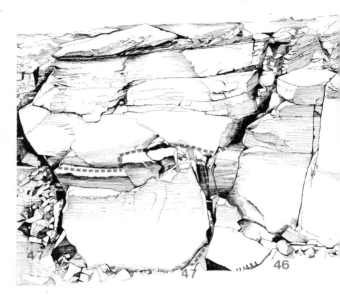

† **48 Hidden in the Midden** 11m E2 5c (1980)
Start at the aforementioned block belays. From the top of these
make dynamic moves leftwards along the break, past a short
crack, to finish up and diagonally leftwards.

49 Deception 9m HVS 5c (1976)
Nine metres left of Great Flake Chimney is a thin crack in a
broken corner; follow it direct. A poor route.

BURBAGE SOUTH

*35m left of the Northern Quarry is another quarried face up which
the first route on the South Edge finds it way.*

THE CLIMBS are described from RIGHT to LEFT.

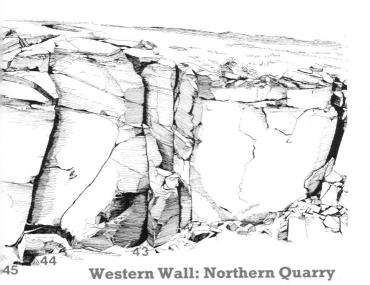

45 44   43

Western Wall: Northern Quarry

1 Saul 12m VS 5b   (1964)
Start at the right-hand side of a smooth wall to the left of a spoil
heap. Climb polished holds to a ledge, crux, mantelshelf onto
the ledge, then walk left for about 3m, before finishing direct.

† **2 Rollerwall** 10m E5 6c   (1987)
Just left of Saul is an obvious line of once-chipped holds which
have now been filled in with cement. Follow these directly to join
the finish of Saul. Short but sharp finger-nasty crimping – ugh!

*** **3 Messiah** 8m E6 6c   (1984)
The formidable right arête of the next buttress will almost
certainly need help from above. It will make exacting demands
on one's technical repertoire (it's bloody desperate!). A Friend
half is also said to be of help.

4 Sling Shot 15m HVS 5b   (1984)
On the left a ramp rises up leftwards into the next route. Follow
the ramp then a horizontal break to gain the top of Goliath.

* **5 David** 8m HVS 4c (1951-1956)
The right-hand of two wide cracks is laybacked past a
chockstone.

* **6 Goliath** 8m E5 6a (1958)
The left-hand crack is one of the hardest offwidths in the country.
Relatively easy climbing allows a shelf to be gained at just less
than half-height. From then on progress is horrendous and
committing. Either wedge yourself inwards then upwards or
layback, probably with your eyes closed, until the top brings
relief. In the unlikely event of a queue, pass quickly on to:

Goliath Area

** **7 Above and Beyond the Kinaesthetic Barrier**

6m E4 6b (1976)

The left-hand arête of the buttress is gained from a hole on the left and then followed direct. A short, yet punishing and technical route which has reached classic status. The arête can be climbed direct all the way, although this is obviously harder, (6c).

8 The Disappearing Bust of Voltaire 6m VS 5a (1977)

Climb the short crack across from and facing Above and Beyond.

* **9 Dork Child** 8m E1 5c (1976)

Down and left is a long slabby arête. Climb this, then the wall above with a long reach at the crux. Finish just left of the arête.

10 Goblin 8m D   (1957-1965)
The corner just left is taken to a ledge, followed by the wide
crack above.

*Nine metres left is a prominent arête rising the full height of a
larger buttress. To the right of this the ground slopes up to a large
boulder, above which is a short arête:*

† **11 Midget Tart** 5m E4 6b   (1987)
Step off the boulder and pull onto the short arête. Follow this to
the top with a degree of trepidation: are you put off yet?
Originally climbed with side-runners, it has been soloed to give
a short but serious route. Destined for obscurity?

12 We Ain't Gonna Pay No Toll 9m E5 6b   (1987)
Climb the steep wall down and to the left, a traditional boulder
problem, until it is possible to traverse a thin break leftwards to
join Pebble Mill on its small ledge. Finish up that route. Another
poor eliminate.

* **13 Pebble Mill** 11m E5 6b   (1976)
Head and shoulders above the rest. Climb the left-hand side of
the arête to the obvious horizontal break (the crux for tall
climbers), then swing up and right to a no-hands rest on small
ledges. Pause for a while then, before your courage leaves you
or it goes dark, make a long reach for a distant horizontal break
(the crux for short climbers). An alternative start is to layback the
arête on its right-hand side. This is slightly harder but feels
infinitely less committing. The ledge before the last hard section
is big enough to stand around on. If you look hard enough you
can always see rain clouds gathering in the west, which is as
good an excuse as any for a top rope!

14 Wazzock 9m S   (1964)
Climb the crack which bounds the face on its left.

15 The Birth of Liquid Desires 6m HVS 5a   (1977)
Another surreal gem; this one goes directly up the wall left of
Wazzock.

16 Lino 6m HVS 5b   (1964)
Nine metres left is a steep slab with a small overhang at the top.
Climb the right-hand arête of the slab as closely as possible.

* **17 Limmock** 8m HVS 5b (1964)
Polished holds lead up the centre of the slab to a small flake, and
a long reach for the horizontal break. Move slightly left then go
up past the overhang to finish. Not to be missed.

18 Broddle 6m VS 4c (1964)
Ascend the left-hand arête of the slab.

Down and left of this buttress are some good problems on
obvious boulders.
Some 32m left is a dark hole containing a short buttress.

19 Doddle 8m M (1957-1965)
Start at the right-hand edge of the slab and climb direct. A
harder variation finishes left between two overhangs.

The roof crack appearing out of the hole at the start of the
previous route is worth doing.
*75m farther on, a path crosses the edge. Just left of the path is an
undercut buttress rising from a hollow.*

20 Walker's Pulpit 9m VS 4b (1934-1951)
From the path follow large ledges leftwards to a pulpit. Finish by
making a long reach from the top of the pulpit. This can be
avoided by continuing the traverse, making the route VD.

21 Parson's Crack 9m VS 4b (1957-1965)
From the left-hand side of the hollow, climb a thin slanting crack
to a ledge. Gain the pulpit on its left and finish as for Walker's
Pulpit, or move left, S.

† **22 Booby Prize** 9m E3 6b (1982)
Starting right of the large corner, climb the centre of the wall
past a huge reach (not in situ) to finish direct. Originally a real
sand-bag route at HVS.

** **23 The Drainpipe** 9m S 4a (1957-1965)
The corner crack just left is strenuous but well-protected.

24 The Staircase 9m HS 4a (1934-1951)
Follow a line of cracks just left of the arête. The difficult middle
section can be avoided by climbing the wall on the left. Don't be
put off just because it looks harder; it isn't. The arête itself yields
a poor VS climb.

25 Ribbed Corner 8m M (1951)
Follow either of the cracks left of the protruding ribs and
continue up the shallow chimney above.

26 Unfinished Symphony 8m HVS 5b   (1974)
From the top of the lower rib, climb the widening crack in the left wall of the corner. Strenuous but well-protected.

* **27 No Zag** 8m HVS 5a   (1957-1965)
Four metres left is a rightward-curving flake in the centre of the wall. Follow this to a horizontal break, then move right to finish up the awkward crack. Strenuous, and a good test of jamming skills.

28 Zig-Zag 9m VS 4c   (1957-1965)
As for No Zag to the break; traverse this leftwards, round the arête, until a finish up the gully wall is possible.

29 Less Bent 6m S   (1965-1978)
Climb the arête left of the curving flake to meet and follow Zig-Zag.

The next buttress has two wide cracks on its left and a thin one on the right.

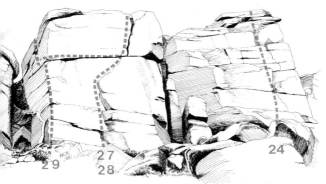

Nosferatu Area

30 Nick Knack Paddywack 8m E2 6b   (1982)
On the extreme right of the wall is a short flake; make a hard
move up this to a horizontal break. Hand-traverse left to a good
foothold and climb the wall direct; hard for the short.
The direct start, **Old MacDonald**, 6a, (1982). Pull up from the
foot of The Knack, then move up and rightwards to reach the first
break of N.K.P. at its left-hand end.

* **31 The Knack** 8m E1 5c   (1971)
Make hard moves up the wall to reach a thin crack, which,
although it eases somewhat towards the top, still commands
respect.

32 Nathaniel 9m HVS 5b   (1951)
This hideous bulging fissure is the right-hand of two wide cracks.
Climb it to a resting ledge and prepare for battle.

33 The Attitude Inspector 9m E4 6c   (1979)
The overhanging wall and arête left of Nathaniel. A dynamic start
above an ankle-snapping boulder (sounds great doesn't it) leads
to a ledge and protection (chockstone in Nathaniel). Climb the
wall above to finish.

* **34 Reginald** 9m VS 4b   (1951)
Climb large blocks to the steep corner chimney which has good
holds but is strenuous. Move right where it narrows.

* **35 Nosferatu** 11m E6 6b   (1980)
Utterly desperate. From a fallen monolith climb the left-hand
side of the arête with a very hard move/jump to gain a ledge.
Move right and finish up the hanging arête. The monolith isn't
the only thing to have fallen off this route, so be warned!

* **36 Sorb** 9m E2 5c   (1976)
From the left-hand arête of the buttress climb up to a long pocket
which leads to a ledge. Finish straight up with a phenomenal
reach (harder) or move left to finish on the arête.

*Down and to the left a large block, which has many boulder
problems, leans against the edge. The next route is at its
right-hand edge of the block.*

37 The Big Dipper 18m HVD   (1957-1965)
From a block gain and climb the slab. Descend the other side.
Step onto an exposed rib and climb it to a short finishing crack.
The polished corner right of the rib is harder and less amusing.

38 Pie and Chips 6m E1 6a   (1987)
The wall right of Pythagoras, starting at an obvious good hold.

39 Pythagoras 6m HS 4b   (1957-1965)
The right-hand corner of the box-like recess.

40 Shooting Star 6m HVS 5b   (1978)
The wall between Pythagoras and Surprise is climbed without
recourse to either route. Strenuous but protectable.

41 Surprise 6m VD   (1957-1965)
The wide left-hand crack is quite pleasant.

42 Movie Star 8m HVS 5a   (1978)
Swing onto the face left of Surprise, via a large hold three metres
up that route, and climb the wall, moving right to finish up the
arête. More suited to a sleazy down-town cinema than the West
End.

43 Castor 8m S 4a   (1957-1965)
Left again are twin cracks high up; this is the right twin.

44 Pollux 8m HS 4b   (1957-1965)
The left-hand twin is often dirty.

45 Vulcan 9m VD   (1957-1965)
Just left, gain a sloping ledge by a rising leftwards traverse.
Climb the corner and finish up a crack right of a small slab.

46 The Iron Hand 9m S   (1957-1965)
The crack just left, starting at a small pedestal.

47 Dowel Crack 8m VS 4c   (1964)
The impressive corner crack has a hard upper section.

48 Fade Away 8m E1 6a   (1982)
From the ledge at the foot of Dowel Crack, lean out left on to the
face and climb up the left-hand arête to a large hold. Move
slightly left and go up the wall, passing a large pocket to finish.
Unprotected and dirty but escapable in its upper reaches.

49 Macleod's Crack 8m VD   (1934-1951)
The crack just left is hardest at the start. **Lapwing Variation**, HS,
goes rightwards from the bulge onto the wall, passing a pocket.

50 Recurring Nightmare 8m E5 6b   (1982)
Climb the rib on the left to a frightening finishing move. The lack
of gear and the obligatory bad landing should help to
concentrate the mind. If it doesn't, then don't say you haven't
been warned!

51 Ladder Gully 9m M   (1934-1951)
The obvious gully just to the left.

Connolly's Variation, 10m, M, (1934-1951). From the ledge
half-way up Ladder Gully, crawl through the cave on the left into
a crevasse. Climb out by a pleasant slab.

Just left is a coffin-like recess with a short wall on its right.
Both the arêtes on the short wall are 5b, although the right-hand
arête can be done on its right-hand side at 6a.

52 Gog 11m S   (1951)
The crack in the right-hand corner of the recess is taken to a
swing right to finish up a slab and large ledges on the left. No
push-over.

53 Magog 11m HVS 5a   (1951)
The left-hand corner of the recess is climbed to a large ledge.
Finish up the creaking flake above.

54 Slow Ledge 11m VS 4c   (1965-1978)
From the left-hand arête of the recess, move up and left to a
ledge. Finish as for Magog.

The wall on the left overhangs slightly and is a little undercut. A
powerful and often frustrating problem follows this wall to the
obvious ledge.

* **55 Captain Sensible** 8m E1 5b   (1977)
Left of the left-hand arête of Magog Buttress is a line of thin
flakes. Follow these to a tricky finish. A mini-classic.

† **56 Bath-house Pink** 8m E4 6c   (1987)
Just left is a desperate-looking blank slab. Unfortunately it not
only looks desperate, but it is. Good luck!

*The next few buttresses are the largest and most imposing on the
edge. The right-hand buttress,* **THE KEEP**, *contains the next few
routes.*

* **57 Keep Crack** 11m VS 5a   (1960-1965)
The corner crack leads to a large platform. Finish up a short
crack behind a pedestal. A tough nut to crack, but it is probably
a tougher crack to nut.

·* **58 The Knock** 9m E5 6a   (1975)
The arête left of Keep Crack gives bold, elegant and poorly
protected climbing. Start slightly left of the arête and follow good
finger holds until a 'span' out right to the arête is possible. Move
up quickly to the break. This unfortunately provides an excellent
place not only to stop but also to get pumped and gripped whilst
desperately seeking holds above. Either get rescued, jump off,
or close your eyes and do the scary move for the top. It is
possible to place small wires in the break which may or may not
protect the last move.

† **59 Who's There? Titan's Grandma** 6m E3 6b   (1982)
On the ledge above The Knock, a short wall and slab on the left is
climbed up its centre. Nuts placed in the crack behind the
pedestal stop one falling all the way to the ground – but not to
the ledge.

† **60 Ron. Ring Home!** 9m E5 6c   (1986)
The wall left of The Knock provides a testing sequence of moves
on thin holds. Unfortunately (or fortunately) it is escapable. The
exact relationship with the next route is not yet clear.

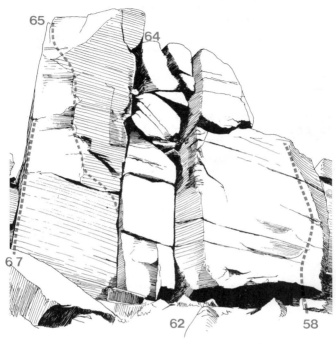

The Keep

† **61 The Searing** 9m E3 6c   (1987)
Climb the right-hand side of the very blunt right arête of the next
route to a curving crack. Follow the crack to better holds and a
mantelshelf. Runners in the highest break on the arête protect
the crux.

*** **62 Byne's Crack** 14m VS 4b   (1934)
The right-hand of the two imposing cracks gives classic jamming
up to a niche at half-height. It then widens out and a little
laybacking leads to the top.

63 Combined Heroes 14m E2 5c (1983)
Climb the right arête of the next route, then move right along the
break to below thin leftwards-slanting parallel cracks; climb
these until it is possible to crawl into the hole on Brooks' Crack.
Move right into Byne's Crack and finish up this. Poor and
contrived.

∗ **64 Brooks' Crack** 14m HVS 5a (1934)
Climb the steep leftward-facing corner below the left-hand crack
until an awkward pull leads to the start of the crack proper.
Higher up, the crack is both strenuous and sustained.

On the left is a magnificent hanging prow; 'as seen on TV'.

† **65 Parthian Shot** 15m E9 7a (1989)
Follow Brooks' Crack for 6m, move left then with a huge dyno
gain the hanging flake above (side-runners used on the first
ascent). Place very poor small nuts in the loose flake, then press
on to the top and the crux. Very serious, hard climbing giving a
totally committing route of the highest calibre. One of the most
serious routes in the country. Worth three stars and one or two
daggers of anybody's money! (It is also possible to start from the
left and avoid the dyno.)

66 Easy Traverse 14m HVS 5b (1969)
And why not? Traverse the buttress rightwards along the
obvious break from half-way up Brooks' Crack to finish up the
corner of Keep Crack. Another route which is destined to be
forgotten.

The left-hand wall of The Keep gives **Byne's Flake**, a short
layback. Above is an impressive wall taken by The Braille Trail.
First however is:

† **67 Blinded by Science** 8m E4 6a (1979)
Climb the right-hand side of the short arête below The Braille
Trail past a sloping break. Traverse left to exit at the top of
Byne's Flake.

∗ **68 The Braille Trail** 10m E7 6c (1984)
An audacious route combining technically demanding climbing
with poor peg protection across the wall right of Byne's Flake.
From the flake, traverse right (two poor hand-placed pegs in
slots) to gain a sloping rest ledge on the arête (first crux).

Andy Pollitt on first ascent of Masters of The Universe, Burbage South Quarry.
Photo: Neil Foster.

Swallow hard and climb up the wall to a crack (second crux) just left of the arête. Follow this to finish. Now considerably harder than when originally climbed as some pebbles have come away.

The cracks left The of Braille Trail are HVS 5a.

69   Tower Chimney   11m   M   (1934-1951)
The chimney in the back left-hand corner of the amphitheatre leads to a finish under the chockstone.

On the left is a large buttress, **THE TOWER,** *which has an obvious niche below the top.*

70   Yoghurt   14m   E3   6b   (1980-1983)
The right-hand arête of The Tower is taken to a ledge by hard moves above a bad landing. Walk off rightwards or finger-traverse leftwards into The Boggart and finish up this. Needs a direct finish.

** **71   The Boggart**   12m   E2   6b   (1960-1965/1975)
Running down from the aforementioned niche are twin cracks. From the right-hand of these, a horizontal crack runs right to meet a thin crack starting above the ground. Hitherto this was gained by *'using a shoulder insert a small nut in the indefinite crack and step into the sling.' – 1965.* Nowadays reach this by hard fingery climbing, then move up and go left along the horizontal to the start of the bigger right-hand crack. Climb this to the niche and the top. Thankfully the upper crack, though pressing, is much easier.

72   Boggart Left-hand   12m   E4   5c-6a   (1976)
The left-hand crack below the niche is reached, or not as the case may be, from the base of Tower Crack. E2 with a runner in Tower Crack.

* **73   Tower Crack**   12m   HVS   5a   (1957)
The right-hand of three cracks just left of The Tower leads to a small ledge. Finish up the obvious layback flake on the right.

74   Tower Climb   12m   HS   (1934)
Climb either, or both, of the other cracks to the ledge. Follow a chimney for three metres then finish up a diagonal crack on the right wall.

Keith Sharples, The Simpering Savage, Burbage South.
Photo: Ian Smith.

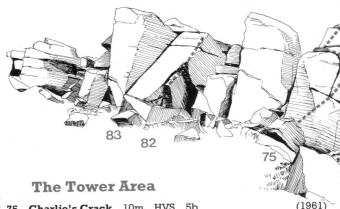

83   82   75

The Tower Area

* **75 Charlie's Crack**   10m   HVS   5b   (1961)
The sickle-shaped crack up the bulge and slab on the left is
gained with difficulty from the boulder on the left. Follow this to
finish with lethargy. This route has been claimed by more
climbers than almost any other route. This should now be
considered the definitive line and name!

† **76 Life Assurance**   10m   E6   6b   (1986)
Start as for Charlie's Crack but continue via thin smears up the
slab above. A serious route; using a 100m sprinter for a belayer
may prove to be a sound policy.

77 Lethargic Arête   8m   S   (1951)
Climb the slab just left of the arête using a short thin crack to a
ledge. Finish more easily up the crack above.

78 Mad Llehctim   6m   E3   6b   (1984)
Some thin moves lead precariously up the slab left of Lethargic
Arête. Etiuq etarepsed and it is considerably harder to crack
than the puzzle!

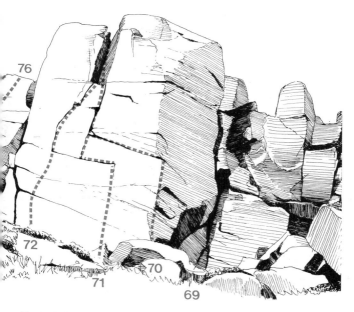

To the left is a narrow leaning buttress containing a ramp.

79 Press-on 8m E2 6a   (1987)
Follow the ramp leftwards on to a large ledge. Continue up the small side-wall on the right (the left wall of the buttress).

80 The Gutter 8m HVS 5a   (1977)
Climb the short, painful crack just left of the narrow upright buttress to a large ledge. Continue more easily up a crack in the back right-hand corner of the ledge.

81 Rombald's Staircase 6m M   (1957-1965)
From the foot of the narrow buttress follow steps leftwards.

* **82 Gable Route** 8m HVS 4c   (1977)
Left again is a wide crack with a slab on its right. This delightful little gem is the right arête of the slab starting at a large flake.

·* 83 Roof Route 8m VS 4c (1934)
The wide crack itself gives an unrelenting struggle. Climb it
'using a left leg jam.' – 1951. If you cruise this, head straight for
Curbar and Left Eliminate; you have begun your career as a real
crack climber!

84 Chimney Route 8m HVD (1965-1978)
Just left of a steep buttress is an unusual flake chimney. Keep
well out from the back.

85 The Thistle Funnel 8m VD (1964)
18m left is a blunt arête split by a widening crack. From the
ledge finish just right of the arête. For **The Connection**, VD,
(1965-1978), mantelshelf left out of the funnel on to a ledge and
traverse left to finish up Abu Simbel.

86 Abu Simbel 6m M (1964)
Five metres left, twin cracks lead pleasantly to the top.

87 Triglyph 6m VS 4b (1964)
The right-hand of two wide slanting cracks, six metres left, is
strenuous.

* 88 Every Man's Misery 6m VS 5a (1957-1965)
The wider left-hand crack is exhausting. You will not see the
lycra-lads on this one!

89 Kleg 6m HVS 5b (1972)
Climb the centre of the wall right of Midge and traverse
rightwards to finish above Every Man's Misery. Also known as
Boulder Child.

* 90 Midge 6m El 5c (1972)
Two cracks rise from a dismal recess. This is the right-hand
crack.

* 91 The Gnat 6m HVS 5b (1966-1969/1972)
The other overhanging crack in the angle gives a fine tussle.

92 Split Nose 6m VS 5a (1957-1965)
Step off the boulder just left and jam the crack splitting the nose.
The continuation crack is on the other side of the block and it
provides a short layback problem.

18m farther left is a small buttress with a hollowed-out base.

93 Wagger's Wiggle 6m D (1952)
Step onto a pedestal and continue up the crack above.

27m left is another small buttress with two curving cracks forming a lens of rock in its upper section.

94 Lens Crack 6m S   (1957-1965)
Climb the left-hand crack. *'The right-hand crack is an easier if less difficult finish.' – 1978.*

95 Breathless 6m HVS 5b   (1965-1977)
Start at a boulder at the left-hand arête of the buttress and follow the side wall just left of the arête. A long reach is needed to finish.

96 Renobulous Bongetl 8m E5 6a   (1982)
Climb the unprotected arête across the gully left of Breathless starting on the left and finishing with a long reach above a bad landing. Falling from this would be like diving into a funnel fitted with cheese grater sides.

97 Short Crack 6m VD   (1965-1978)
Climb the crack just to the left of 'what's its name'.

98 Slantside 6m M   (1965-1978)
The block-filled chimney and its arête six metres left.

99 Dominican 6m VD   (1977)
The crack in the corner three metres left.

100 Friar's Wall 6m VS 4b   (1977)
Climb the next wall just right of its blunt arête.

101 Little Pig 6m S   (1977)
The crack just left of a protruding rib. Its easier litter mate two metres left is VD.

† **102 The Alliance** 6m E4 6b   (1987)
"A Lib-Lab pact using the left and right arête to stay in the middle." Reputed to be harder for the short.

103 Chockstone Layback 6m HVD   (1957-1965)
At a cleft, swing up under a huge jammed boulder on jams. Layback up its left-hand edge and continue up the slab above.

* **104 Home Cooking** 7m E4 6c   (1984)
The arête to the left is started on its leaning left-hand side until a nasty, awkward move right enables the right-hand side to be followed more easily. Keeping on the left-hand side a bit longer apparently reduces the grade to 6a and there is gear!

* **105 Big Bad Wolf** 8m E5 6b   (1982)
Climb the overhanging wall just left, starting from a boulder on
the left. Move right on the first break and make a 'mean' move
up, trending rightwards to finish just right of the arête. Brutish in
the extreme! Award yourself 2 days cruising on limestone E5s
after a successful ascent of this.

106 Sublime Indifference 6m E2 6a   (1984)
Nine metres left is a short buttress with a ramp running from
right to left up the lower part of the face. When the ramp fades,
make a hard move to get established on the centre of it and
continue via one more awkward move to the top.

107 Clark's Route 6m HVS 5b   (1965-1978)
The wall and left arête of the face.

Nine metres left is a small face.
No Name Crack, VD, (1934-1951), follows the centre of this face.

14m farther on is a buttress split by a wide crack.

108 Fat Man's Misery 6m S   (1934-1951)
Ascend the crack making use of a flake on the left-hand wall.

109 Prow Crack 6m S   (1957-1965)
A clean crack by a small nose 18m left.

110 Pebble Crack 6m HVS 5a   (1957-1965)
45m left is a buttress with an upper section split by a slanting
crack. This is reached from a small corner on its right.

*Farther left is a small buttress with a clean break at half-height
leading leftwards to a steep arête.*

† **111 The Little Rascal** 9m E4 6c   (1986)
Without using a boulder, start up a small groove at the
right-hand side of the buttress to gain the break, crux. Follow
this leftwards to a hard move up the final arête.

CARL WARK

O.S. ref. SK 259815

by Keith Sharples

SITUATION and CHARACTER

Carl Wark is a flat-topped summit lying midway between Higgar
Tor and the Toad's Mouth Bridge on the A625. The natural crags
to the north and east have been fortified on the west by ancient
man. Facing east, Carl Wark gets the early morning sun.
However, the crag has hitherto failed to attract the number of
climbers that frequent the other crags in the Burbage Valley, it
being limited both in height and extent. Nevertheless, there are
some impressive routes here and the crag does offer solitude for
the climber wishing to get away from it all. Its east-facing aspect
and lack of popularity does mean that some of its lesser-climbed
routes carry a covering of lichen. It seems that these days, one
must choose between climbers or lichen!

APPROACH and ACCESS

Carl Wark is best approached from the southern end of the
Green Drive; see the Burbage Quarries and South Edge notes for
details of car parking and bus services etc. About 100m north of
the gate at the southern end of the Green Drive a path branches
off leftwards towards Carl Wark. Cross the Burbage Brook then
head straight up to the crag following a good footpath all the way.

100m left of where the path crosses the brook is a small outcrop
featuring two cracks.

THE CLIMBS are described from LEFT to RIGHT.

† **1   Guplets on Toast**   6m   E3   6c   (1985)
The wall left of Slanting Crack has a hard pebbly start and,
unfortunately, a filthy finish.

2   Slanting Crack   6m   VS   4c   (1977)
The slanting crack at the left-hand end of the outcrop.

3   Rumble Groove   6m   VS   4b   (1977)
The overhanging crack to the left of the grotto.

The slab on the right offers some sport.

The path to the main crag divides shortly before reaching the rocks and the first route is on the nose of the buttress above the fork.

4 Lookout Ledge 6m D   (1957-1978)
Climb the arête of the first buttress finishing to the left.

† **5 Sensory Overload** 6m E1 5c   (1991)
Take the arête on the right, finishing with a precarious slap for the top.

6 Boulder Crack 6m D   (1934-1951)
Take the recessed crack two metres right, finishing direct.

7 Ingle Nook 6m D   (1957-1965)
Climb the blocked chimney at the back of the alcove and finish up the wide crack.

8 Lump Wall 6m D   (1957-1965)
The crack two metres right to a ledge; finish up the wall via the lump.

9 Leaning Crack 8m S 4c   (1934-1951)
Climb the narrow crack and wider continuation two metres right of Lump Wall.

10 Corner and Crack 8m S 4b   (1957-1965)
Starting two metres right again, go up the angled corner and a tricky crack through the overhang above.

11 Broken Buttress 8m VD   (1934-1951)
Climb the arête three metres right again, then move left and finish up the obvious crack.

To the right are a few problems; a crack, a corner, a chimney and an arête, all of which are about VD.

The next recorded route is 30m right.

12 Carl's Buttress 6m S 4b   (1934-1951)
Climb the slab on its right side. Variations are also possible.

20m right is a small buttress.
The first little problem follows the corner on the left (with the aid of a starting block). The second problem is the gloomy corner on its right. Both are VD.

The next climbs are 80m farther right, facing Higgar Tor.

13 Layback Crack 7m VD (1934-1951)
Below and right of a fluted capstone is an obvious corner crack
with a choice of finishes.

Eight metres right is a scarred arête.

14 2b or not 2b 7m HVS 5b (1983)
Traverse the obvious break leftwards from the next route until
almost at the arête. Pull up past the rock scar to finish up a scoop
in the back wall.

15 Chockstone Crack 8m HVD (1957-1965)
Just right again is a crack with a chockstone at 3m.

15a Chocks Away 8m HVS 5a (1987)
Climb the wall right of Chockstone Crack and finish up the short
scoop above.

*15m right is a wall with a crack at its centre leading to a triangular
block and a chockstone chimney on its right.*

16 Art of Silence 5m E3 6a (1982)
Climb the blunt rib two metres left of the crack. The crux is
reaching left at the top.

17 Orange Juice Wall 12m HS 4b (1964)
From a boulder, climb the centre crack, then take the left-hand
branch. Mantelshelf on to a ledge and finish up a short chimney.

† **18 Six Pack** 12m E3 6a (1985)
Follow the right-hand branch from Orange Tree Wall to climb
the steep head-wall using a small flake and an outrageous reach.
Originally climbed using a pebble which has since been broken
off.

* **19 Lime Juice Chimney** 11m D (1900-1920)
A classic. Pass the chockstone on the inside or the outside.

20 Tower Wall 10m HVS 5b (1965-1978)
A thin crack leads to a hand-traverse leftwards at 4m. Make a
difficult move up to finish in a groove left of the arête.

† **21 Lost World 10m E6 6c (1985)
Climb the thin crack of Tower Wall and finish directly up the
perplexing wall above. Good protection in the horizontal break.
Well-hidden and well-hard!

22 Tower Crack 8m VD (1934-1951)
Climb a crack just to the right to a ledge. Finish up a corner.

23 Last Crack 7m HVD   (1965-1978)
Two metres to the right, climb the next crack.

HIGGAR TOR (Also Higger Tor)

O.S. ref. SK 256819

by Keith Sharples

*'This hill – "The Hill of God" – is a little north of Carl's (sic)
Wark. There are small rocks here which give amusing
problems, and one vicious crack near the huge Leaning
Block which may repay attention.'*

Eric Byne, Sheffield Area Guidebook, 1951.

SITUATION and CHARACTER

Of all the crags in the Burbage Valley, Higgar Tor occupies the
most prominent position. The famous 'Leaning Block' is clearly
visible from all the roads around the Fox House pub. In contrast,
the block is hidden from view from the north by the hillside and
is difficult to locate on first acquaintance.

Although Higgar Tor is included in the Burbage Valley section it
actually overlooks the Hope Valley. Its elevated position on the
moor, at 430m above sea level, means that it is very exposed to
the weather. Westerly winds are funnelled down the Hope Valley
and rake the tor as they rise over Hathersage Moor. This,
together with the sunny south-west facing aspect of the tor,
means that it dries quickly after rain. One could perhaps dispute
the fact that The Rasp ever gets wet! Nevertheless, one or two
stubborn streaks do persist on some climbs. It is best to visit on
calm sunny evenings when its position will offer relief from the
balmy and/or midge-ridden conditions often found on other
crags in the area in the middle of summer.

The tor itself consists of rough gritstone, the like of which dreams
are made. It will shred skin from a carelessly placed handjam
with consummate ease. There is very little loose rock here, and
only occasionally does a thin flake break off.

The 'Leaning Block' overhangs some four metres in its
fifteen-metre height. Once beneath the block, its angle tends to
fool even the regular visitor. Only when the block is seen in

profile from close quarters can its true steepness be appreciated. To either side of the block the crag is reduced in height to some ten metres and in angle to merely vertical! The routes have traditionally followed cracks, though in recent years the walls in between have been climbed.

APPROACHES and ACCESS

The easiest approach is from the Sheffield/Ringinglow to Hathersage road which runs just to the north of the tor. From Sheffield continue past Burbage North and the turn off to Stanage and begin the descent down to the A625 and Hathersage. Limited parking is available on the right-hand side of the road oppposite the new path to the tor.

Just after the stile, a path contours around the hillside. Alternatively, if one is approaching from Hathersage, follow the main Hathersage to Sheffield Road, the A625, past the Millstone pub until Millstone Edge is clearly visible. A road then leads off to the left which is sign-posted to Ringinglow. Follow this to beneath the tor, then continue up the road a little way until it starts to level off. Park here and follow the path for five minutes around the hillside and then up to the tor. The tor can also be reached from the south. Follow the Carl Wark approach until on top of that crag. Continue on to the tor by following a well-used footpath. Twenty minutes should be sufficient from the Burbage South car park.

THE CLIMBS are described from LEFT to RIGHT.

45m left of the Leaning Block there is a small buttress with an undercut left-hand arête.

1   Hathersage Climb   6m   VS   4c   (1957-1965)
Pull over the overhang and climb the wall just right of the arête.

* **2   Tossing a Wobbler**   6m   VS   4c   (1982)
Go up the short corner just to the right, toss the wobbler, then continue up the wall above.

Left of the Leaning Block is a long steep wall.

3   The Warding   6m   VD   (1957-1965)
The crack at the left-hand end of the wall.

4   Aceldama   7m   E3   6a   (1980)
Two metres right, climb the wall direct. Poorly-protected.

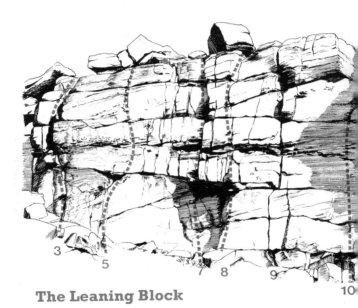

The Leaning Block

* **5   The Mighty Atom**   8m   E3   5c   (1975)
Take the easiest line up the wall to a broken flake, then make a
cunning move leftwards to finish. Protection is well below the
crux, so care is advised lest you split the atom!

6   Brillo   8m   E1   5c   (1987)
Follow the left arête of the cave then the thin crack directly
above.

13 14

18

* **7 The Riffler** 8m HVS 5a (1957-1965)
From the small cave on the right, move directly up the wall
finishing up a small corner. Strenuous but well-protected.

8 The Cotter 8m HVS 5a (1957-1965)
Climb the wall just right of the small cave.

9 The Rat's Tail 8m VS 4c (1957-1965)
The crack one metre right of The Cotter.

10 The Reamer 8m VS 4c (1964)
The arête on the left-hand side of the gully, and the thin crack above, lead to a large ledge.

11 Leaning Block Gully 9m D (1957-1965)
Steeped in tradition and lots of other things. Go up the gully, exit outside the first chockstone and finish up the flake on the left wall. The gully bed itself provides an easy descent route.

* **12 The Sander** 12m E4 6b (1976)
The steep right wall of the gully is started by bridging the gully. In fact the next moves are so problematical that this is as far as many climbers get. Still it is good bridging practice. Get established on the left-hand side of the right arête of the gully, then by an initially perplexing but, once solved, obvious sequence climb the wall left of the arête.

The next few routes are on the overhanging front face of **THE LEANING BLOCK**. It is steep and uncompromising country where any weakness in a climber will be quickly and severely revealed.

·* **13 Surform** 15m HVS 5b (1958)
Follow the flake on the left-hand side of the face until it is possible to move left into a shallow recess. Go left again to a rounded finish.

† **Bastard Cut**, E4 6a, (1991), takes Surform for 4m then goes left on a large jug and follows the shallow groove above to rejoin Surform where it traverses left.

† **14 Prince's Dustbin** 12m E4 6b (1988)
Follow Surform to the ledge, then move wildly right on to the hanging tooth. Continue, using rugosities to the break then finish directly by a hideous mantelshelf. Eccentric and exciting.

·* **15 The Rasp** 14m E2 5b (1956)
The classic route of the crag is a steep line of flakes up the centre of the face. Start as for Surform and move right, where that route goes left, to gain a niche of sorts. As you throw in the obvious Friend, spare a thought for the first ascensionist who threaded the break. Suitably protected, make some strenuous moves to gain the flakes above, crux, and follow these to the overhung niche below the top. Rest for a while, then exit right, to the break in the skyline.

16 Arnold Schwarzenegger Stole My Body

15m E4 6a (1988)

Follow the previous route to where it goes right and Surform goes left. Climb straight up (bet you would never have guessed that) past a large green jug to finish up Flute of Hope.

** **17 The Rasp Direct** 12m E3 6a (1975)

A fine alternative on the original line. Start up the thin crack beneath the crux on the original. Continue up this to the final niche. Pull over the capping roof with a hideous nose-grinding mantelshelf. As good a place as any to start your free-fall career!

*** **18 Bat out of Hell** 12m E5 6a (1979)

A difficult and strenuous route up the face right of The Rasp. Start up a small arête by a shallow corner near the right edge of the face. Move left and climb a short vertical crack to a break and good protection. Now it gets tough. Hard moves up the faint flake above gain a break. Now you have an option. Either get pumped trying to get a Friend in the break above, or throw caution to the wind and get on with it. Finish by swinging slightly right to better holds then climb the last few moves of The Rasp.

*** **19 Flute of Hope** 20m E4 6a (1971/1977)

Climb The File for 4m, traverse left to the arête, and then go left again along a descending break. Alternatively, and perhaps more sensibly, follow the previous route to this point. Continue up the short vertical crack, then move left for 3 metres along a hideous break into The Rasp. Follow The Rasp up to the top niche until it is possible to move out left. Finish, with your heart in your mouth, over the bulge.

* **20 Pulsar** 12m E5 6c (1980)

By far the most demanding route on the crag, taking the right-hand side of the overhanging face of the block. Climb the arête left of The File to the third horizontal break. Move two metres left along the break to finish direct up the wall. Seldom climbed.

*** **21 The File** 10m VS 4c (1956)

Round the right-hand arête of the Leaning Block is a fine clean crack which provides superb jams.

To the right the wall diminishes in height.

† **22 The Raven** 9m HVS 5a (1980)

The blunt arête right of The File.

* 23 Paddock 7m VD (1964)
From a block at the centre of the face, move left and climb a
series of cracks.

24 Greymalkin 7m S (1964)
Climb the indefinite cracks to the right of Paddock.

25 Hecate 7m VD (1964)
Climb a shallow corner near the right-hand arête, by a huge
boulder, to gain a ledge. Finish easily rightwards.

* 26 Rock Around The Block
37m E3 5a,6a,5c,4c (1982-1983)
A girdle of the left wall and the Leaning Block.
1. 10m. Step from a block at the left edge of the wall and traverse
on good holds to a harder move up thin cracks just right of the
Mighty Atom. Continue more easily to a belay on the arête of the
gully.
2. 10m. Move up and fall across the gully then follow a horizontal
crack to good jams and runners on the arête. Move right across
the ridiculously-angled wall to gain the niche of Surform.
3. 10m. Shuffle along the upper line on distinctly indifferent holds
to excellent jams just before the arête. Belay round the corner.
4. 7m. Follow the horizontal break as far as one desires before
going easily up the back of the block.

The short back wall of the Leaning Block contains several easy
ways up (or down).
Right of the Leaning Block is a bay.

27 Wotan's Crack 5m S 4a (1957-1965)
Follow the thin polished crack in the back of the bay.

*The first buttress right of the bay has an overhang towards its
right-hand end.*

28 Chance Encounter 7m VS 5a (1982)
Start two metres right of the left arête. Pull up to reach a slanting
crack. Climb this and the arête above.

29 Sickle Overhang 6m VS 4c (1957-1965)
The overhang right of Chance Encounter is taken direct.

Right: Nigel Prestidge bouldering at Mother Cap.
Photo: Richie Brooks.
Overleaf: Colin Binks on The File, Higgar Tor.
Photo: Chris Craggs.

Ten metres right is a V-shaped arête. Left of this is a scooped slab taken by the next route.

† **30 Jupiter Slab** 7m E1 6a   (1990)
After a difficult start to get established in the scoop, easier moves lead diagonally right to the ledge and the finish of Jupiter's Arête.

31 Jupiter's Arête 6m VS 4c   (1957-1965)
The arête is climbed via a ledge on the left.

32 Jupiter's Crack 6m HVD   (1957-1965)
Ascend the crack to the right of Jupiter's Arête.

Ten metres right is a detached arête with an overhanging capstone.

The left wall is split by three cracks: **Doddle**, VD, (1978-1983), is the left-hand crack; **Walkover**, HVD, (1978-1983), is the centre crack which is finished on the right; **Piece of Cake**, VD, (1956-1965), is the right-hand crack.

Farther right is a buttress capped by a fluted overhang.

33 Achilles' Heel 12m E2 5c   (1960-1965)
Climb the fluting to the right, up to the roof. Traverse right to a ledge and finish easily. **Laze**, E1 5c, (1975), is a direct finish.

34 Canyon Climb 6m D   (1957-1965)
Just right of the canyon, at the back of the buttress, is a chimney. Climb into it and exit on either side of the capstone.

35 Zeus's Crack 6m S   (1957-1965)
Follow the wide crack to the right of the leaning rib.

36 Root Decay 9m E4 6b   (1988)
Climb the wall right of Zeus's Crack with a hard start to a break, Friends. Move slightly right and press on to finish. Bad landing; spotter advised.

37 Stretcher Case 9m E2 5c   (1979)
Climb the vague rib on the long wall right of Zeus's Crack.

38 Splint 8m HVS 5a   (1979)
The arête on the right of Stretcher Case.

The continuation wall gives three routes:

Nigel Slater 'crimping' on Wall Street Crash, Millstone Edge.
Photo: Keith Sharples.

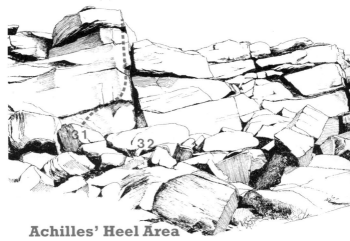

Achilles' Heel Area

39 Loki's Way 7m S 4a   (1964)
Climb the crack just right of the arête, moving on to the front face
to finish.

40 Fricka's Crack 6m VS 4c   (1964)
The thin crack to the right.

41 Jade Tiger 6m HVS 5b   (1984)
Climb the wall right of Fricka's Crack using the right arête.

42 Freya's Climb 6m VD   (1964)
The broken corner to the right again.

† **43 Pippin** 6m E1 5c   (1987)
Right again is a short wall which has a deep horizontal break and
a roof above. Climb the wall, then attack the crack in the roof
above.

*On the eastern side of Higgar Tor, and facing Burbage North, is a
collection of small buttresses and boulders.* The north-facing right
wall of the largest buttress is taken up its centre by **Krush
Regime**, E3 6b, (1985). This is best approached by following the
new path from the car-park to the top of the tor. The buttress is
visible to the left after a hundred or so metres.

South-west of Higgar Tor are two minor outcrops.

WINYARDS NICK

O.S. ref. SK 252813

The pile of boulders that thinks it's a crag. This chaotic jumble of rough gritstone blocks provides endless boulder problems of all grades. The 'crag' reaches 5m in places and as some landings could be terminal, a rope may be advisable in places.

OVER OWLER TOR

O.S. ref. SK 251808

by Jon Lawton

> *'Sorry this is a bit late, I wrote it on the way to the airport in London! I'm off to Madagascar for two months.'*

Wrongly described in the previous guidebook as Winyards Nick (which actually lies a little farther North) this isolated bouldering spot atop the moor behind Millstone is easily visible from Stanage Edge and the A625 Fox House road.

The rocks are weather-beaten grit, reaching 9m in places and covering an area similar in size to Robin Hood's Stride. The tor dries quickly in this exposed location and is an excellent spot for an evening's bouldering, especially after a day on the Millstone cracks. A rope is advisable.

Access is via a stile and path at the far North (left-hand) end of Millstone or by a path past Mother Cap from the Surprise View car-park on the A625.

These rocks have certainly been climbed on before and Malc Baxter recorded several climbs in the 1960s. However, other lines were recorded in 1991 by J Lawton with J Middlebrook.

THE CLIMBS are described from LEFT to RIGHT, starting on the overhanging buttress which is split by twin cracks.

1 Skydiver 7m VS 4c   (1960s)
Climb the obvious overhanging flake then span the wall above.

2 F-Plan 8m HVD   (1960s)
The narrow fissure beside the roof on the right.

* **3 Green Light on Go** 9m E1 5b   (1991)
The obvious roof is climbed via a sharp pocket (Friend) on its right-hand side and flat holds on the wall above.

To the right an obvious flake jutting out from the edge provides a fun hand-traverse – **Free Fallin'**.

Next is a short wall with two big pockets at its top. **Right Eye**, 4a, goes up from the boulder, while **Left Eye**, 4c, starts just left of the boulder.

4 Breaststroke 7m M   (1991)
The big cleft to the right is fun and has a squirmy exit at the back, while outside the cleft on the front it is VD.

13m right past another small buttress is:

5 Elephantitis 6m 5c   (1991)
Climb the rib on the left face of the next buttress from a hole in the buttress to a rounded finish.

6 Zorro 7m D   (1991)
Climb the arête and an obvious slanting crack on the right face of the same buttress.

Just right the mass of the main tor is disappointing as it is composed of many short and easy-angled faces. *Farther right is the best and most obvious feature* – Over Owler Pinnacle. *This is bounded on its left by a deep chimney, M, and immediately left again a deep crack which is:*

7 Aviator 9m VD   (1991)
A worthwhile climb up the deep crack with an exit left of the capstone.

8 Transglobe 9m HVS 5a   (1991)
Climb the left-hand side of the front face of the pinnacle via an obvious crack in the upper section. Pleasant.

† **9 Aeroflot 9m E1 5c   (1991)
Climb the lower wall to the break then the right arête of the pinnacle using a thin seam. Friends and micros protect. Excellent.

The back of the pinnacle has a short crack, **Propellor**, 4b.
The next large buttress to the right has some extra rock leaning against its base.

10 Balloon 10m HS   (1991)
A good climb up the arête with pockets and a thin flake.

11 Vienetta 10m D   (1991)
Climb the arête and right wall.

On the next big buttress on the pocketed wall facing Millstone is:

12 Plop 8m HVS 5a   (1960s)
Climb the arête with increasing difficulty.

13 Plip 7m VS 4c   (1991)
Climb the wall via pockets.

In addition there are assorted boulder problems of all grades including a desperate overhanging crack in the large block on the far right-hand end of the crag.

MOTHER CAP QUARRY   O.S. ref. SK 251805

Past the entrance track to Millstone Edge, round the Surprise View bend and a short distance back on the moor top is a large car-park on the left (going towards Fox House). From the back of the car-park a prominent footpath leads up on to the moor passing Mother Cap and leading on to Winyards Nick. A short distance from the car-park is a small quarry on the left. The quarry contains a prominent arête. The undercut wall left of the arête is taken from the right by **Flat Cap**, E1 5c, (1991) and more directly by **Andy Capp**, E1 6a, (1991). **Dog Brush**, HVS 5c, (1990), goes from the arête rightwards using a ramp to a ledge and a finish on the left of the crack above. The crack together with the same finish as the previous route is HVS 5a whilst the crack with a finish on the right is VS 4c. The wall right again is **Night Cap**, E2 6a, (1991).

MOTHER CAP   O.S. ref. SK 252805

An excellent and curiously square-shaped pinnacle prominently stuck on the moor top south-east of Over Owler Tor and by the side of the footpath from the Surprise View car-park, from which the top of the tor can be seen.

The climbs are described anti-clockwise. The north face (uphill) has nothing listed as it is more discontinuous than its neighbours. All the climbs are about 7m in length.

The west face (nearest the path) has:

1   Blue Cap HVS 5a   (1991)
Climb the right-hand side of the left arête with a difficult move after the break on to a rather bald top.

2   Elf Cap E2 6a   (1991)
Climb carefully up the centre of the face moving slightly rightwards towards the break. Finish in the centre of the wall above the break. Graded for side runners.

3   Oyster Cap E2 5c   (1991)
The right-hand arête gives absorbing climbing. From the break move leftwards and finish with further interest as for Elf Cap.

The south face (downhill) has:

† **4   Conan the Librarian** E3 6b   (1986)
Take the best line up the face to suit.

5   Milk Cap VD
A short crack on the right of the face leads to the ledge and a short wall which also gives the easiest way off the top.

6   Ink Cap VS 4c
Pull over the overhang on the right arête and continue with a difficult move to the ledge. Or, slightly harder, climb the short wall to the right on the east side.

BURBAGE VALLEY LIST OF FIRST ASCENTS

Pre-1900   Ernest A Baker and his companions in the Kyndwr Club scrambled over Carl Wark, Higgar Tor and the Mother Cap.

1900-1920   **Lime Juice Chimney**   James W Puttrell.

Incredibly the Burbage Edges were woefully ignored until:

1932   **The Dover and Ellis Chimney, Hollyash Crack, Dover's Progress, Great Crack**   Harry Dover, Gilbert Ellis.
An impressive opening gambit from one of the finest teams operating on gritstone at that time. The 'Chimney' is still rated Extreme today.

1932   **Brooks' Layback**   Rupert Brooks, Eric Byne, Jack Macleod.

1932   **Amazon Crack**   Jack Macleod, Rupert Brooks, Eric Byne.

1932   **Stomach Traverse, Triangle Buttress Arête, Overhanging Buttress Arête, Ash Tree Wall, Twin Chimneys Layback**   Eric Byne, Rupert Brooks, Jack Macleod.

1933   **The Knight's Move**   Gilbert Ellis, Harry Dover.
A hard route for its time. Curiously missed out of the 1951 and 1956 guidebooks.

In 1933 members of the Sheffield Climbing Club produced many new routes and published a guidebook to Burbage Valley in the 1934 Mountaineering Journal.
Routes whose first ascent details are unknown include:
Route 2, Route 3, Twenty-Foot Crack, Triangle Buttress Direct, Triangle Crack, Leaning Wall, Monkey Corner, Overhanging Buttress Direct, Burgess Buttress, Burgess Face, Green Slab, Slanting Crack, Slanting Gully, Chockstone Climb, Wall Chimney, Wall Corner, Ash Tree Crack, Bilberry Crack, Bilberry Face, The Big Chimney, Left Twin Chimney, Right Twin Chimney, Split Slab, Falstaff's Chimney, Falstaff's Innominate, Falstaff's Crack, Bilberry Wall, Left Twin Crack, Right Twin Crack, Wobblestone Crack, Holly Bush Gully, Left Studio Climb, Right Studio Climb.

1934   **Brooks' Crack**   Rupert Brooks.

1934   **Byne's Crack**   Eric Byne.

1934   **Fox House Flake** (*née* Creeping Crack)   Frank Burgess, George Walker.

1934   **Tower Climb**   Byron Connelly, Bert Smith.

1934   **Roof Route**   Jack Macleod.

1934   **Mutiny Crack**   Eric Byrom, Douglas Milner.
Byrom and Milner refused to repeat Stomach Traverse and instead recorded Mutiny Crack: a better proposition altogether.

At this time Frank Burgess climbed many of the routes on Carl Wark. After 1934 access again became a problem as the keepering of the moors was stepped up.

1948 July   **Obscenity**   G (Nip) Craven, Rowland Pitts.
Missed out of the 1951/1956 guidebooks.

Publication of the 1951 Sheffield Area guidebook.
Other routes whose first ascent details are unknown include:
**Route 1, Triangle Buttress Girdle, Ad Infinitum, Side Face, Ash
Tree Girdle, Leaning Block Crack, Green Chimney, Jetty
Buttress, Phillipa Buttress, Black Slab Arête, Black Slab, Black
Slab Variations, Sentinel Chimney, Sentinel Crack, Ring Climb**
(*née* Ring Wall), **Ring Chimney, Green Crack, The Big Chimney
Arête, Alpha Crack** (*née* Alfa Crack), **Omega Crack, Scarred
Buttress Climb, Amazon Gully, Greeny Crack, Quarry Gully,
The Shattered Cracks, Giant's Staircase, Broken Crack, Curving
Chimney, Perched Block Route** (*née* Perch Block Chimney), **The
Great Flake Route, Walker's Pulpit, The Staircase, Macleod's
Crack, Ladder Gully, Connolly's Variation, Tower Chimney, No
Name Crack, Fat Man's Misery, Boulder Crack, Leaning Crack,
Broken Buttress, Carl's Buttress, Layback Crack, Tower Crack.**

1951 Jan.	**Ribbed Corner, Valk Corner, Isolated Buttress, Scoop Crack** Joe Brown, Merrick (Slim) Sorrell.
1951 May	**Cranberry Crack** Albert Shutt.
1951 Sept.	**Lethargic Arête, Gog, Magog, Valhalla** Joe Brown, Slim Sorrell. *Valhalla was Brown's most significant route from this 'crop'. The instability of this area finally brought about eventual collapse in 1980. But the story lives on ..... see later.*
1951 Sept.	**Reginald, Nathaniel** J R (Nat) Allen, Nip Underwood.
1952 Nov. 8	**Wagger's Wiggle** C W Ashbury, Eric Byne.
1953 Aug. 21	**Peter's Progress** Peter Biven.
1956 Nov.	**The File** Don Whillans, Joe Brown, Nat Allen.
1956 Nov.	**The Rasp** (1pt) Joe Brown, Don Whillans. *This route by Brown represented a level of difficulty that had hitherto never been achieved. It was one of the hardest routes on gritstone at the time. It is apparent that both Brown and Whillans were trying the route together and that either of them might have been successful. In the event Brown succeeded first; though he did use a resting sling. The first free ascent is not known.*
1956 Autumn	**Still Orange** Dave Gregory, Ron Townsend.
1951-1956	**Pulcherrime** Dave Gregory, Barry Fairest and others. *Climbed whilst truanting from King Edward's School. Pulcherrime is a poor translation of 'fairest'. Gregory recalls that it was Fairest who had first go, but it was the team that gave the route its name.*
	David and **The Old Bailey** were claimed during this period by different parties.
	Publication of the 1957 Further Developments guidebook. Other routes whose first ascent details are unknown include: **Monkey Wall, Bracken Crack, Wayward Wall, Potter's Pride.**
1957 March	**Tower Crack** (*née* Night Climber's Crack) Geoff Sutton, Tony Moulam.
1957 June 19	**Detour** Ron Townsend, M Padley.
1957 July 8	**Leaning Wall Direct** Ron Townsend, M Padley.

1958	**Rose Flake** Sheffield University Mountaineering Club party.

Previously top-roped in 1952 by Pete Cargill and Donald Wooller.

1958 **Surform** Joe Brown.

1958 **Millwheel Wall** Len Millsom (solo).

1958 **Goliath** Don Whillans (solo).
Goliath is still a very formidable route which is rarely climbed. Currently it is graded E5. At that time it was almost certainly the hardest route in the country, although it was almost certainly climbed with protection from inserted chockstones. Altogether a typical Whillans affair!

1958-1959 **The Chant** Alan Clarke.
After a failure by a party comprising Dave Gregory, Andrew Brodie and George Kitchin, Clarke completed the first ascent. Clarke offered no name, but The Chant refers to a Gregorian Chant.

1961 **Charlie's Crack** Charlie Curtis.
Incorrectly called The Sickle in the 1983 guidebook.

1964 Summer **The Grogan** Gerry Rogan.
Dave Gregory and Andrew Brodie were failing in their efforts when Rogan came along after work. He climbed the route in his work boots and a tattered, mortar-stained Burberry.

1964 Summer **Wollock, Evening Wall, Lino, Limmock, Broddle, Wazzock, Orange Juice Wall, Dowel Crack, Triglyph, The Thistle Funnel, Abu Simbel** Dave Gregory, Andrew Brodie, George Kitchin.
Limmock was named as the assembled party thought that you would have to be supple to do it. To quote a phrase of Kitchin's father.... "He were that limmock, he could fit in a roll of lino". Dowel Crack was so called because a section of thick wooden rod was wedged in it.

1964 Summer **Loki's Way, Fricka's Crack, Freya's Climb, Paddock, Greymalkin, Hecate.** Dave Gregory, George Kitchin (various leads).

1964 Summer **The Reamer, Diversion, Saul, Creaking Flakes, Gardener's Wall, The Ramp** Dave Gregory, Andrew Brodie.
All climbed during guidebook work.... and Gregory is still writing thirty years on! A gargantuan appetite for one of the most thankless jobs in climbing.

1960-1965 **Wednesday Climb** Pat Fearnehough.

1960-1965 **Long Tall Sally** Alan Clarke.
First free ascent after a previous unrecorded pegged ascent.

1960-1965 **Hades, The Cock, Achilles' Heel** Gerry Rogan.

1960-1965 **Keep Crack, The Boggart** (2pts) Alan Clarke.
Clarke used a shoulder and a nut for aid to force the first ascent of the latter.
First free ascent in 1975.

Publication of the 1965 Sheffield Froggatt Area guidebook. Other routes whose first ascent details are unknown include:
Little Plumb, Baseless, Steptoe, Burgess St., Dead Tree Crack, Stepped Crack, The Grazer, Lie Back, Ringo, Snow Flakes, December Climb, Split Slab Crack, Grotto Slab, Grotto Crack,

First Crack, Farcical Arête, Left Recess Crack, Right Recess Crack, Thrall's Thrutch, Right Fin, April Fool, Spider Crack, End Buttress, End Slab, Bracken Crack, Spyhole Crack, Dunkley's Eliminate, Twin Cracks, Broken Wall, Shale, Corner Chimney, Sand Chimney, Goblin, Doddle (the south Burbage one!), **Parson's Crack, The Drainpipe, No Zag, Zig-Zag, The Big Dipper, Pythagorus, Surprise, Castor, Pollux, Vulcan, The Iron Hand, Rombald's Staircase, Every Man's Misery, Split Nose, Lens Crack, Chockstone Layback, Prow Crack, Pebble Crack, Lookout Ledge, Ingle Nook, Lump Wall, Corner and Crack, Chockstone Crack, Hathersage Climb, The Warding, The Riffler, The Cotter, The Rat's Tail, Leaning Block Gully, Wotan's Crack, Sickle Overhang, Jupiter's Crack, Piece of Cake, Canyon Climb, Zeus's Crack.**

1966-1969	**The Gnat** (some aid) Alan Clarke. *First free ascent in 1972.*
1969 March 25	**Skive** (A1) S Chadwick, B Briggs. *One of the bolted routes on the Cioch.*
1969 May 10	**Easy Traverse** Al Thewless, C A Plant.
1969	**Boney Moroney, Zeus** Jack Street. *The latter route was reputedly called Tramlines by Street. Originally there was a peg runner. Later that year it was claimed as Zeus by Tom Proctor. Although Street was the first ascensionist, Proctor's name stuck.*
1970	**The Fin** (some aid) Tony Barley. *First free ascent in 1971.*
1971 June	**Banana Finger** Ed Ward-Drummond (solo).
1971 July 4	**Flute of Hope** (2pts) Ed Drummond, Hamish Green-Armytage. *Typically, Ward-Drummond was eager to try the hardest problems around, and, in so doing, brought his controversial style to the Peak District. Both these routes were significant; the latter for the climbing, and the former its verbose description. Unfortunately he used two aid slings to force Flute of Hope. First free ascent in 1977.*
1971 Oct. 29	**Now or Never** John Allen, Neil Stokes.
1971 Nov.	**The Knack** John Allen, Neil Stokes.
1971	**Sentinel Indirect** John Allen, Neil Stokes.
1971	**The Fin** Neil Stokes, John Allen. *First free ascent.*
1972	**Noble Rot, The Verdict** Ken Jones.
1972	**Midge** Neil Stokes, John Allen.
1972	**Tiptoe** Chris Craggs.
1972	**The Gnat** Neil Stokes. *First free ascent.*
1972	**Kleg** John Allen, Neil Stokes.
1974	**Unfinished Symphony** John Allen, Steve Bancroft.
1975 July 29	**The Mighty Atom** Steve Bancroft, John Allen.

1975 Aug. 4	**Silent Spring**	Steve Bancroft, John Allen (alternate leads). *On the first ascent no bolts were clipped, only 'natural' gear was used.*
1975 Nov. 30	**The Rasp Direct**	Steve Bancroft, John Allen. *The initial crack had previously been climbed by John Allen.*
1975	**Burssola, Laze, The Boggart, The Knock**	John Allen (solo). *Whilst Laze was originally graded HVS 5a, it was the first free ascent of The Boggart and his ascent of The Knock that were impressive.*
1976 April 9	**Boggart Left-hand**	Steve Bancroft, Chris Addy.
1976 April	**Sorb**	Dennis Carr, Al Parker, D Sinclair. *Now changed due to a rock-fall, although the original grade still stands.*
1976	**Meddle**	Dennis Carr, Jon de Montjoye.
1976	**Connoisseur's Crack** (*née* Sniper)	Nicky Stokes, John Allen.
1976	**Above and Beyond the Kinaesthetic Barrier, Pebble Mill**	John Allen (solo). *Both of these routes were chipped after pebble(s) came off (the former before the ascent).*
1976	**Dork Child**	John Allen, Nicky Stokes. *See the first ascent details for Usurper (Curbar Edge: 1977) for details of how this route was named.*
1976	**The Sander**	Jerry Peel. *A somewhat obscure, though netherthless hard, route.*
1976	**Deception, Coldest Crack**	Mick Fowler, John Stevenson.
1977 Jan. 12	**Little White Jug**	Andy Hall, Keith Sharples.
1977 June 7	**The Rainmaker**	Keith Sharples, Liz Blakemore.
1977 July 2	**Remergence**	Steve Bancroft, Neil Stokes. *Named in deference to Steve's nth comeback.*
1977 Summer	**Tharf Cake**	John Parkin, Dave Gregory. *Tharf Cake is another name for 'parkin'.*
1977 Aug. 4	**Captain Sensible**	Steve Webster (solo).
1977 Sept. 7	**The Penultimate**	Keith Sharples (solo).
1977 Oct. 22	**The Gutter**	Dave Gregory, Mark Vallance.
1977 Oct. 22	**Gable Route**	Mark Vallance, Clive Jones, Dave Gregory.
1977 Oct. 26	**Slanting Crack**	Dave Gregory, Dominic Lee, Jeremy Lee.
1977 Oct. 26	**Rumble Groove, Dominican, Little Pig**	Dominic Lee, Dave Gregory, Jeremy Lee.
1977 Oct. 26	**Friar's Wall**	Dominic Lee (solo). *Dominic Lee's first new routes, climbed in black pumps. Much more is to be heard of Dominic in the years to come.*
1977 Autumn	**Ivy Tree, Oak Face**	Dave Gregory, Andrew Brodie.
1977 Autumn	**The Disappearing Bust of Voltaire, A Phenomenological Problem, The Birth of Liquid Desires**	Clive Jones (solo).
1977 Autumn	**Agnostic's Arête**	Clive Jones (solo).

1965-1977	**Breathless** Anon.	

Later claimed as Mirror Wall by Mark Vallance in 1977.

1977   **Flute of Hope**   Ron Fawcett, Geoff Birtles.
First free ascent.

1977   **The Sentinel**   Dennis Carr, Ted Rogers, Tony Cowcill.

1965-1977   **All Quiet on the Eastern Front**   Ed Ward-Drummond (solo).

1978 Oct. 11   **High Flier, Slide-away, Submission**   Gary Gibson (all solo).
Some of these routes were omitted from the 1983 guidebook and have been claimed many times since.

1978   **The Irrepressible Urge, Early Morning Performance, All Stars' Goal, Red Shift, Furiously Sleepin', The Screamer, Rhapsody in Green, The Edging Machine, Shooting Star, Movie Star, Prince Tarquin**   Colin Banton.

1978   **Approach**   Colin Banton (solo).
This route was then described as being on the left of April Fool and graded HVS 5b. The 1978 guidebook subsequently described it on the right of this route.

1977-1978   **The Curse**   Anon.

1965-1978   **Poisoned Dwarf**   Alan 'Richard' McHardy, Terry King.

Publication of the 1978 Froggatt Area guidebook.
Other routes whose first ascent details are unknown include:
Ash Tree Variations, Bilberry Arête, Ace, Ender, Endste, Less Bent, Slow Ledge, Chimney Route, The Connection, Short Crack, Slantside, Clark's Route, Tower Wall, Last Crack.

1979 April/May   **Bat out of Hell**   Paul Bolger.
A fine solution to a long standing problem.

1979 Aug. 11   **Pretzel Logic**   Dave Jones, John Codling (both led).
A direct finish, Cartwheel Wall was added in 1985.

1979   **Rise 'n Shine**   Phil Baker, Nick Fenwick.

1979   **Stretcher Case**   Chris Craggs, Colin Binks.

1979   **Splint**   Colin Binks, Chris Craggs.
Appropriately named since Chris broke his leg skiing two weeks after the ascent of these routes.

1979   **Crow Man Meets the Psychotic Pheasant, Rumblefish**   Mark Stokes (solo).
Crow Man ... was also climbed by Gary Gibson as The Arête of Cold Gloom on 24 April 1979.

1979   **The Attitude Inspector**   Mark Wilford, Derek Bolger (both led).

1979   **Blinded by Science**   Chris Gore.

1973-1979   **Cardinal's Backbone**   John Allen, Mark Stokes, Nicky Stokes.

1980 July 4   **Nosferatu**   Andy Barker, Pete Lowe.
An un-sung desperate: even Barker couldn't repeat it in 1985. A rock-fall to the left has made the landing much worse. Originally climbed with a side-runner in a pocket on the left, placed from the now defunct block.

1980 Sept. 12	**Arme Blanche, Windjammer**	Gary Gibson (solo).

Arme Blanche was climbed without taking the direct start.

1980 Sept. 22 **Pulsar** Jonny Woodward (unseconded).

1980 Oct. 27 **The Raven** Gary Gibson, Dave Tempest, Richard Kerr.

1980 Oct. 27 **Aceldama** Gary Gibson (solo).

1980 **Hidden in the Midden** Paul Mitchell, Dave Greenald.

1980 **Flaked Out** Paul Mitchell, Ian Jones, John Kirk.

1981 May **The Simpering Savage** Paul Mitchell, Andy Barker.
Tried over some time with both climbers coming close to success.

1981 July 10 **Arme Blanche** Gary Gibson, Derek Beetlestone.
Climbed direct but with a side-runner, although this was eliminated by Gibson some months later.

1981 Aug. 14 **G.B.H.** Andy Barker, Paul Mitchell.
Apparently Barker was spurred into action by Mitchell who told him that Graham Hoey was after the line. Hoey, on the other hand, has no recollection of this at all!

1982 Jan. **The Busker, Monk On** Steve Bancroft.
Steve often had a monk on.

1982 March **Fade Away** Paul Mitchell.
Later claimed by Mark Mitchell (no relation to Paul) in 1982 as The Knick.

1982 April 25 **Knick Knack Paddywack** Andy Barker, Paul Mitchell.

1982 April **Old MacDonald** Andy Barker (solo).

1982 May 8 **Bashed Crab meets Dr Barnard** Paul Mitchell.
It is said that you will need a transplant from the good doctor when you see the gear.

1982 May 12 **Disbeliever** John Arran, Andrew Osborne.

1982 May 22 **Tossing a Wobbler** Jim Rubery, Dave Gregory.

1982 May 22 **Chance Encounter** Dave Gregory, Jim Rubery.

1982 Aug. 4 **Big Bad Wolf** Paul Mitchell.

1982 Aug. 4 **Who's There? Titan's Grandma** Paul Mitchell.
Titan's Granddad is an extremely wide crack in a boulder down by the Green Drive which is climbed from a sitting position on the ground.

1982 Aug. 4 **Renobulous Bongetl** Andy Barker (solo).
On the first attempt Barker was pulled over the top clinging to Martin Veale's arm. Another attempt had him going left into the gully, landing on a large stone and safety!

1982 Aug. 18 **Recurring Nightmare** Andy Barker (solo).

1982 Nov. 7 **R9** Dennis Kerr (on-sight solo).

1982 **Booby Prize** Andy Barker (solo).
A quote from Barker ... "This needs up-grading as it is rather a large sand-bag".

1982 **Art of Silence** Steve Bancroft, John Allen.

1980-1983	**Odin's Piles** Paul Mitchell.

Mitchell re-ascended the gap where Brown's Valhalla once stood.

1978-1983	**Small Arctic Mammal** Mark Millar (solo).
1980-1983	**Yoghurt** Daniel Lee (solo).
1982-1983	**Rock Around The Block** (1pt) Chris Craggs, Colin Binks.

Originally done with 1 rest point; later freed by Craggs.

1982-1983	**Groat** (née Al's Arête) Al Rouse, Richard Haszko.

*Publication of the 1983 Stanage Millstone guidebook.
Other routes whose first ascent details are unknown include:*
Route 1.5, **Route 4**, **Lost in France**, **Pickpocket**, **Doddle** (the
Higgar Tor one), **Walkover**.

1983 March 9	**Combined Heroes** Paul Evans, Doug Kerr, Jon Handley.
1983 Oct. 7	**Nicotine Stain** Al Rouse (solo).
1983	**2b or not 2b** Nick White (solo).
1984 April 21	**Survivor's Syndrome** Richard Davies (on-sight solo).
1984 April	**Sublime Indifference** John Allen.
1984 Easter	**Nice and Tasty** Paul Pepperday, Chris Hayles.
1984 Easter	**Longest Day** Chris Hale, Paul Pepperday.
1984 April 20	**Life in a Radioactive Dustbin** Paul Mitchell (unseconded).

*It took Mitchell three moves, including a swinging 'one arm' to get both
hands on a hold on the lip. Bob Berzins could reach it from the ground,
but was too gripped to do the next move.*

1984 Aug. 26	**Jade Tiger** Richard Davies (on-sight solo).
1984 Oct. 10	**Hell for Leather** John Allen (solo).
1984 Oct. 13	**Blind Date** Al Rouse.

*Al's finest hour. Eventually climbed in sections after many attempts.
Soon after the first ascent, the boulder which just allowed a desperate
'splits' bridge to begin the route strangely migrated towards the crag
making the start easier. This boulder has now gone altogether, thereby
making the start appallingly difficult.*

1984 Oct. 16	**Ai No Corrida** John Allen, Mark Stokes.
1984	**Messiah** Jerry Moffatt (unseconded).

*Very impressive and seldom repeated.
Jerry knew Johnny (Dawes) had tried it but summer temperatures
meant that conditions weren't favourable. Jerry had also inspected it
and, although he felt that the top would 'go', he thought the bottom
looked like it might be a 'project'. One day as a storm was brewing it
was very windy and the temperature was just right. "It took about two
hours to find someone to go out and give me a belay. Anyway I soloed
up to put the gear in, then lowered off, rested five minutes and then did
the route first try – much to my surprise".*

1984	**The Braille Trail** Johnny Dawes (unseconded).

*Soon lost 'crucial' pebbles: top-roped by many but again rarely
repeated.
Previously cleaned by Andy Barker after Pete Lowe said he wanted to*

climb it. Lowe's name was to be Klaw Kinski. Barker recalls that the idea lasted about as long as it took him to abseil down and clean it.

1984	**The Disposable Bubble**	Johnny Dawes (solo).

1984   **Home Cooking**   Johnny Dawes (on-sight solo).

1984   **Mad Llehctim**   Paul Mitchell (solo).
Top-roped first.

1984   **Sling Shot**   Chris Craggs, Colin Binks.

1985 March 4   **West Side Story**   John Allen (solo).
The first significant route on Burbage West. Climbed after many visits, West Side Story was claimed as the first named 7a on Peak District gritstone!

1985 April 22   **The Sphinx**   John Allen (solo).

1985 April 24   **Offspring**   Johnny Dawes (unseconded).

1985 June 12   **Sunlight Caller**, **Boggle Boothroyd**   M J Bridges.

1985 June 15   **Lost World**   John Allen, Steve Bancroft.
A remote gem; originally called Roman Orgy.

1985 June/July   **Pest Control**   Greg Griffith (solo).

1985 Aug.   **Rockers**   Al Rouse, Steve Sustad.

1985 Sept. 9   **Yabadabadoo**, **Answer the Phone**   Graham Hoey (solo).

1985 Sept. 19   **Small is Beautiful**   John Allen.
"It's the last time I tell John about a possible new route" ... quote from Barker.

1985 Sept. 19   **Ring my Bell**   John Allen, Steve Bancroft.

1985 Sept. 19   **The Gargoyle**   Steve Bancroft, John Allen.
... is not one of Steve's nick-names.

1985   **Manatee Man**   Paul Pritchard.

1985   **Safe Bet**   John Allen (solo).
Named Safe Bet by Greg Griffith who claimed it later in 1985.

1985   **Six Pack**   Steve Bancroft, John Allen.
Not another of Steve's nick-names.

1985   **Krush Regime**   Greg Griffith (solo).

1985   **Barry Manilow**   Steve Bancroft (solo).

1985   **Cartwheel Wall**   D Wilson.

1985   **Guplets on Toast**   Jonathan Wyatt (solo).

1986 May 18   **Life Assurance**   John Dunne, Dean Eastham.

1986 Aug. 5   **The Little Rascal**   Johnny Dawes (solo).
Subsequently climbed without the boulder at the start.

1986   **The Keffer**   Kevin Thaw, Neil Beverly.

1986   **Ron. Ring Home!**   Ron Fawcett (solo).
Named by the Editor on behalf of Ron.

1986   **Conan the Librarian**   Johnny Dawes (solo).

1986	**Shark's Fin Soup** John Bull (solo).
1978-1987	**The Enthusiast** Nick Hallam (solo).
1987 April 19	**The Alliance** Pete Oxley (solo).
1987 June 23	**Too Good to be Forgotten** Keith Sharples (solo).
1987 June 23	**Pie and Chips** John Allen (solo).
1987 June 23	**Press-on** John Allen, Dave Fearnley.
1987 July 4	**Bath-house Pink** John Allen (solo).
1987 July 12	**Midget Tart** John Allen (unseconded). *Climbed with a side-runner. Later climbed without the side-runner in* *September 1987 by Pete Oxley, as Piano Play.*
1987 July 12	**We Ain't Gonna Pay No Toll** John Allen (solo).
1987 July	**Rollerwall** Ron Fawcett (solo). *Finally, a desperate solution to a long-standing micro-route. Previously* *chipped in the early Seventies by an unknown climber and* *subsequently cemented in by Andy Barker.*
1987 Autumn	**Brillo** Chris Craggs, Dave Spencer.
1987 Oct. 12	**Chocks Away** Malc Baxter (solo).
1987	**Stockbroker in the Woodpile** Paul Mitchell, Paul Evans.
1987	**The Searing** Pete Oxley
1987	**Short Fat Bar Star** Malc Taylor, Terry Godum. *A subtly-named route (both before and after censorship!) and one* *which is rumoured to have been previously climbed by John Allen.*
1987	**Pippin** Malc Baxter (solo).
1988 April 7	**Masters of the Universe** Andy Pollitt (unseconded)
1988 June 5	**Grooveamarionation** Stuart Mackay (unseconded). *Top-roped first.*
1988 June 12	**Prince's Dustbin** John Allen, Martin Veale.
1988 Aug. 15	**Gymnipodies** John Allen (unseconded).
1988 Oct. 14	**Arnold Schwarzenegger Stole My Body** Nigel Prestidge, Mike Lea.
1988 Oct. 26	**Root Decay** Mike Lea, Nigel Prestidge.
1989 April 18	**Living in Oxford** Johnny Dawes (solo). *Dawes, returning to his native gritstone, records a route of* *uncompromising seriousness. Top-roped prior to the first ascent.* *Named by the Volume Compiler who had tried repeatedly to contact* *Dawes during the preparation of the guidebook.*
1989 Aug. 22	**Crystal Tips** Chris Horsfall (solo).
1989 Sept. 19	**Parthian Shot** John Dunne (unseconded). *A major route climbing one of the 'last great problems'. Totally serious*

Regent Street, Millstone Edge.
Photo: Dave Wilkinson.

and very hard climbing with some side gear. A top-roped ascent by Johnny Dawes had previously been the subject of a video shown on TV.

1989	**Nefertiti** John Allen (unseconded). *A long-standing line which still awaits a direct start.*
1990 April 25	**Jupiter Slab** Malc Baxter (solo).
1990 Oct. 7	**En Passant** Al Evans (unseconded).
1990 Oct. 14	**Dog Brush** Malc Baxter (solo).
1991 Jan. 13	**Sensory Overload** Stephen Robinson.
1991 May 12	**Middle-aged Mutant Ninja Birtles** Steve Bancroft, Dave Nicol, John Cullen.
1991 May	**Captain Invincible** Sean Myles (unseconded). *A fantastic achievement.*
1991 July	**Night Cap**, **Flat Cap**, **Andy Capp** D Kerr (solo)
1991 Aug. 14	**Balloon** Malc Baxter.
1991 Aug. 29	**Elf Cap**, **Milk Cap**, **Ink Cap** Gavin Taylor, Malc Baxter.
1991 Aug. 29	**Oyster Cap**, **Blue Cap** Malc Baxter, Gavin Taylor.
1991 Sept. 10	**Bastard Cut** Martin Veale, Chris Craggs.
1991 Sept. 21	**Ring Piece** Jim Rubery, Chris Craggs, Colin Binks, Graham Parkes (all led).
1991 Sept. 30	**Route 2.5**, **Base over Apex** Jim Rubery, Chris Craggs (solo). *Both undoubtedly done before.*

Publication of the 1991 Froggatt guidebook.
Other routes whose first ascent details are unknown include:
Little Brown Thug.

Keith Sharples on Jermyn Street, Millstone Edge.
Photo: Ian Smith.

MILLSTONE EDGE

O.S. ref. SK 248801 to 248807

by Keith Sharples

'Here the piton and etrier can be used without shame; no raised eyebrows or supercilious glances will be cast at the ringing sound of hammer on peg; for here, on these great smooth exposed walls, no one could sense a defilement which would be felt on such natural Edges as Stanage or Gardoms. Considerable boldness, skill, technique and endurance are necessary factors, for some of the routes are likely to take as long as three or four hours, and thus are not to be treated lightly.'

Eric Byne,
Further Developments in the Peak District, 1957.

SITUATION and CHARACTER

Millstone Edge is one of the most impressive quarries in the Peak District. It runs due north from a point approximately 100m north of the bend in the A625 Fox House to Hathersage road. When travelling towards Hathersage, the view from this bend, known locally as Surprise View, is quite spectacular.

Millstone Edge is the most recently worked of the old quarries in this guidebook. Some holds are still suspect and the quarry is notorious for the 'chest of drawers' structure at the top of the crag where the rock is thinly bedded. This 'loose' rock has been responsible for various injuries over the years. The finishes above this band are often loose and sandy and should be treated with respect. Belays at the top of the crag are scarce and a long rope to the base of the concrete fence posts is usual. Millstone faces south-west and therefore gets the sun from late morning. Most of the routes dry quickly especially as its dominating position makes it open to the wind. If none of the bays is sheltered, then a visit to Lawrencefield should be considered. Unfortunately some of Millstone's walls retain a green lichen which is slow to dry and this adds little to the frictional qualities of the already smooth rock.

APPROACHES and ACCESS

The SYT No. 272 stops at the Surprise View. Trains from Sheffield and Manchester stop at Hathersage and Grindleford. Cars may be parked at a large lay-by on the Fox House side of Surprise View or at a smaller one at the start of the track to the edge, just next to the Surprise View.

The edge is owned by Sheffield City Council and is managed by the Estates Department. Permission has not been given for climbing activities and climbers do so at their own risk.

HISTORY

Millstone Edge did not attract the early pioneers in the way that the natural edges of the Peak District did. In the 1920s the active climbers, George Bower, Reg Damms, Jack Macleod and Eric Byne amongst them, visited but climbed and recorded very little. The uncompromising steepness of the relatively featureless rock, coupled in the main with the lack of protection, was probably responsible for the lack of interest.

Development began in earnest however in the mid-to-late Fifties, although very few free climbs were added. Of the routes; *Great Slab* by Alan Maskery and *Flapjack* by Jack Soper, were typical of the style of the day. These routes followed slabs and corners respectively and as such they broke no new ground. George Leaver however, put *Petticoat Lane* up a steep, open wall which still retains some friable rock.

However, the vast majority of the new routes climbed at that time were artificial routes. They followed thin cracks in the vertical walls and often special pegs had to be home-made to fit the cracks. Peter Biven and Trevor Peck started the ball rolling with numerous impressive ascents, including *Great North Road*, *Regent Street*, *Jermyn Street*, and *Coventry Street*. Their artificial routes culminated in 1956 with an ascent of the then ultra-thin hairline crack of London Wall. This was led by Peck in a four-hour session and was said to be one of the hardest climbs on the crag at that time. Others were active in this period as well. *The Great West Road*, *Twikker*, and *Pinstone Street* were climbed by Dave Johnson with support coming from members of the Sheffield University Mountaineering Club.

By 1956 Millstone was an aid climbing venue, par-excellence. The acceptance of routes being 'pitoned to death' was in stark contrast to the rest of the routes being climbed on Peak District gritstone. There was at that time no established ethic regarding the use of pegs in the quarries. However, Joe Brown and Joe Smith, both very active throughout the Peak District, visited Millstone in 1957 and free-climbed *Great North Road* to give a stunning pitch. *Plexity* was also added by the same team, followed by *Dexterity*, an excellent route from Harold Drasdo.

Almost overnight the development of new aided routes ceased. The new routes which were then climbed were more traditional in style. *Remembrance Day* by Ted Howard, *Gimcrack* by Bas Ingle, *Crew Cut* and *Great Portland Street* by Alan Clarke, *Satan's Slit* by John Loy and *Watling Street* by Len Millsom were all climbed in the period up to 1965. They illustrate the developing nature of the climbs at Millstone at that time. The 1965 guidebook went to press with these and many more routes included. Large numbers of aided routes had been added for which few first ascent details were known. Sadly this remains so to this day.

A new and talented group of climbers took over the crag's development in the late Sixties. Terry King freed *Regent Street* in 1968 to produce a brilliant pitch and one which was a number of years ahead of its time. Today it is one of the most popular climbs of its grade and often has teams queuing for a turn. *Gates of Mordor* was climbed by Phil Burke, though sadly he was forced to use an aid point at the top of the crack. Mancunian Al Evans, climbed a lot with another Peak District activist, Keith Myhill, at the end of the Sixties. During this period Evans reduced the aid on *Pinstone Street* to one point as well as doing the first free ascent of *The Great West Road* (first pitch), and making the first lead of a previously top-roped problem, *Windrête*.

Events at that time were however totally eclipsed by the ascent of *Green Death* by Chesterfield climber, Tom Proctor. This followed a corner which had hitherto been thought unclimbable without recourse to aided means. It was very bold, the token protection being a poor peg at three-quarters height, and technically at least as difficult as any route in the country at the time. It was repeated by Proctor in 1974, after a good peg had been drilled and cemented in, and the feat was televised to the nation. Later, Proctor was to get a fine double when he was first to lead the route in winter. More technical, though shorter and much less serious, was the left arête of the Embankment; now called *Technical Master*. Myhill seems to have first claim on this one, though many others claimed it in the Seventies.

Proctor, climbing with the Sheffield-based Geoff Birtles, continued his campaign with *Knightsbridge*. This was described as being 'free with minimal protection', something of a Proctor hallmark. Visiting American climber, 'Hot' Henry Barber, freed *Brimstone* whilst John Allen, climbing with Neil Stokes, did *Keyhole Cops*. In 1974 Lancashire's Hank Pasquill did *Xanadu*, but it was Richard McHardy who stole a march when he did *Edge Lane*. Proctor was not pleased as he also was preparing for an ascent. Ed Ward-Drummond, a controversial climber at that time and one who was increasingly making his mark in the Peak District, was equally displeased when Allen freed *London Wall*. Drummond, whose fingers would not fit into the crack, was astounded. Proctor responded to these 'goings on' with *Great Arête*, another very bold undertaking. Many other routes were climbed that year (1975), but probably none so impressive as any of those mentioned.

1976 was equally as busy. The aid on *White Wall* was cut to one point by Jim Reading who then saw Steve Bancroft immediately dispense with that as well. It was however a new team from London, Mick Fowler and John Stevenson, who climbed the most routes that year. *London Pride* and *Blind Bat* were their best efforts by far.

The next few years passed relatively quietly; only perhaps *The Snivelling* by Bob Millward, and *Tea for Two* by Ian Riddington, are worthy of specific mention. A 'big' route was long overdue. In 1982 Ron Fawcett provided just that when he freed an old aid line to give *Scritto's Republic*. Climbed just before the 1983 guidebook went to press, the route was hailed as 'a contender for the hardest pitch on gritstone'. This may have been true at that time but after both the old bolts had 'died the death', it was soloed in 1988, albeit after top-roped practice and with an impressive landing 'mat'.

A number of impressive new routes were added in 1983, some from old hands and others from newcomers. *Wall Street Crash* and *Monopoly* were climbed in somewhat controversial style (the latter using pre-clipped side-runners) by Johnny Dawes. However, it was Ron Fawcett who set the cat amongst the pigeons when, as most people were plucking meat off the turkey at the Christmas table, he climbed *The Master's Edge*. It was a very significant route and one which represented a leap in standards. It remains today, one of the most coveted of gritstone routes.

In 1984 Fawcett followed Master's with *Clock People*, the obscure *Meeze Brugger* and the even more obscure *Jermyn Street Direct Finish*. Dawes, for his part, climbed *Adam Smith's Invisible Hand* and *Perplexity*. Though not quite matching Master's, these routes are nevertheless very impressive and it is indeed lamentable that the latter has been effectively destroyed by mindless hold chipping since Dawes' ascent. It is unrepeated in its 'butchered' state.

1985 was a quiet year, probably the pick of the new routes being Mark Leach's *Adios Amigo*. This was actually climbed after Leach 'copped out' of a go at Master's. New route activity in 1986 was at a very low ebb, but things picked up a little in 1987. Leach struck again, this time with the bold *The Bad and The Beautiful*. Allen Williams was busy too; *Frank Sinatra Bows Out* and *Blood and Guts on Botty Street* were climbed at that time. Little of worth has been added since and things are quiet as this guidebook goes to press.

It is difficult to see just where any major new routes can be added at Millstone (famous last words) but what however is certain is the importance of the quarry and the quality of climbing found there. It is without doubt, one of the major crags of its type in the country.

THE CLIMBS are described from RIGHT to LEFT.

On the right of the track are several small bays, each of which has varying amounts of 'climbable' rock.

The first routes proper are in a large bay, on the right of the track, approximately 100m from the car park. A slab is split by three cracks.

1 Pip 8m S (1959)
The right-hand crack is taken direct.

† **2 Beneath the Pavement Lies the Beach** 8m E4 6a (1986)
Climb the slab between Pip and Squeak through the centre of the first overhang then finish over the cracked nose above.

3 Squeak 8m VS 5b (1959)
The central crack has an overhang at mid-height.

4 Wilfred 8m S (1957-1965)
Start up Squeak but avoid its overhang by the crack on the left,
then step back up right above.

5 Annabella Superstella 8m E2 6b (1986)
The slab just left of Wilfred.

6 Helping Hands 8m E1 5b (1985)
Climb the slabby wall left again with a mantelshelf move at two-
thirds height which provides the crux. Finish up easy ledges.

*The corner to the left is broken and gives a convenient descent
route which trends leftwards.*

7 Frond Crack 7m VD (1957-1965)
On the wall left of the corner a flake crack leads to two cracks
and a large ledge. A continuation crack, S, can be used to
lengthen the route.

8 Crane Fly Climb 8m S (1957-1965)
The arête left of Frond Crack has a large scar. Climb this (the
arête not the scar), then step right to a ledge and go up to a
larger ledge. Finish above or walk off to the right.

*The face to the left is of better rock and gives the best climbs in this
bay. There is a large ledge running along the wall at just over
half-height; escape can be made to the right or up the short walls
above.*

† **9 Blood and Guts on Botty Street** 8m E5 6b (1987)
Climb the right arête of the next buttress.

10 Street Legal 8m E2 5c (1978)
Climb the wall just left of the arête passing a small hanging flake.

11 Giant's Steps 8m VD (1957-1965)
This is the first of the three prominent corners on the wall,
starting from a pedestal-like rock.

12 Midrift 8m VD (1957-1965)
The second corner is similar to, but smoother than, the first.

Juniper, 5b, (1978), is the left arête of this corner.

* **13 Hell's Bells** 8m HS 4a   (1963)
The third, and smoothest, corner is a pleasant foretaste of the
corner climbing available at Millstone.

14 Chiming Cracks 8m HS   (1959-1961)
Just to the left are twin parallel cracks. Follow these direct.

Thorpe Street, HVS 5a, (1976), follows the wider crack on the left.

15 Flank Crack 8m VD   (1957-1965)
Start at the foot of Chiming Crack but climb onto the wide ledge
on the left. Climb the crack in the angle to the large ledge.

16 Crossways 11m HVD   (1957-1965)
Go up Flank Crack to the first ledge, then traverse a long way left
before climbing the corner to the top of a projecting buttress on
the left.

*Two routes split the wall above the traverse of Crossways. Both are
friable in places.*

17 Flared Bottom 12m HVS 5a   (1977)
Climb the right-hand crack and the broken wall above.

18 Straight Leg 12m VS 4b   (1977)
Ascend the left-hand crack.

19 Key's Climb 16m HVS 5a   (1957-1965)
Climb the short chimney below the final corner of Crossways to
a hard exit. Go up the Crossways corner until moves right can be
made on to a slab below a roof. Turn the roof on the right.

20 Butter-ess 8m HVS 5b   (1959)
To the left is a projecting buttress which is split by a crack. This
is difficult near the bottom and gets even harder at the top.

21 Piper's Crack 12m VD   (1957-1965)
Climb the corner crack left of the projecting buttress, moving
right to finish.

22 Bent Crack 13m HS   (1963)
The thin crack left of Piper's Crack is climbed direct.

*The next bay left is considerably more impressive than the small
quarries you have just passed. The largest wall is dominated, at
half-height, by a cave which gives this area its name;* **THE
KEYHOLE CAVE AREA**. *In the wall to the right is a similar
shaped, but less impressive cave, above which is a slabby area of
rock. The unstable slope above the lip of the quarry at this point*

should be treated carefully, especially as ropes can dislodge loose stones. The right-hand corner of the bay is the easy way down for all routes in this area of the edge.

23 Pot Leg Wall 15m HVS 5c (1976)
Right of the descent is a broken buttress containing a series of discontinuous peg cracks. These are most difficult low down.

All the King's Horses, S, (1965-1978), used to find its way up the broken rocks (immediately to the right of the descent) but the rocks are now too unstable even for some of the King's Men. May they RIP.

24 Trio Crack 15m S (1957-1965)
Left of the descent, a corner crack is reached by an earthy corner.

* **25 Oriel** 15m VS 5a (1957-1965)
The awkward jamming crack left of the corner leads into the cave. Traverse right onto a slab and ascend this.

† **26 Wash and Brush Up** 7m E1 6b (1985)
The brushed wall just left of Oriel provides difficult bouldering to the cave. Ironically it is seldom clean.

27 Charing Cross Road 25m HVS 5a (1956/1967)
Just left of Oriel is a slanting peg-crack which, in common with the majority of the climbs in this area, is often very sandy. Follow the crack to the cave, or start up Happy Wanderer. Above, two peg-scarred cracks lead out of the cave. Take either crack to finish; the right-hand crack is the harder.

28 Happy Wanderer 25m VS 4c (1957-1965)
The narrow crack left again leads to the left-hand side of the cave. From the cave traverse left to finish up Gimcrack.

29 At-a-cliff 25m HVS 5a (1977)
Starting two metres right of Gimcrack, climb the crack and then the overhang above to the top.

Wings of Steel, E3 5c, (1979), takes the ill-defined line to the right.

** **30 Gimcrack** 24m VS 4c (1962)
A hand-jamming crack leads up the wall and trend leftwards into the obvious hanging corner above. The unstable slope above is 'studded' with small projecting blocks which are easy to

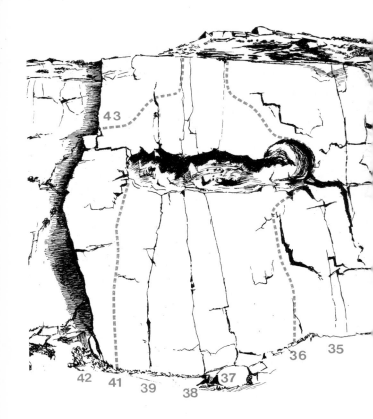

dislodge on to your belayer. Unless you have good insurance, or a ready supply of partners, take care!

* **31 The Whore** 20m HVS 5b (1975)

Left of the previous route the wall becomes steeper and more continuous. A thin crack snakes up to the overhang and the start of the major difficulties. Unfortunately swearing at the overhang

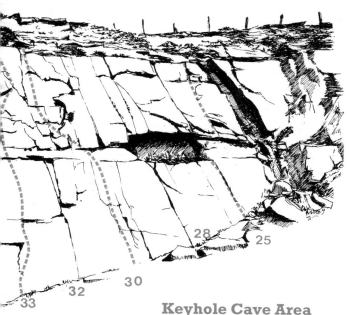

Keyhole Cave Area

is unlikely to help the strenuous layback moves which are
needed to reach the easier finishing crack.

* 32 Shaftesbury Avenue 20m HVS 5a (1956/1967)
Left again, and a prominent feature on the wall, is a fist-wide
crack. Elegantly, or otherwise, jam this to a slight roof which
must be overcome before easier climbing leads up the cracked
wall to the top.

*** 33 Wall Street Crash 20m E5 6b (1983)
Climb the thin crack in the centre of the wall left of Shaftesbury
Avenue to its end and balance frantically up the rugosited wall
above, past a peg and two bolt heads. Finish either up the ramp
variation to Regent Street, or grab a conveniently pre-placed
abseil rope. Superb crimping, at its best when un-chalked.

Unfortunately, it is usually necessary to pre-place rope slings or wires on the old bolt heads.

34 Regent Street Variant 25m E4 6a   (1975)
Effectively a direct start plus an indirect finish to the next route. Starting two metres right of Regent Street hard bouldery moves lead up to, then through, the bulge into the bottom of the shallow groove (bold and pumpy). Continue until below the final crack then take the steep ramp system on the right. Well it was 'billed' as an indirect finish!

* **35 Regent Street** 20m E2 5c   (1956/1968)
A 'real' gem; don't walk past this one, even if you have done it before! A good warm-up for the finger-cracks hereabouts. Easy finger-jamming up the crack left again leads up quickly to a small overhang which 'guards' the slabby wall above. Place some runners, anything from a Rock 1 to a Rock 9, then get over the roof. Move easily up to the bigger roof above, but swing right under this until it is possible to pull onto a small ledge at the bottom of the final crack. This is the meat of the route. Crank up this confidently to the ramp above; recover your composure and finish up the 'ball-bearings' above.

A poor eliminate up the wall between Regent Street and Jermyn Street has been climbed with side-runners, † **Appletree Yard**, E4 6a, (1988).

* **36 Jermyn Street** 25m E5 6a   (1956/1975)
Just left again a thin peg-scarred crack and a rib lead, with a bit of luck, into the right-hand side of the cave. Above is a rather unstable arête up which you have to teeter. Half-way through teetering, slot in a small nut in a thin crack on the right, then from the top of the arête, launch leftward along the lip. Once at the end of the hand-traverse summon what is left of your nerve to pull boldly on to the wall above. Continue leftwards to finish up Coventry Street.
The **Direct Finish**, E5 6b, (1984), leads off up the head-wall above the unstable arête to finish via the thin twin cracks. The earlier route is sometimes climbed with side-runners in Regent Street in which case the route is E4.

* **37 Coventry Street** 22m E5 6b   (1956/1976)
The thin finger-jamming crack in the centre of the face leads, with interest, to a good resting ledge below an all-too-obvious hard section just below the cave. Attack this with determination,

harder for those with big fingers, and get established in the cave. Step right, then climb up to and over the roof, bong runner. Holds on the left are useful. Finish direct up the easier upper crack. 6b for the first bit and E5 for the top roof but definitely no tick unless the top roof is done as well.

* **38 Piccadilly Circus** 20m E2 5b,5c (1957-1965/1976)
1. 10m. The natural finger-crack left again leads pleasantly to the cave.
2. 10m. Escape from the left-hand end of the cave to finish up The Rack. No original climbing but it is the easiest way up the wall.

* **39 Oxford Street** 22m E3 5a,6b (1956/1969)
'Follow the crack to a hard landing in the cave. The overhang is most thrilling and takes hours.' – 1957.
1. 10m. Just left is a natural hand-jamming crack. Follow this to the cave.
2. 12m. Desperately climb the overhang just right of the belay to an easier finish. Reach is a considerable advantage.

† **40 Littleheath Road** 9m E3 5c (1976)
From the belay on Oxford Street climb the rather rusty-looking overhang and crack directly above the belay. A seldom repeated route which is best not discussed in polite circles!

* **41 The Rack** 20m E5 6a (1957-1965/1976/1982)
The overhanging wall left of Oxford Street is climbed directly and is pretty strenuous and sustained. Sadly it is also a little friable. A Friend in Oxford Street, and another ready to drive you to hospital, may help to calm your nerves until the in-situ peg is reached. Unfortunately the route is close to Oxford Street in a couple of places.

*** **42 Adam Smith's Invisible Hand** 20m E6 6b (1984)
The left arête of the wall provides a formidable challenge, but at least one which is protected; providing of course you trust the old, hollow bolts which are threaded with boot-laces! Climb the arête on its right-hand side past the three bolt-heads until a swing left allows a peg to be reached. Continue more easily to the large ledge above. Traverse off, or finish as for Skywalk.

* **43 Skywalk** 25m HS (1957-1965)
Starting on the left of the arête climb the corner to the second ledge on the right. Traverse around the arête on the right onto the wall above the cave. Traverse right and finish up Oxford Street – exposed.

Two girdle traverses have been done across the Keyhole Cave area; one across the lower wall and one across the upper wall.

Transmetropolitan, E3 5c, (1988), is a poor traverse from 3m up Regent Street across the lower wall to finish up the last few feet of The Rack.

* **44 Keyhole Cops** 50m E2 5a,5c (1973)
1. 25m. Follow Oriel then meander leftwards above the overhang to a belay in the corner.
2. 25m. Move left round the corner then follow the ramp to the Regent Street peg. Go down leftwards past some old bolts into Jermyn Street. Follow this, then make a final traverse into Skywalk.

45 Ekel 20m S (1957-1965)
Climb the large corner at the right-hand end of the next wall.

* **46 Brixton Road** 25m HD (1951-1957)
Climb a jagged crack left of Ekel to a wide ledge. Go up the corner on the left moving onto a small arête for the final section.

† **47 Metal Rash** 25m E1 5b (1978)
Climb the wall left of Brixton Road to ledges then follow the thin crack to the right.

48 Bow Street 20m HVS 5b (1956/1967)
Three metres left of Brixton Road, climb the thin steep crack to join and finish up Brixton Road.

49 Petticoat Lane 25m HVS 4c (1956)
Climb a thin crack left of Bow Street to a horizontal fault, then traverse 5m left and move up right to a narrow ledge. Finish up the wall above moving right. Some friable rock, but don't let that put you off. A direct has been reported (1979), but nobody seems to know where it goes, thank God.

50 Brittle Road to Freedom 20m E1 5b (1978)
An eliminate line parallel to, and two metres left of, Petticoat Lane. Equally, if not more, stunning.

51 Alopecia 18m HVS 5a (1957-1965)
The thin crack left again demands care owing to friable rock. Well-named!

52 Old Kent Road 25m VD (1951-1957)
From the left-hand end of the wall move diagonally right up an obvious ledge to the top.

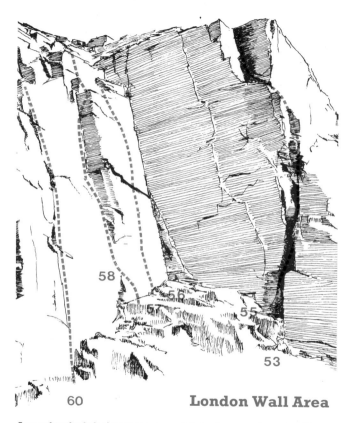

London Wall Area

Around to the left, the quarry completely changes character. Steep, solid walls are split by 'soaring' cracks. Many of the routes here are amongst the best in the Peak District.

* **53 Lambeth Chimney** 22m VS 4b   (1951-1957)
The broken chimney right of London Wall and the continuation
arête are followed until an exposed step left into the final groove.

54 Badly Bred 24m E1 5c   (1977)
From six metres up Lambeth Chimney move left to a ledge, then
move up to the base of a groove, and finish up the technically
absorbing arête on the right.

* **55 London Wall** 22m E5 6a   (1956/1975)
The thin finger-jamming, peg-crack which snakes its way up the
right wall of the big corner is one of Millstone's best-known, and
finest climbs. The initial crack often takes scalps, but two pegs
help to protect (the climbing, not your hair). In the early Eighties
this section was thought to be so hard that chalk was often
pre-placed by abseil! Easier finger-jamming leads to a
reasonable resting ledge below the final crack. Don't just stand
there, start cranking and don't stop. A capital tick for those who
get that far.

* **56 The Mall** 22m VS 4c   (1951-1957/1957)
The big corner is a classic climb of its grade, but it is
considerably harder, and less pleasant, after rain, when it
becomes sandy.

* **57 White Wall** 22m E5 6b   (1969/1976)
The line of peg holes up the wall left of The Mall is followed with
considerable difficulty, particularly in the middle section. One
peg is in situ on the upper wall. Well-protected where it matters
providing one is tall enough to place the gear. A soft touch at this
grade.

* **58 Great Portland Street** 20m HVS 5b (1951-1957/1963)
The left-facing groove is gained by a tricky mantelshelf and is
followed directly by some superb bridging. An alternative start
has been made up the wall and flake a few metres left, 5b.

† **59 Monopoly** 21m E7 6b   (1983/1984)
A thought-provoking lead up the bold wall left of Great Portland
Street. Originally led at E5 with side-runners, it has now been led
with a low peg (not in situ). Not to be under-estimated.

Right: Geoff Radcliffe on Oxford Street, Millstone Edge.
Photo: Keith Sharples.
Overleaf: Shaun Hutson on early repeat of Adam Smith's at Millstone Edge.
Photo: Ian Smith.

*** **60 Bond Street** 22m HVS 5a   (1951-1957/1957-1965)
The hand-jamming crack of the crag. From the ledge the upper
arête of Covent Garden can be used as a finish. A good
introduction to the grade and well-protected by 'cow bells' or
Friends.

† **61 Scruples** 22m E5 6b   (1987)
Climb Bond Street until established in the first sentry-box.
Arrange protection, then move boldly leftwards to climb the
bulge and slab. A peg runner in situ at the time of the first ascent
is now missing and the placement has been broken.

62 Rake's Progress 25m E1 5c   (1957-1965/1965-1978)
A thin crack in a small corner left of Bond Street leads to the top
of a pedestal. Climb the wall and groove above to a large ledge.
Finish as for Covent Garden.

** **63 Covent Garden** 25m VS 4b,4b   (1956)
1. 15m. Climb the wall up the left-hand side of the pedestal via
easy ledges. Move up on to the arête and follow it to the top of
the pedestal. Climb the wall and groove above to a large ledge.
A 5a variation passes a shot-hole then follows the arête.
2. 10m. Move left across the steep face to the left. Finish up the
superbly exposed arête. Suspect rock.

† **London Marathon**, E5 6c,6b, (1988), is a left-to-right traverse
from Covent Garden, taking a stance in The Mall, then moving
across to London Wall before finishing up Badly Bred.

* **64 Lotto** 25m E1 5c   (1957-1965/1975)
Ascend the next route to the obvious ledge. A faint groove, with
a thin crack-line in the back, starts from the right-hand end of the
ledge. Follow this to the arête, then swing on to the front face and
move up to beneath the small roof above. Hand-traverse
leftwards, back around the arête, until it is possible to finish up a
short, wide crack. There are rumours of a more direct version.

* **65 Whitehall** 25m HVS 5a   (1951-1957/1969)
The corner of the bay is followed directly with most difficulty
above the ledge.

Previous Page: Mike Lea 'puffing' on Scritto's Republic, Millstone Edge.
Photo: Dave Simmonite.
Left: Steve Hartland, down the Great North Road, Millstone Edge.
Photo: Martin Whitaker.

Embankment Wall Area

Immediately left of Whitehall is the smooth **EMBANKMENT WALL** *up which several finger-jamming classics find their ways.*

`*` **66   Embankment 4**   22m   E1   5b   (1951-1957/1975)
The first crack just left of the previous route. A small ledge, more of a good foot-hold really, at about five metres is a good place to stop and review your finger-jamming technique. The continuation crack proves to be a little harder and the moves into a shallow groove a little bolder. Once gained, the groove gives easier climbing, although the move leaving the groove does tend to catch out those who are tiring.

`*` **67   Time for Tea**   20m   E3   5c   (1974)
Two metres left is one of the few 'natural' cracks on the wall. Climb this to its termination then move leftwards, with a degree of confidence, to gain a small ledge in the middle of the wall. Finish either straight up or leftwards into Embankment 3. The original, and still frequently climbed, route goes right from the top of the crack, E1 5b, (1974), crux, to finish up Embankment 4. This is a three-star combination in itself. A modern variation is:

`*` **68   Tea for Two**   20m   E4   6a   (1982)
Follow Time for Tea to the top of the crack then continue confidently, or more likely gibber upwards like an idiot, with some difficulty.

`*` **69   Embankment 3**   25m   E1   5b,5b   (1957-1965/1970/1975)
1. 15m. The peg-crack in the centre of the wall leads, with even more excitement above half-height, to the terrace.
2. 10m. Finish up the thin crack which splits the wall just left of a shallow corner.

`*` **70   Scritto's Republic**   15m   E7   6b   (1951-1978/1982)
A hard and technical pitch up the tenuous peg-crack in the blank-looking wall to the left of Embankment 3. The bolts which previously protected the crux have broken off leaving it unprotected until above the crux. Small wires however protect the easier upper section.

`*` **71   Embankment 2**   25m   HVS   4c,4b   (1957- 1965/1965-1978)
1. 15m. Left again are two parallel cracks. Both cracks lead to the terrace; the route takes the left-hand crack throughout. The right-hand crack is HVS 5b, (1965-1978). Using the two together is likely to confuse the issue, so make your choice and stick to it!
2. 10m. Finish up the aforementioned shallow corner right of Embankment 3.

72 Who Wants the World? 10m E5 6a   (1981)
The upper wall right of Embankment 1 is hard, reachy and
initially unprotected. Fortunately the climbing soon eases.

*Returning back to the lower wall, an obvious dog-leg crack right of
the arête is taken by:*

* **73 Embankment 1** 27m E2 4c,5c   (1957-1965/1975)
1. 12m. Follow the crack to its top, then swing right past a piece
of iron to gain and follow a slight groove/crack to the terrace.
The overhanging flake which leads off leftwards from the top of
the initial crack can also be climbed at about the same grade.
This VS pitch is often done in its own right.
2. 15m. Finish directly above up the thin peg-crack.

The lower arête on the left of Embankment Wall gives a very
interesting problem. **Technical Master**, can be climbed on
either side at 6b or even one-handed (the left) at E4 6c on the
right! Just left, the layback crack is taken by **Technical Baiter**,
5b, and the arête left again by **Master Chef**, 6c. Farther left a
hanging flake provides **Deaf Dog**, a tall man's 5b.

*Above Technical Master, the final route starting from the terrace,
is:*

** **74 Blind Bat** 30m E4 5c   (1965-1972/1976)
Takes the wall just right of the left arête of the upper wall. Start
by placing a nut four metres up pitch 2 of Embankment 1. Climb
the wall between Embankment 1 and the arête, with long
reaches to a peg. Move up on sloping holds then step left
towards the arête. Finish right of the arête.

Starting back at ground level, several metres left of Technical
Master is:

* **75 Quality Street** 30m E5 6b,6a   (1983)
1. 10m. Climb directly onto the smooth ramp just right of Great
North Road with difficulty. From its top lurch right for a jug and
climb directly to the large ledge.
2. 20m. Follow the arête on the left to reach a small groove.
Climb this, moving left at the lip of the capping roof to finish
direct.

*** **76 Great North Road** 35m HVS 5a   (1956/1957)
This 'Cenotaph Corner' of Millstone is climbed directly and is
best done in one runout.

* **77 By-pass** 40m HVS 4b,5a (1963)
1. 20m. Start as for Great North Road and climb a slanting crack
with large dangerous blocks in the left wall to the huge ledge.
2. 20m. Traverse right at either of two possible levels to finish up
Great North Road.

The next two routes start from the big ledge at half-height.

* **78 Watling Street** 15m E3 5b (1957-1965)
From the ledge of By-pass climb the prominent arête left of Great
North Road. A high-enough side-runner in Great North Road
reduces the grade to HVS.

* **79 Clock People** 15m E6 7a (1984)
Ridiculously technical moves are needed to start the thin crack in
the wall left of Watling Street. Slightly easier, but very sustained,
climbing remains. The small nut protection at the top is said to
be a little 'doubtful'.

* **80 Detour** 40m E2 5c (1975)
Start 5m left of By-pass and climb slabby rock to reach a thin
crack. Climb this to the huge ledge. Traverse right into Great
North Road. Move up to the overhang and pull round this, then
move straight out onto the exposed arête to finish.

* **81 The Hunter House Road Toad** 15m E5 6b (1985)
Follow Detour to the base of a thin crack leading slightly
rightwards. Follow this desperately, past two pegs to the huge
ledge. Powerful and mean.

82 The Scoop 35m D (1951-1957)
Climb the slab on the left to the huge ledge. Finish up the corner
at the back. Provides a superb glissade in winter.

83 Scoop Crack 32m VS 4b (1957-1965)
Climb a shallow corner in an arête between the slab of The
Scoop and Knightsbridge. From the huge ledge, finish up the
obvious crack in the centre of the back wall.

* **84 Knightsbridge** 35m E2 5b,5c (1951-1957/1973)
1. 16m. The rarely-climbed green corner left of The Scoop leads
to the huge ledge.
2. 19m. A thin peg-scarred crack above the ledge is climbed
directly by excellent moves. It is most difficult in the middle
section but it is adequately protected.

*** **85 The Master's Edge** 18m E7 6b (1983)

A stunning route up the square-cut arête left of Knightsbridge. Difficult moves lead up the right-hand side of the arête with a particularly serious move to reach the shot holes, (Amigo and Tricam 2½ protection). Continue boldly to a final 'heart in the mouth' lunge for a jug, then a comparative romp to finish. Long falls from the final hard move seem to be *de rigueur*.

*** **86 Green Death** 18m E5 6b (1969)

The impeccable smooth corner left of The Master's Edge. After a hard, and getting harder, start, easy climbing leads to a steepening at a bulge. An awkward move, particularly for the short, enables the peg to be clipped and the corner to be followed to the top. Superb. A super direct start is possible in the corner 6c/7a. Alternatively, an indirect start traversing in from two metres up Edge Lane, is possible, 6a.

*** **87 Edge Lane** 18m E5 5c (1974)

The impressive clean-cut arête left of Green Death provides another totally committing route of superb quality. Progress up the arête is best achieved in stages, as it is possible to stand in balance in several places. The crux comes at the top.

*** **88 Great Arête** 16m E5 5c (1975)

The fourth horror-show hereabouts. This pitch is conveniently placed to act as a second pitch to any of the three previous routes! Belay on the ledge at the top of the previous three routes. The right-hand arête of the bay is followed, first on the right, then on the left. Any thoughts that you could jump off on to the ledge should be abandoned before you start! The small nut protection at about 2m is a bit of a joke.

† **89 The Bad and the Beautiful** 15m E6 6c (1987)

If you have survived encounters with death on the previous few routes, try this for size. The wall left of Great Arête is climbed carefully or not at all. *'You can fall but don't bounce!'*

*** **90 Great West Road** 38m E2 5b,5b (1956/1969/1975)

1. 19m. Climb the peg-scarred groove left of Edge Lane directly past a peg at 12m to the large ledges. An E1 variation goes left from the peg then up awkward ledges to the belay.
2. 19m. The big arête on the left leads impressively past an old bolt to an exposed and serious finish.

The wall to the right of the top pitch of Great West Road is **The Ginger Sponge and Custard**, E3 6a, (1983).

Green Death Area

·* **91 Adios Amigo** 15m E5 6b (1985)
'From a few metres up Xanadu do a way-out stem to gain some
shot-holes to the right. Ascend these then crank like a disease to a
nothing finger edge from which a bucket can be reached'. Hmmm!
The short will need to dive. An Amigo and Tricam protect once
out on the wall. Side-runners in and around Xanadu, together
with a third rope to curtail the swing, seem to be the minimum
necessary protection to start the route.

† **92 The Trumpton Anarchist** 12m E5 6c (1988)
Climb the bold wall above the previous route and left of the top
pitch of Great West Road starting at a faint flake. Several pegs
are said to offer some protection.

·* **93 Xanadu** 35m E3 5c,5b (1969/1974)
1. 18m. Climb the blank square-cut corner at the back of the bay
to a good ledge. Very difficult for the short. A nut slot which
previously gave good protection on this pitch is sadly no longer
with us – tough, although a hex (remember them?) can be put in
a shot-hole on the left.
2. 17m. Continue up the corner crack to a small ledge below the
top then traverse right along a break. Finish up the arête.

·* **94 Xanadu Original** 45m HVS 4c,5b (1969)
An earlier method of doing Xanadu is to do the first pitch of
Myolympus and pitch 2 of Xanadu.

* **95 Jealous Pensioner** 25m E4 5c (1978)
Climb the centre of the wall left of the first pitch of Xanadu on
good shot-holes to an obvious ledge and a poor peg. Step
slightly right, and with all the friction and commitment you can
muster, follow a slight rib up to a large ledge above where relief
is instant.

* **96 Under Doctor's Orders** 25m E2 5c (1951-1957/1987)
The thin crack in the arête left of Jealous Pensioner is followed
directly, past a peg, to a ledge. As you approach Crew Cut,
swing out right and mantelshelf on to a good ledge to finish.

·* **97 Crew Cut** 25m VS 4c (1963)
The smooth and impressive crack left of the shot holes offers
little in the way of route finding difficulties! It is usually
laybacked although it is possible to do *'Yosemite-style*
off-widthing' at around 5.10!

* **98 Yourolympus** 14m VS 4c   (1969)
From the large ledge at the top of Crew Cut, follow a rightward-slanting crack up the wall past a small ledge to a larger one. Move left along this and finish up the arête. A good top pitch to Crew Cut.

* **99 Myolympus** 40m HVS 4c,5b   (1969/1969)
1. 21m. From the resting ledge two-thirds up Crew Cut, traverse right across a slab into Xanadu's corner. Climb this to the ledge.
2. 19m. Take a line diagonally left of Xanadu, then finish directly up a thin crack.

* **100 Stone Dri** 15m E2 6a   (1976/1978)
The corner left of Crew Cut gives a fierce and technical problem which is fortunately short and safe. Regrettably, it has been chipped.

The short shot-holed flake two metres left is **Nib Nob**, HVS 5b, (1982).

To the left, a scree slope comes down from the top of the crag. This is used as the easy way down for this part of the crag. Left of this a short wall overlooks the scree.

101 Instability 15m S   (1962)
From a large boulder on the scree climb a thin crack to a grassy ledge, then move left and finish up a shallow scoop.

102 Rotten Row 16m VD   (1957-1965)
Follow the easy-angled ridge left of Instability.

103 Gripe 15m S   (1962)
The crack left of Rotten Row leads to a large grassy ledge. Finish up a wide shallow crack.

● **104 Mopsy** 15m 007   (1957-1965)
The next chimney is, at present, extremely loose and must be recorded as unjustifiable.

† **105 Piledriver** 16m E3 5c   (1976)
The arête on the left which is very close to Mopsy, has recently had a rock-fall, and is probably best avoided for both these reasons.

A poor eliminate, **Sea Creature**, E4 6a, (1984), follows the thin crack right of Billingsgate until a traverse left leads into that route to finish.

* **106 Billingsgate** 18m HVS 5b (1951-1957/1969)
*'Very hard free climbing, requiring one or two finishing pitons.' –
1957.* The open groove now gives an elegant and absorbing
climb with good protection from small wires.

107 Findus 18m HVS 5b (1983)
Start just left of Billingsgate and climb into and up an obvious
groove, finishing at the same point as Quiddity.

* **108 Quiddity** 16m HVS 5a (1957-1965)
Climb the rib between Billingsgate and Crusty Corner.

* **109 Crusty Corner** 15m S (1957-1965)
Climb a prominent V-shaped groove just right of a peculiar flake
of rock which leans to the left.

110 Keelhaul 15m VS 4c (1957-1965)
The peculiar flake is reached by a short corner. Layback round
the flake and climb to a ledge. Finish up the wall above keeping
to its left-hand edge.

* **111 Winter's Grip** 17m E6 6b (1983)
The arête left of Keelhaul is climbed on the left. Utterly gripping
at any time of the year. Rumoured to accept two hand-placed
peg runners in which case the grade may be generous at E6.

112 S.S.S 18m VS 4b (1957-1965)
Round the arête left of Keelhaul climb the larger corner to join
Keelhaul for the final few moves.

113 Neatfeet 17m VS 5a (1977)
Follow the arête left of S.S.S.

114 Flapjack 24m VS 4b (1956)
Climb the shallow stepped corner at the left-hand edge of the
projecting buttress. Move right and go up to a mantelshelf on a
ledge. Follow a wide shallow groove to a ledge then a short thin
crack.

115 Optimus 18m HVS 4c (1978)
Climb the pleasant arête left of Flapjack, avoiding the bulge on
the right.

116 Black Crack 24m S (1963)
Climb the crack in the right-hand corner of the recess left of the
projecting buttress.

110
109
108
106

Billingsgate Area

117 Shady Wall 25m VS 4c (1957-1965)
Climb the wall two metres left of Black Crack to a grassy ledge.
Continue past a small niche, then move left to a shallow groove
to finish.

Twikker Area

118 Helliconia Spring 20m HVS 5a (1983)
Start as for the previous route and follow this until it is possible to
move right to a thin crack which splits the tower. Follow this to
the top.

* **119 Diamond Groove** 30m HVS 5b (1957-1965)
Climb a thin crack about 5m left of Black Crack to a ledge on the
right. Continue up a corner in the middle of the face and climb
this, crux, to a wide ledge. Finish up the wall above.

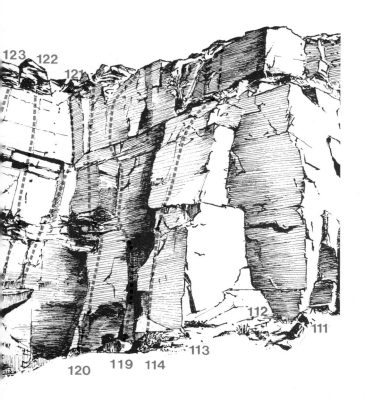

* **120 Pinstone Street** 28m E2 5c (1956/1969/1969-1978)
Start just right of the angle of the bay. Follow the peg-scarred
crack over the overhang to a ledge. Finish direct. A good pitch
despite its appearance.

*There is a large cave in the left wall of the bay. The cave can be
reached by a HS pitch leading to its left-hand side and is the
starting point for four routes.*

121 Lubric 30m HVS 5b (1957-1965)
From the right-hand side of the cave, climb out right to reach a
small ledge in the corner. Easy moves lead to a second ledge
below the final, and often greasy, corner.

* **122 Twikker** 28m E3 5c (1956/1975)
The lip of the cave on the left is split by a fine crack. This gives
strenuous and thuggy climbing, but remember, don't let
technique get in the way of strength! Continue directly up the
crack which, after another unfortunately small roof, leads to a
slab and less thuggish climbing to the top. There are two
alternative, and much harder, ways of entering the cave to begin
Twikker. The **Direct Start** is 5c and follows the
rightward-curving flake which leads to the right-hand end of the
cave. The **Direct Start** is harder still at 6b. This takes the wall
below the flake to finish at the same point as the direct start. Both
are little more than extended boulder problems.

* **123 Erb** 30m E2 5c (1957-1965/1975)
The thin crack three metres left of Twikker's upper section. Gain
this crack from the left-hand side of the cave and climb it to the
top. Easier and not quite so fine as Twikker.

* **124 Lyon's Corner House** 35m HVS 5a (1956/1957-1965)
Follow Erb to the lip of the cave but continue traversing left up
on to the face. Climb the wall diagonally leftwards to the arête on
large but awkward holds. Finish up the arête. Or, from the ledge
on the face, climb a thin flake crack to a small overhang.
Hand-traverse left to join the arête.
For **The Direct Start**, 5a, (1957-1965), climb the arête and crack
below and left of the cave directly to the ledge on the wall.

Instant Coffee, 4c, (1957-1965). Climb a crack in the centre of
the wall left of the arête for about 4m, then hand-traverse
rightwards to join Lyon's Corner House at the arête.

125 Mean to Me 35m HVS 5b (1980)
Start as for Instant Coffee. Climb the crack in the wall to a
corner/groove and go up this to a jug. Then step right on to the
wall, go up to a ledge and finish up the wall left of Lyon's Corner
House.

Mark Leach soloing the top pitch of Great West Road, Millstone Edge.
Photo: Neil Foster.

Acheron, VS 4c, (1963), is buried somewhere in the corner of the bay.

* **126 Frank Sinatra Bows Out** 15m E5 6b (1987)
A good scary wall climb. Climb the wall to the ledge and an unusual peg; though a Friend backs this up. Difficult moves above lead to a sloping ledge. Scramble desperately on to this, ground-fall potential, then either traverse off or continue up the easier though loose wall above.

* **127 Eros** 15m HVS 5b (1957-1965/1969)
Climb the flake crack in the centre of the left wall of the bay to finish directly up unstable breaks. The original free version, **Vulcan's Variant**, HVS 5a, (1968), finished leftward and is slightly easier but less logical.

* **128 Meeze Brugger** 15m E5 6b (1984)
Step off the block just left of Eros and trend leftwards past a good Friend to a prominent jug and 'iffy' wires. Now make hard moves to stand on the jug. A final awkward move leads to easier but looser ground.

† **129 Breeze Mugger** 15m E5 6b (1990)
Start just left of Meeze Brugger, beneath a hole at 4m. Climb directly to the hole, good wires, then continue direct to easier ground. Finish by swinging out on to Windrête.

* **130 Windrête** 14m E2 5b (1969)
Left of the previous route is a prominent arête which appears to terminate in the usual Millstone 'pack of cards'. Start on the right of the arête, then follow it to top. The crux is low down, but interest is maintained.

On the left of Windrête is a large bay, the bottom half of which is an immense slab – **THE GREAT SLAB**. *Several routes lead up this to a variety of finishes which have varying degrees of looseness.*

131 Cake Walk 20m HS (1957-1965)
Start at the right-hand edge of the Great Slab and climb easily up to its top. Traverse left to a crack in the centre of the wall and climb this and a chimney.

Adios Amigos to Neil Travers, Millstone Edge.
Photo: Chris Wright.

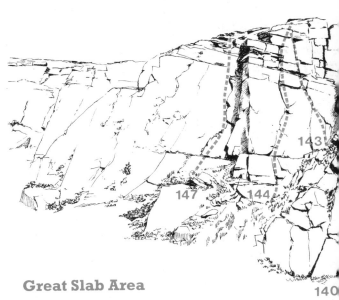

Great Slab Area

132 Bun Run 20m HVS 5a   (1969)
Climb to the top of the slab via a thin crack near its right-hand
edge. A hanging crack right of a curved flake leads to a finish up
a shallow corner.

133 Lorica 20m VS 4c   (1957-1965)
As for Bun Run to the top of the slab. Climb the curved flake to a
good ledge. Finish as for Bun Run.

134 Sex Dwarfs 10m E3 6b   (1982)

A thin line three metres right of The Great Slab requires
squeaky-clean boots. Rapidly becoming very polished. Finish by
sliding, or falling, down the route or by climbing down Cake
Walk.

135 Dino 13m E4 6b   (1984)
An even thinner, independent, line starting as for Sex Dwarfs.
Follow a parallel line just right of Great Slab which leads slowly,
and without relent, to the break. Finish as for The Great Slab or
traverse off to the right.

* **136 The Great Slab** 28m HS 4a   (1952/1957)
Climb the crack in the middle of the slab until a move up right
leads to easier climbing to its top. Follow a crack in the centre of
the wall and then move right to gain a chimney which leads to
the top (as for Cake Walk).

137 Election Special 15m E4 6b   (1987)
Climb the slab between The Snivelling and Great Slab to a peg;
missing at the time of writing. Continue over the overlap to a
belay. Side-runners in The Great Slab are usual at this grade.

* **138 The Snivelling** 15m E5 6a   (1978)
A unique slab climb, just left of the chiselled holds on The Great
Slab. Climb the slab slightly leftwards then move directly on
very poor holds to a large hole and Hex. 10 or Friend 4. Exit
directly. Easy on a top-rope, but just try leading it on-sight.

139 Velvet 20m E2 5c,5b   (1984)
A worthwhile route up the slab left of The Snivelling.
1. 10m. Climb the slab two metres right of the corner taken by
Svelt to a junction with that route at a small roof. Follow Svelt until
it is possible to belay in the break above.
2. 10m. Take the thin groove above the belay to a roof, then
hand-traverse left to finish up a grassy groove.

* **140 Svelt** 20m HVS 5a   (1962)
Climb the smooth corner at the left-hand side of the slab to a
ledge on the right. Finish up the wide shallow groove above. A
better finish up the left-hand groove is 4c.

A pointless but enjoyable girdle of the slab, **Gibbering Heap**, E3
5c, (1984), is possible. Follow Velvet to the roof on Svelt, then
traverse delicately right passing the large hold on The Snivelling
to finish across Sex Dwarfs and down Cake Walk.

141 Crumbling Cracks 20m HS   (1957-1965)
Start at the bottom left corner of the slab. Climb a groove in a
narrow projecting rib of rock, finishing on the front of a small
buttress on the left.

142   Creaking Corner   18m   VS   4c   (1957-1965)
Left of a loose area of rock is a corner. Climb this and finish up a
wide crack on the left.

143   Evening Premiere   19m   HVS   5a   (1976)
Left again is an obvious left-slanting crack which joins Wuthering
Crack near its top.

* **144   Wuthering Crack**   18m   HVS   5a   (1957-1965)
Climb the Y-shaped crack in the left wall of the bay, passing a
triangular block, to a friable finish.

145   The Pittsburgh Enigma   15m   E4   5c   (1985)
Scramble up loose blocks to the foot of the arête left of
Wuthering Crack and climb up and right to a peg. Continue up
the arête, past a second peg on the left, to finish up poor rock.

● **146   Dune Crack**   10m   Suicidal   (1957-1965)
A dangerous route up the thin sandy crack in the corner left of
Wuthering Crack, with a particularly 'exciting' step left at the top.

147   Dune Flake   10m   S   (1957-1965)
The flake to the left is better, but exercise care at the top.

148   Sudden Impact   11m   E1   5b   (1984)
Climb the thin crack left of Dune Flake.

149   Flaky Pastry   12m   VD   (1957-1965)
Start near the foot of Dune Flake and climb diagonally leftwards
to finish near the top left-hand corner of the wall.

150   Rough Puff   10m   VD   (1957-1965)
Some loose cracks near the left edge of the wall.

151   F.A.T.D.   14m   S   (1969)
Climb the arête between Rough Puff and Bowling Green.

The next bay has a peculiar pinnacle, **THE CIOCH**, *leaning
against its left wall.*

152   Bowling Green   14m   VD   (1959)
From ledges to the right of the bay, climb a wide, shallow groove
to finish at the top right-hand corner of the wall.

† **153   Slime Crime**   18m   E4   6a   (1983)
Slippery climbing up the slab between Bowling Green and
Eartha trending slightly right then left.

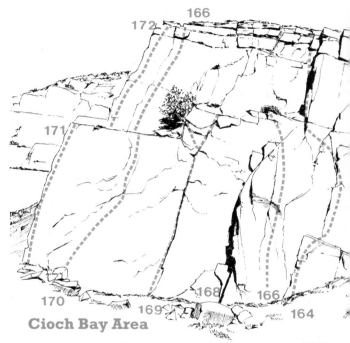

Cioch Bay Area

* **154 Eartha** 18m HS 4a   (1957)
Start just to the right of a wide crack in the right wall of the bay.
Climb delicately to a ledge at 6m, then move right to finish up a
flake crack in the centre of the wall.

* **155 Only Just** 23m E1 5b   (1959)
Climb Eartha to the ledge, then a shallow groove just left of
Eartha to the top. Usually nuts are placed in Eartha.

156 Shamrot 16m S   (1957-1965)

'Will become more pleasant with use.' – 1965. The wide crack just left of Eartha leads to a large grassy recess. Finish up the loose corner.

* **157 Cornerstone Climb** 17m S (1952)
Delicately climb the slabby angle of the bay by its right-hand edge. Finish by moving right to avoid the loosest rock.

† **158 Strait Jacket** 9m E5 6b (1989)
Climb the right-hand side of the slab, just left of the previous route, to an obvious nut placement. Move left via two small pockets then finish direct.

159 Eskimo Blue Day 16m VS 4c (1971)
The crack two metres to the left of Cornerstone Climb.

* **160 Boomerang** 24m S (1957-1965)
On the left wall of the bay, first climb a left-slanting break, then a right-slanting break. Traverse right and take the easiest line to the corner. Very loose at the top.

161 Brumal 20m VS 4c (1957-1965)
As for Boomerang to the right-slanting break at 6m. Move up right, then go back left into a slanting crack. Finish left from the ledge.

† **162 Diamond Daze** 20m E3 5c (1983)
Climb the slab left of Brumal to join Boomerang.

On the left is **THE CIOCH** *itself.*

163 Cioch Diagonal 22m HVD (1956)
Follow the first break of Boomerang to the top of The Cioch. Finish up the wall above, about three metres left of the corner.

* **164 Close Shave** 30m S (1956)
Start just right of The Cioch and climb thin corner cracks to its top. Finish up the corner at the back of the shelf.

† **165 The Hacker** 20m VS 4c (1983)
Follow a curving peg-scarred crack two metres right of Supra Direct to a short vertical crack with two ancient pegs. Follow the crack which leads to the crux on the wall above. Finish up the overhanging wall to the right of Supra Direct.

* **166 Supra Direct** 20m HVS 5b (1957-1965/1975)
The peg-scarred crack on the front face of The Cioch to the shelf. Finish up the thin crack near the left-hand end of the wall above.

A poor eliminate, **Frigged Anonymously**, E2 5c, (1985), has been climbed between Supra Direct and Mayday.

* **167 Mayday** 22m HVS 5a (1957-1965)
The left arête of The Cioch is climbed to the ledge. The arête on
the right is then followed to the top.

168 Cioch Corner 22m S (1956)
Climb the corner on the left of The Cioch to the shelf, then take
any finish to the top.

** **169 Dexterity** 20m HVS 5b (1957)
The fine jamming crack in the wall left of The Cioch. Arm
yourself with Hex's 9 to 11, or Friends 2 to 4, and lay siege to the
crack. Once level with a slight roof at about 10m, you can
cop-out by moving easily left onto the shelf. It is best however to
eschew all traversing off and carry on direct. Finish up the wall
above the ledge.

* **170 Dextrous Hare** 16m E3 5c (1957-1965/1976)
In the middle of the wall to the left is a thin peg-crack which
leads to the base of a small hanging corner. Once gained, the
corner is followed easily to the ledge above.

* **171 March Hare** 30m E2 5b (1957-1965/1975)
The arête left of Dextrous Hare is climbed initially on the left
wall, then by moving right on to the arête proper. Finish up the
crack just right of the upper arête. The wall just to the left can
also be climbed.

* **172 April Arête** 16m HVS 4c (1957-1965)
Gain the shelf by any of the previous routes. Climb the
square-cut arête, on the left of the shelf, on its right-hand side.
The old aided start up the flake/groove left of March Hare, now
free at 6b, was previously *'climbed by placing a piton high in the
flake whilst standing on the second man's shoulder. Stand in a sling
suspended from the piton and so gain the shelf.' – 1965.*

173 Fluted Corner 12m HS 4a (1957-1965)
Climb the grassy corner round the corner.

174 Dolorous Gard 11m E2 5b (1982)
The sharp arête four metres left is climbed on its left-hand side.

175 Bamboozle 10m VS 4c (1957-1965)
Climb the groove left of Fluted Corner to the large rounded
overhang. Climb round this then go diagonally right to the rib.

176 Slack Alice 10m E1 5c (1982)
Climb the thin crack through a bulge.

North Bay Area

178

179

180

182

*The gully in the corner of the next bay, **NORTH BAY**, has been affected by a large rock-fall.*

177 Spider Crack 15m VS 4c   (1957-1965)
On the right wall of the debris. Start in a groove below a crack. Climb to a block then move right to reach the crack itself and follow this to the top.

178 The Web 16m VS 4c   (1951-1957)
Climb to the groove left of Spider Crack. Go up the groove and the edge on the right to a large grassy shelf and an easier finish.

*An extensive rock-fall on the left has taken with it the upper sections of **Chaos**, (1957-1965), and **Derision**, (1957-1965). The flake crack just left, which was once the start of Derision, is now the start of the next route.*

* **179 Soho Sally** 28m HVS 5b   (1975)
From the ledge at the top of the flake, climb the open groove above until forced onto the airy left-hand arête. Climb this to a broken finish.

·* **180 Saville Street** 28m E3 6a   (1957-1965/1975)
A fine route. A short, but awkward, crack leads onto the ledge. Attack the splendid crack above. The overhang is the hardest section but a positive approach pays dividends with the sloping holds that lurk in the niche above.

† **181 Scumline** 28m E5 6b   (1969/1984)
Climb the thin, scarred crack left of Saville Street until it fizzles out. Swing desperately left to join and finish up the next route.

182 Commix 28m E2 5c   (1957-1965/1976)
Start in the corner on the left of Saville Street. Go up a short corner to the ledge (or walk under Plexity). At the right-hand end of the ledge is a shallow groove which slants leftwards and overhangs in its middle section. Go up this for three metres then move right to a thin peg-scarred crack. Climb this until it is possible to mantelshelf into a niche. Climb the wall and a short loose corner.

183 Southern Comfort 22m E3 5c   (1957-1965/1976)
A more direct, but less pleasant, version of Commix which goes straight up the overhanging groove which Commix avoids.

A rightward-trending hand-traverse from the ledge at the start of Commix has been climbed. Follow a line of pockets into Saville Street, † **Owzaboutthatthen**, E4 6b, (1988).

Well to the left of an easy gully is a short wall.

† **184 Fat and Jealous** 9m E5 6c (1989)
Climb the centre of the wall past a peg – missing at the time of writing.

† **185 Salinela Sunset** 10m E4 6a (1987)
Left again is an arête. Climb it on its right-hand side with a final move left using a jug.

Returning to the main crag the next few routes start off the big ledge above the floor of the bay which is reached by scrambling up the short gully.

* **186 Rainy Day** 20m VS 4b (1957-1965)
Climb the corner crack that starts halfway along the right-hand back wall of the big ledge, then move on to a ledge on the left. Continue past an overhang and finish up a short steep crack above.

* **187 Day Dream** 20m VS 4b (1957-1965)
Start just left of Rainy Day on the projecting rocks. Follow an indefinite crack-line and shallow corner to join Rainy Day at the final short crack. Finish up this.

* **188 Remembrance Day** 22m VS 4c (1959-1961)
Climb the crack in the left-hand wall of the bay to an earthy ledge on the right. Finish up the groove above.

*** **189 Plexity** 22m HVS 5a (1957)
Climb the overhanging crack in the middle of the left wall of the bay to a recess. Finish up the steep crack above by stepping in from the right.

Six metres left of Plexity is an arête; the substance of the next route:

† **190 Perplexity 24m E6 6c (1957-1965/1986)
Another 'Dawes desperate'. Climb the steep arête via a series of bold moves to the overhang. Step right to climb the groove and a thin crack right of the upper arête to finish. Now sadly chipped and unrepeated in its present state.

North Wall Area

201   200   199

* **191 London Pride**   25m   E5   6b,5c   (1957-1965/1976)
1. 15m. Left of Perplexity is a scarred crack. Climb the crack,
hard at first but fortunately well-protected, until easier, but alas
poorly-protected, moves lead past a small overhang at about 5m.
Finding a hidden peg above should be your next priority. Once
found and clipped, calm down, then traverse right to the arête
and a bolt belay. The state of the bolts leaves plenty to be
desired and you may wish to continue without belaying. On the
other hand you may not wish to continue at all!

2. 10m. Traverse 5m right and climb a groove just left of Plexity.
Go up the groove to an overhang. Go over this and climb the
crack in the wall above.

A direct finish has been claimed above London Pride's first pitch.

† **Which way up Robitho**, E4 6b, (1988), follows the obvious

hanging groove left of the arête. It has three pegs but very few holds.

* **192 Gimbals** 18m HVS 5b   (1957-1965/1976)
Start up the corner left of London Pride, move right at the small overhang and finish up the wall above.

* **193 Estremo** 16m HVS 5a   (1957-1965)
Climb the S-shaped crack just left of Gimbals. At the overhang move left into a corner. Layback up this to the top.

194 Cauldron Crack 15m E3 5c   (1957-1965/1976)
Climb the right-hand side of the arête, just left of the S-shaped crack, to the overhang. Move left onto the face to a leftward-slanting crack. Follow this to the top.

195 Freight Train 15m E4 6a   (1988)
From the overhang on the previous route swing out on to the hanging arête, 'iffy' peg but good wires to the left, then continue by swinging round onto the other side, and up past another peg. Finish direct.

196 Hacklespur 15m HVS 5b   (1957-1965)
Climb the prominent chimney/groove.

197 Pin Prick 15m E2 5c   (1957-1965/1977)
Climb the system of thin cracks just left of Hacklespur.

* **198 Gates of Mordor** 15m E3 5c   (1969/1969)
Left of Pin Prick are two cracks which merge after about 6m. Climb the right-hand crack/groove to the small overhang. Continue up the crack above to an awkward finish. Strenuous.

199 Satan's Slit 13m HVS 5b   (1964)
The next crack to the left forks after 3m. Climb the crack then move right into the main crack. Climb this past a recess.

For those terminally obsessed with this area, yet another rightwards traverse, † **Anything is Possible in Cartoons**, E4 6b, (1988), follows Satan's Slit for 3m, then goes right, crux, to a peg and so into Gates of Mordor.

Right: Greg Cunningham on Erb, Millstone Edge.
Photo: Ian Smith.
Overleaf: A snowy Great Slab, Millstone Edge.
Photo: Martin Whitaker.

** **200 Brimstone** 13m E1 5b (1957-1965/1973)
Left of the previous route is a thin peg-scarred crack. Awkward, rather than hard, moves get you established at a good horizontal break. Place as many runners as you can, then press-on to the top.

201 Scrimsel 12m VS 4c (1957-1965)
Climb the next prominent crack to the left. The initials CB are carved on the wall by its side halfway up.

To the left, a peg-scarred crack gives a short problem.

202 Brindle 8m VS 4c (1957-1965)
Left again is a short prominent crack. Climb this taking care near the top.

MILLSTONE EDGE LIST OF FIRST ASCENTS

Early 1920s	*George Bower did a few routes up now forgotten weaknesses. He then retreated to Stanage Edge.*
Late 1920s	*Reg Damms, Jack Macleod and Eric Byne also visited but again only left one un-recorded route before leaving.*
	The edge lay dormant for some time.
1952	**Cornerstone Climb, Great Slab** (some aid) Alan Maskery. *First free ascent of Great Slab in 1957.*
1956 Sept.	**The Great North Road** (A2) Peter Biven, Trevor Peck. *First free ascent in 1957.*
1956 Sept.	**Petticoat Lane** George Leaver, Kit Twyford. *Climbed on the same day as Great North Road – towards the end of September.*
1956	**Lyon's Corner House** (A3) George Leaver, Kit Twyford. *First free ascent unknown (1957-1965).*
1956	**The Great West Road** (A3) Dave Johnson and Sheffield University Mountaineering Club party. *First free ascent in 1969-1975.*
1956	**Twikker** (A2 and VS) Dave Johnson and SUMC party. *First free ascent in 1975.*
1956	**Pinstone Street** (A2) Dave Johnson and SUMC party. *First free ascent in 1975-1976.*
1956	**Flapjack** Jack Soper.

Previous Page: Jim Curran on April Arête, Millstone Edge.
Photo: Ian Smith.
Left: Johnny Dawes on the first ascent of Perplexity, Millstone Edge.
Photo: Neil Foster.

1956   **Bow Street** (A2)   Frank Fitzgerald, Beeley.
First free ascent in 1967.

1956   **Close Shave**, **Crazy Paving** (No longer described), **Cioch Corner**
Alan Clarke, Ben Wilson, Ted Howard.

1956   **Cioch Diagonal**   Alan Clarke.

1956   **Shaftesbury Avenue** (A1)   Peter Biven, Trevor Peck.
First free ascent in 1967.

1956   **Regent Street** (A2)   Peter Biven, Trevor Peck.
*The 1957 Recent Developments guidebook credited Regent Street to
George Leaver and Kit Twyford.*
First free ascent in 1968.

1956   **Jermyn Street** (A2)   Peter Biven, Trevor Peck.
First free ascent in 1975.

1956   **Coventry Street** (A3)   Peter Biven, Trevor Peck.
Micro pegs were necessary.
First free ascent in 1976.

1956   **Oxford Street** (A3)   Peter Biven, Trevor Peck.
First free ascent in 1969.

1956   **Covent Garden**   Peter Biven, Trevor Peck.

1956   **Charing Cross Road** (A1)   Peter Biven, Trevor Peck.
First free ascent in 1967.

1956   **London Wall** (A3)   Trevor Peck, Peter Biven.
*Climbed using especially thin pegs for the then hairline crack. The
ascent took about four hours.*
"The hardest climb on the crag ... a thrilling and spectacular route".
First free ascent in 1975.

1956   **The Girdle Traverse** (Aid)   Peter Biven, Trevor Peck.
*Obviously a frantic year with several teams working hard. In the event,
Peter Biven and Trevor Peck established an effective technique and
almost entirely dominated the development, especially so in the
Keyhole Cave area.*

*Publication of the 1957 Further Developments guidebook. Other routes
mentioned whose first ascent details are unknown include:*
Billingsgate (A1 & VS), **Hammersmith Road** (A2, wedges),
Knightsbridge (A1 wedges), **The Scoop**, **The Embankment** (A1,
now called Embankment 4), **Whitehall** (A1), **Bond Street** (A1), **Great
Portland Street** (A3), **The Mall** (A2), **Lambeth Chimney**, **The Old
Kent Road**, **Brixton Road**.

1957   **Supra Direct** (A1)   Parnassus Climbing Club party.
First free ascent in 1975.

1957   **Great North Road**, **The Mall**   Joe Brown, Joe (Morty) Smith.
First free ascents.

1957   **Plexity**   Joe Brown, Morty Smith.

1957   **Dexterity**   Harold Drasdo.

1957   **The Great Slab**, **Eartha**   Al Parker, Peter Bamfield.
First free ascent of Great Slab.

1959 Summer	**Pip**, **Squeak**, **Bowling Green** Al Parker, Peter Bamfield.
1959	**Butter-ess** Al Parker, Bob Brayshaw. *Omitted from the 1965 guidebook.*
1959	**Only Just** Ernie Marshall, Wilfred (Wilf) White. *Omitted from the 1965 guidebook.*
1959-1961	**Remembrance Day** Ted Howard.
1959-1961	**Chiming Cracks** Alan Clarke.
1962	**Gimcrack** Barry (Baz) Ingle.
1962	**Instability** John Loy.
1962	**Gripe** Harry Wood.
1962	**Derision** Clive Rowland. *Omitted from the 1965 guidebook).*
1962	**Svelt** Al Parker, Martin Boysen (alternate leads).
1963	**Crew Cut**, **Bent Crack**, **Hell's Bells**, **Great Portland Street**, **Windrête** Alan Clarke. *Whilst Windrête was only top-roped, Clarke's ascent of Great Portland Street was the first free ascent.*
1963	**Acheron**, **Black Crack** Don Morrison.
1963	**By-pass** John Loy.
1963	**Duo Crack**, **Michaelmas Crack**, **Michaelmas Corner** (no longer described) Harry Wood.
1964	**Satan's Slit** John Loy.
1957-1965	**Watling Street** Len Millsom. *Omitted from the 1965 guidebook.* *Until recently known as Brush Off.*
1957-65	**Wlfred** Alan Clarke, John Loy.
1957-65	**Frond Crack**, **Crane Fly Climb** John Loy (solo).
1957-65	**Piper's Crack** John Loy.
1957-65	**Crossway** John Loy.
1957-65	**Torridon Corner**, **Humpty Dumpty** Don Morrison, John Loy.
1957-65	**Trio Crack** John Loy, Don Morrison, Harry Woods.
1957-65	**Happy Wanderer**, **Oriel** John Brailsford.
1957-65	**The Rack** (Hard A2 & HS) *'Tanky had something to do with this. A sky hook was used on one move and Tanky fell out of his etriers.'* *First free ascent in 1982.*
1957-65	**Skywalk** John Loy, Alan Clarke.
1957-65	**Ekel** John Loy. *Ekel is German for dirty.*
1957-65	**Lotto** (A1 & HS) John Loy, J Widdowson. *First free ascent in 1975.*

1957-65	**Embankment Routes** (A1 & VS) probably Biven and Peck. *First free ascent in 1975.*
1957-65	**Scoop Wall** (A1) probably John Conn. *First free ascent in 1969.*
1957-65	**Scoop Crack** John Loy, Alan Clarke.
1957-65	**Rotten Row, Mopsy** John Loy (solo).
1957-65	**Quiddity** John Loy, Don Morrison.
1957-65	**Crusty Corner** John Loy (solo).
1957-65	**Keelhaul** Alan Clarke, John Loy.
1957-65	**S.S.S.** Jack Soper. *S.S.S. is an irreverent geological term meaning shit and small stones.*
1957-65	**Flapjack** Jack Soper.
1957-65	**Shady Wall** Alan Clarke, John Loy.
1957-65	**Diamond Groove** John Loy, Alan Clarke. *'1 peg runner by the loose block – we didn't have wires in those days. I was also wearing mountain boots.'*
1957-65	**Lubric** Alan Clarke, John Loy. *'Alan led this on sight – no pre-cleaning or inspection – I thought that he was mad.'*
1957-65	**Erb** (A1 & VS) Alan Clarke. *Named after his son who was a few days old.* *First free ascent in 1975.*
1957-65	**Instant Coffee** John Loy (solo).
1957-65	**Lorica** possibly John Conn.
1957-65	**Crumbling Cracks** Alan Clarke, John Loy.
1957-65	**Creaking Corner** John Loy (solo).
1957-65	**Wuthering Crack** Alan Clarke, John Loy.
1957-65	**Dune Crack, Dune Flake** John Loy (solo).
1957-65	**Flaky Pastry, Rough Puff** John Loy.
1957-65	**Shamrot, Boomerang** John Loy (solo).
1957-65	**Brumal** John Loy, Harry Woods.
1957-65	**May Day** Alan Clarke, John Loy.
1957-65	**April Arête** Alan Clarke, John Loy (AL) *'We started this by a hanging flake on the side wall below the final arête using combined tactics.'*
1957-65	**Fluted Corner** John Loy (solo).
1957-65	**Bamboozle** Ted Howard, Pat Fearneough. *'This was one Wednesday afternoon. It was the only time that I saw Pat really struggle on a route, but he really had to fight on the layback. When he reached the top he pulled a telephone out of his pocket – it was this that had jammed and given the trouble. The phone was to be*

installed in someone's house the following morning..... the scratches only showed if you looked hard.'

| 1957-65 | **Spider Crack**   Don Morrison, John Loy. |

1957-65   **The Web**   John Loy, A Nother.
Done in pouring rain.

1957-65   **Chaos, Derision**   probably Clive Rowlands.

1957-65   **Saville Street** (A2)   probably Reg Pillinger.
Note the name – a Sheffielder's answer to the London street names.
First free ascent in 1975

1957-65   **Commix** (A2 & VS)   John Loy.
4 pegs were used on the overhanging section of the groove. Harry Woods failed to follow so the leader top-roped the route to retrieve the gear.
First free ascent in 1976

1957-65   **Rainy Day**   Alan Clarke, John Loy.

1957-65   **Day Dream**   John Loy, Alan Clarke.

1957-65   **Estremo**   Ted Howard with probably the Gillotts.

1957-65   **Hacklespur** (aid)   Alan Clarke, John Loy.
Freed by Loy in 1962.

1957-65   **Scrimsel**   Alan Clarke, John Loy.

1957-65   **Brindle**   John Loy (solo).

The 1965 Sheffield Froggatt guidebook went to press with the crag having reached so-called maturity. Many other climbers, including W Ward, K Rhodes, Ted Howard, Clive Rowland and Les Gillott, were also active during this period. Who did what is not clear but the guidebook also contained the following uncredited routes.
Giant's Steps, **Midrift**, **Flank Crack**, **Key's Climb**, **Cold Comfort**, **Alopecia**, **Rake's Progress** (A1 & VS), **Eros** (A1), **Cake Walk**, **Sweater** (A1), **Gimbals** (A1), **Cauldron Crack** (A1), **Pin Prick** (A1), **Brimstone** (A1).
Numerous shorter and scrappier routes were also included and are not described in this edition.

1967 April 19   **In Memoriam** (1pt)   Paul Grayson, Jack Firth.
A rurp and a drilled peg runner were used.
Later claimed by Keith Myhill, Al Evans. Now the top pitch of Great West Road.
First free ascent in 1975.

1967   **Charing Cross Road**   Anon.
First free ascent.

1967   **Shaftsbury Avenue**   Jim Campbell.
First free ascent.
Rumour has it that although many people thought that they had made the first ascent, no-one was willing to argue with 'Big Jim'.

1967   **Bow Street**   Alan (Richard) McHardy.
First free ascent.

1968 Sept.   **Vulcan's Variant**   Al Evans, Keith Myhill.

1968	**Regent Street** Terry King.	

Regent Street Terry King.
First free ascent, a brilliant lead, ahead of its time.

1969 April 17 **Xanadu** Keith Myhill, Al Evans (alternate leads).
This original line started up Crew Cut, then traversed into the main corner along easy ledges. The direct start, eliminating all this traversing, was added by Hank Pasquill in 1974.

1969 Aug. 24 **Gates of Mordor** (1pt) Phil Burke.
Second failed to follow. The aid point was used at the top of the crack. First free ascent in 1969.

1969 Aug. 24 **Bun Run** Al Evans, Nick Elliott.

1969 Sept. **Devil's Delight** (1pt) Keith Myhill, Nick Elliott.
An aid peg was used at the top. First free ascent in 1973 as Brimstone.

1969 **Eros**, **Myolympus** (1pt) Paul Grayson.
First free ascent of the former and the top pitch of the latter with 1 nut for aid. The first free ascent of this was in 1969.

1969 **Yourolympus** Dave Gregory, Andrew Brodie.

1969 **Edge Lane** (aid) Paul Grayson.
Top pitch only. Now the top pitch of Great West Road. Freed by John Allen.

1969 **Great West Road** Al Evans, Keith Myhill.
First free ascent. Only the first pitch was climbed by following the left-hand variation. The direct finish was added later by Keith Myhill.

1969 **Whitehall** Keith Myhill, Al Evans (alternate leads).
First free ascent.

1969 **Billingsgate** Steve Chadwick.
First free ascent.

1969 **Gates of Mordor** Hank Pasquill.
First free ascent. Tentatively re-named as Bolton Crack and graded HVS!

1969 **Myolympus**, **Windrête** Al Evans, Z Dyslewicz.
First free ascent of the former and the probable first lead of the latter although Pete Crew was also strongly rumoured to have soloed it at the time.

1969 **Pinstone Street** (1pt), **Scoop Wall** Al Evans, Z Dyslewicz.
1 peg used to rest on the former route. Only the first pitch of the latter was climbed.

1969 **White Wall** (A1) Anon.
First free ascent 1976.

1969 **Green Death** Tom Proctor, Keith Myhill.
A stunning new route up rock hitherto not thought to be suited to free-climbing. The start was originally made from a pile of stones. Green Death and Proctor received instant fame in 1974 as the BBC televised the second ascent. Following his first ascent, on which the peg fell out after a gentle nudge, Proctor drilled out the peg placement and cemented in the current peg for posterity. Green Death hinted at the

Proctor routes that were to follow in the Seventies. Later, Proctor was to be the first person to lead the route in winter conditions.

1969	**F.A.T.D.** Anon.	

1969   **Nostrils** (A1) R Buckley, Al Thewless.
Climbed with pegs and 7 bolts!
First free ascent of the first section in 1984 as Scumline.

1969   **Oxford Street** Phil Burke, John (Jus) RQ Jeany.
First free ascent.
Later claimed, er'ron'eously, by Fawcett and Pete Livesey.

Late 1960s   **Technical Master** Keith Myhill.
Later claimed by Ron Fawcett, Ed Drummond and John Allen.

1970   **Embankment Route 3** Ken Jones.
First free ascent of pitch 2 only.

1971 Mar. 17   **Eskimo Blue Day** R Hayward, R Sedgewick.

1965-1972   **Blind Bat** (A2) Les Bonnington.
First free ascent in 1976.

1972 May   **The Snake** (no longer described) Ken Jones, Bill Birch, Paul Nunn.

1973   **Brimstone** Henry Barber.
First free ascent of Devil's Delight.

1973   **Knightsbridge** Tom Proctor, Geoff Birtles.
First free ascent, after an earlier attempt by the same team had failed to get rid of the aid entirely. Described at the time as 'free with minimal protection'.

1973   **Keyhole Cops** John Allen, Neil Stokes.
First appearance of Allen et al. at Millstone.

1974   **Edge Lane** Alan (Richard) McHardy, Bill Birch, Neil Stokes, John Allen, Steve Bancroft.
McHardy caused quite a controversy as he placed two pegs to protect his on-sight lead. Proctor and Birtles had, in contrast, top-roped the line in preparation for an intended solo ascent.

1974   **Time for Tea** Ken Wilkinson, R Thomas.
First free ascent of a combination of cracks in the Embankment Route 4 area.

1974   **Xanadu** Hank Pasquill, P Penketh.
The aforementioned direct start but really the meat of the route.

1975 July 16   **Great West Road** John Allen, Chris Addy.
First free ascent of pitch 2 only.

1975 July 19   **Embankment Route 4** Chris Addy, John Powell.
First free ascent proper.

1975 July 30   **London Wall** John Allen, Steve Bancroft.
First free ascent. A superb free route which resisted the 'pack' until the Eighties. Drummond, vying for the first free ascent, was stunned by Allen's ascent since his own fingers wouldn't fit into the crack!

1975 Aug. 31   **Great Arête** Geoff Birtles, Tom Proctor (AL).
Birtles penduled out of Green Death for the first pitch then handed over to Tom. Tom, it was said, put his 'hard hat on for the first time in years'.

> *Enough said. At the top of the route he announced that the grade was Hard Extreme 6a. The natural successor to Green Death and Edge Lane. The lower arête had to wait some time for its first ascent.*

1975 Oct. 16   **The Whore**   Jim Reading, Clive Jones, D Hyles.

1975 Oct.   **Detour**   Jim Reading, Clive Jones.

1975 Nov.   **Regent Street Variant**   Jim Reading, Mark Stokes.

1975   **Embankment Route 3**   Ed Drummond
First free ascent

1975   **Time for Tea**   Ed Drummond, John Young.
The left-hand variation finish: harder and bolder than the original route.

1975   **Saville Street** (1pt)   Geoff Birtles, Tom Proctor.
Believing that the final aid point at the roof couldn't be eliminated, Birtles watched Proctor follow the pitch. 'The bastard freed it', was Birtles' comment as Proctor climbed right past it.
First free ascent in 1975.

1975   **Saville Street**   John Allen.
First free ascent.

1975   **Soho Sally**   Geoff Birtles, Tom Proctor.

1975   **Erb**, **Lotto**, **Twikker**, **Jermyn Street**   Tom Proctor, Geoff Birtles.
First free ascents.
'Tom didn't have those side-runners in Regent Street when we did it, he just had the iron spike down in the cave!' – Birtles, recalling the first free ascent of Jermyn Street, having seen a photo of Bancroft repeating it with side-runners. Bancroft later said "Believe it or not I didn't see the spike".
Even the spike has gone now: removed by a falling climber!

1975   **March Hare**   Gabe Regan.
The second pitch followed the previously-aided upper section of Supra Direct.

1975   **Supra Direct**   Pete Brayshaw, Pete (Pod) O'Donovan.
First free ascent of the first pitch only.

1975   **Embankment Route 1**   John Allen, Tom Proctor.
First free ascent of the top pitch.

1976 April   **Thorpe Street**   Al Parker, Ted Rogers.

1976 July 4   **Pot Leg Wall**   Neil Stokes (solo).
Climbed by Stokes when his leg was in plaster?

1976 July 27   **White Wall**   Steve Bancroft, Jim Reading.
First free ascent after an earlier ascent the same day by Jim Reading who had reduced the aid to one point, although he did not quite finish the route.

1976 Aug. 1   **Stone Dri** (1pt)   John Regan, Paul Kirk, Iain Hibbert.
First free ascent in 1978.

1976 Sept. 3   **Piccadilly Circus**   Steve Bancroft, Nicky Stokes, Chris Addy.
First free ascent of the finishing crack of The Rack.

1976 Oct. 19   **Littleheath Road**   Mick Fowler, John Stevenson.

1976 Oct. 26	**Piledriver**	Mick Fowler, John Stevenson, Geraldine Abrey.

1976 Nov. 4   **Cauldron Crack**   Mick Fowler, John Stevenson.
First free ascent.

1976 Nov. 4   **Gimbals**, **Evening Premiere**   Mick Fowler, John Stevenson, Geraldine Abrey.
First free ascent of Gimbals.

1976 Nov. 17   **Commix**   John Stevenson, Mick Fowler.
First free ascent.

1976 Nov. 20   **London Pride**   Mick Fowler, John Stevenson.
An amalgamation of the initial section of the old aid route, Apollo, with some new rock.

1976 Nov. 20   **Blind Bat**   Mick Fowler, John Stevenson, Mick Morrison, H Crompton.
First free ascent.

1976   **Coventry Street**   Steve Bancroft, John Allen (alternate leads).
First free ascent.

1976   **Dextrous Hare**   Martin Taylor (roped-solo).
First free ascent using a hanging rope with a strategically placed knot at half-height to protect his ascent. Since then, nut placements have 'appeared'.

1976   **The Rack** (2pts)   Jim Reading.
Both points used for resting only.
First free ascent in 1982.

1976   **Southern Comfort**   John Stevenson, Mick Fowler.
First free ascent.
A remarkable domination of new routes by Fowler et al. after they arrived in the Peak District from 'The Smoke'.
Southern Comfort had its moment of glory when for some 'unknown' reason it was the only route to be awarded the XS(+) grade in the 1978 guidebook.

1977 June 23   **Badly Bred**   Steve Bancroft, Nicky Stokes.

1977   **Thin Lizzy**   Andy Barker, Dave Murfin.

1977   **AC Adaptor**   Dave Murfin, Andy Barker.
Both these routes were in the small quarry adjacent to the road. This section has since fallen down.

1977   **Flared Bottom**   Al Parker, Graham Fyffe.

Publication of the 1978 Sheffield Froggatt guidebook. Other routes whose first ascent details are unknown include:
Straight Leg, **Rake's Progress**, **All The King's Horses**, **At-a-cliff**, **Neatfeet**, **Pinstone Street**, **Pin Prick.**

1978 April 15   **Juniper**   Nick Halliday, Tony Sawbridge.

1978 June 3   **Jealous Pensioner**   Jim Burton, Paul Cropper, Chris Dent.
Rumour has it that this route was stolen from Phil Burke and then named in his honour. On an early repeat attempt Quentin Fisher fell off the headwall soloing, but remarkably landed on the narrow ledge, thereby maintaining his reputation for leading a charmed life.

1978 June   **Stone Dri**   Dave Humphries.
First free ascent.

1978 July 16   **Optimus**   Gary Gibson, Mark (Ralph) Hewitt, Derek Beetlestone, John Perry, Keith Edworthy.

1978 Sept. 24   **The Snivelling**   Bob Millward, Tony Dillinger.
The first ascent employed a side-runner in the corner of Svelt. Original route name censored by the Editor. A second pitch was later added by Loz Francomb and M Harrison in 14 June 1979.

1978 Oct. 1   **Brittle Road to Freedom**   Gary Gibson, Derek Beetlestone, Ralph Hewitt.

1978 Oct. 1   **Metal Rash**   Gary Gibson (solo).

1978 Oct. 29   **Street Legal**   Paul Cropper, Nadim Siddiqui.

1979 July 29   **Wings of Steel**   Paul Cropper, Brian Cropper.

1979 July 30   **Petticoat Lane Direct**   Gary Gibson, Steve Keeling.

1980 Aug. 3   **Mean to Me**   Gary Gibson, Steve Keeling, Derek Beetlestone.

1981 Aug. 29   **Who Wants the World?**   Gary Gibson, Martin Veale, Jon Walker.
Originally climbed with very high side-runners, but these were eliminated by Gibson in 1982.

1982 July 8   **Nib Nob**   Paul Mitchell (solo).

1982 July 8   **Slack Alice**   Paul Mitchell (unseconded).

1982 July 8   **Dolorous Gard**   Andy Barker (solo).

1982 Nov. 8   **Tea for Two**   Ian Riddington, Nigel Riddington.

1982   **The Rack**   Loz Francomb.
First free ascent eliminating the last two aid points. Unfortunately Francomb used side-runners in the adjacent Oxford Street and together with the brittle nature of the rock, to say nothing of the strenuous nature, the route has never become popular. Mark Pretty, left an in-situ peg in 1987 and repeated the route with a side-runner to protect the lower section.

1982   **Sex Dwarfs**   Mark Miller (solo).

1982   **Scritto's Republic**   Ron Fawcett (unseconded).
First free ascent of the thin crackline left of Embankment Route 3. Fawcett 'created' a technical masterpiece just as the 1983 guidebook went to press. After several repeats in the earlier Eighties the old bolts, originally placed by Tom Proctor in shallow drilled-out holes, failed. The first was broken off by an aid-climber, whilst the second was removed by Malcolm Taylor who then replaced the pair with a single bolt. This was subsequently removed by Andy Perkins. The route is now unprotectable until after the crux, unless of course the bolt is back in. The route was however soloed in the late Eighties by Pete Cresswell after extensive top-roped practice. The landing was packed with ropes, duvet jackets, rucksacks and the rear seat of a car and its efficiency tested when he fell off from around the crux. Not surprisingly the route is now sadly ignored.

Publication of the 1983 Stanage Millstone guidebook.

1983 May 12   **Helliconia Spring**   Chris Jackson, Adey Hubbard.

1983 Dec. 6   **Findus**   Al Rouse, Phil Burke.

1983 Dec. 7   **Quality Street**   Al Rouse, Phil Burke (AL).
Unpopular despite its name.

1983 Dec. 7   **Winter's Grip**   Neil Foster (solo).
After top-roping.

1983 Dec. 29   **The Master's Edge**   Ron Fawcett (unseconded).
The ultimate: Ron was unseconded, unfettered and unequalled. Having spent the autumn nursing a broken hand, Fawcett came back with a vengeance. Ron later wrote that it was 'E6 or E7, hard 6b or even harder, I don't know what to grade it'.
Ron reportedly practised some moves but did not top-rope the route in its entirety.
First on-sight ascent from Martin 'Basher' Atkinson in 1986, the first flashed ascent from Shaun Hudson in 1990, though it has still had less than ten ascents up to the time of writing.

1983   **Monopoly**   Johnny Dawes (unseconded).
Originally climbed by Dawes with side-runners, then during a subsequent ascent in 1984, Dawes returned and used a low peg runner for protection. This has since been removed.

1983   **Wall Street Crash**   Johnny Dawes, Nigel Slater.
Pre-placed and pre-clipped wires on old bolt heads were used to protect the first ascent. Suitable slings are now sometimes left in situ.

1983   **Diamond Daze**   Gary Gibson (solo).

1983   **Slime Crime**   Gary Gibson.

1983   **The Ginger Sponge and Custard**   Quentin Fisher.

1983   **The Hacker**   Brian Mosley, Tony Eady.

1984 Jan. 9   **Velvet**   Dominic Staniforth, Nigel Slater (AL).

1984 Jan.   **Clock People**   Ron Fawcett (unseconded).
Yet another desperate route.

1984 Feb. 12   **Sudden Impact**   Nigel Slater, Alastair Ferguson.

1984 April   **Meeze Brugger**   Ron Fawcett (unseconded).

1984 Easter   **Dino**   Paul Pepperday (solo).

1984 July 9   **Gibbering Heap**   Johnny Dawes.
Route name censored by the Editor.

1984   **Sea Creature**   Al Rouse, Andy Bailey.

1984   **Scumline**   Paul Tattersall.
Unrecorded at the time.
First free ascent of the initial section of Nostrils.

1984   **Adam Smith's Invisible Hand**   Johnny Dawes.
The route was named after a photograph Dawes had, on which shadows and a rock formation formed a large hand on the wall left of the arête.
Adam Smith was an economic philosopher who proposed that economies were steered by the 'invisible hand' of what we would now call 'market forces', hence the present-day enthusiasm of right-wing politicians and economists for his work.

1984   **Perplexity**   Johnny Dawes (unseconded).
Yet another Dawes' desperate. Needless to say, the old and rotting bolts weren't tested too severely, so be warned. Free-climbs part of the old aid route, Sweater.
Sadly the route was chipped in 1988 and since then has not had an ascent.

1984   **Jermyn Street: Direct Finish**   Ron Fawcett, Dominic Staniforth.

1985 May 7   **Wash and Brush Up**   Al Rouse (solo).

1985 Aug. 28   **The Hunter House Road Toad**   Mark Pretty, Richie Brooks.

1985   **The Pittsburgh Enigma**   Paul Mitchell.

1985   **Adios Amigo**   Mark Leach (unseconded).
Leach recalls that having borrowed Fawcett's Amigo to attempt the second ascent of The Master's Edge he climbed Adios Amigo instead: 'I only did this route because I was too gripped to do Master's that weekend'.

1985   **Helping Hands**   John Feltrup, Jamie Harper.

1985   **Frigged Anonymously**   Jamie Harper (unseconded).

1986 Sept.23   **Annabella Superstella**, **Beneath the Pavement Lies the Beach**
Mark Delafield, Ivor Delafield.

1987 April 23   **Under Doctor's Orders**   Keith Sharples, Ian Riddington, Geoff Radcliffe, Graham Hoey, Martin Veale.
First free ascent of the initial section of Hammersmith Road.

1987 May 16   **Election Special**   Dominic Staniforth, Dave Tidman.
Top-roped first then climbed with a side-runner in Great Slab and a peg runner en route. The peg has now gone.

1987 July 11   **Scruples**   Paul Evans, Neil Buttle.

1987 July   **Salinela Sunset**   Simon Cundy.

1987 Aug.   **Frank Sinatra Bows Out**   Allen Williams, Jason Myers.
Recently chipped and then filled in!

1987   **Blood and Guts on Botty Street**   Allen Williams (solo).

1987   **The Bad and the Beautiful**   Mark Leach (solo).
Top-roped first.
An obvious gap, previously cleaned and top-roped by Dominic Lee. It is reported that on one of his attempts he retreated from a sky-hook, only for it to rip, depositing him on the ledge. Leach felt that he needed both a 'spotter' and a photographer. In the event Dale Goddard convinced Leach that even if he fell he would stay on the ledge, so Goddard photographed the ascent! Leach said "You can fall but you must not bounce."

1988 Spring   **Transmetropolitan**   Steve Bancroft, Sue Bird.

1988 May   **Appletree Yard**, **Owzaboutthatthen**   Paul Mitchell (unseconded).

1988 June   **The Trumpton Anarchist**   Paul Mitchell, Steve Wright.

1988 Aug.   **Freight Train**   Paul Mitchell (unseconded).

1988 Sept. 10   **Anything is Possible in Cartoons**   Paul Mitchell (unseconded).

1988 Sept.	**Which way up Robitho** Paul Evans (unseconded).
1988	**London Marathon** Steve Bancroft, Harry Venables.
1989 May 18	**Strait Jacket** Paul Reeve *Top-roped first.*
1989	**Fat and Jealous** Dave Pegg.
1990 July 8	**Breeze Mugger** Paul Deardon.

LAWRENCEFIELD

O.S. ref. SK 250795 to 250800

by Bill Gregory

*'The climb starts from the ledge in the corner of the Great
Wall, reached by Jughandle or the Traverse. This ledge may
be termed The Hilt, and a couple of pegs for belaying can
be used. Higher, the leader may well use two more pitons
for running belays. The route is very exposed and a serious
undertaking; without peg protection it would be excessively
severe. It would be pointless to provide Excalibur with the
opportunities of reversing its legendary fate.'*

Reg Pillinger and Albert Shutt,
Further Development in the Peak District, 1957.

SITUATION and CHARACTER

Lawrencefield is an old quarry about 100m south of the bend in
the A625, Sheffield to Hathersage Road, which is known locally
as the Surprise View. On the map the moor above the quarry is
identified as Lawrencefield, whereas the quarry is in fact known
as Bole Hill Quarry. Lawrencefield consists of fairly well
weathered rock, although occasional huge rock-falls do still
occur, especially from the more broken sections. The
massively-bedded gritstone gives a predominance of steep
walls, with some suspect rock. In places the tops, especially in
the region of Great Harry, are suspect and need care. Often, the
only belays are wooden fence posts well back from the edge
although a number of iron stakes are available above the pool.
The few posts that are left are now rotten and extreme care
should be exercised in using them. Although the quarry is 400m
above sea level, it is sheltered and can be a sun-trap during the
winter. In summer frying alive is not unknown, so choose a day
with some breeze. Warning: the giant wood ants are ALWAYS
ravenous.

APPROACHES and ACCESS

Approach as for Millstone Edge, then follow either a footpath on
the Fox House side of the Surprise View and follow the quarry lip
rightwards to an easy descent, or climb the stone wall opposite
the Millstone Quarry track and contour below the first two bays

to the main face. Do NOT lean on the buttress when climbing the stone wall – the other side of it fell down during 1981!

HISTORY

This long-disused, impressive quarry was discovered as a climbing ground in 1952 by Bert Shutt and Reg Pillinger of the Peak Climbing Club, although it must surely have been visited before then. Early routes included *Three Tree Climb, Pulpit Groove* and *Stonemason's Buttress*, the crag's first VS. Activity continued in 1953 with the addition of *Guillotine* to the accompaniment of Joan Shutt's knitting. The *Great Wall Traverse* led to a series of fruitless attempts on the wall itself. In September *Great Harry* was climbed together with *Meringue*, which employed the first aid peg on the crag. This peg was eliminated in 1955 and, about this time, Dave Gregory solved *Limpopo Groove*. The crag's reputation began to spread and Don Morrison, with John Fearon, climbed *Red Wall*, employing a typical Morrison mantelshelf manoeuvre. Pete Biven and Trevor Peck cleaned out *Cordite Crack* and *Excalibur* and found the fine *Delectable Variation* to *Red Wall*. On *Great Peter, Boulevard, Suspense* and *High Street*, however, they found it necessary to use their piton arsenal.

The guidebook was one of the few bonuses from the awful summer of 1956 although it failed to initiate any new climbs. Apart from the aided start to *Suspense*, by Alan Clarke in 1958, little else was achieved until John Loy began work on the next guidebook. During this period *Itslide* and *Sinister Crack* were soloed by Loy; and Morrison, Clarke and Les Gillott did both *S.A.E.* free and the former peg-route up Red Wall to give *Delectable Direct*. A week later the crag was girdled by *Playtex*, a Morrison/Gillott creation.

The 1965 guidebook was published and the crag lay fallow, although *Peg Wall* was converted to *Once-pegged Wall*. All was quiet until 1975 when a new era was heralded by free ascents of the aid routes up Great Wall. *Boulevard* went to Ed Drummond and Jim Reading liberated *High Street*. The aid was eliminated from *Suspense* by John Allen and a four-man team comprising Geoff Birtles, Ernie Marshall, Tom Proctor and Giles Barker created the superb *Billy Whiz* by breaking out left from *High Street*. The hot summer of 1976 was somewhat embarrassing in this sun trap but the old aid was eliminated from *Great Peter* and

Frustration. The following year saw a determined effort from Jim Reading resulting in *High Plains' Drifter* and *Holy Grail* on the Great Wall and the start of a period of slower development.

Since then most new routes have reflected the general increase in the number of climbers operating at a high standard, being either fairly serious or technically very hard. The most notable events have been the evolution of the completely free version of *Suspense Direct*, now known as *Pool Wall*, by Roger Greatrick, and the freeing of *Block Wall* by Dominic Lee. This ascent used two pre-placed pegs which were found to be unnecessary on the second ascent by Jerry Moffatt.

Tony Ryan's route of 1985, *Von Ryan's Express*, was the major route at this time, although Johnny Dawes climbed *The Gordons, The Gordons*. In 1986 Chris Plant gave us the self-libelling pun of the year, *Heavy Plant Crossing*, which he climbed with Mark Pretty. It now seems that Lawrencefield is more or less worked out as far as major new lines are concerned. There are no remaining aid points and future new lines must surely be eliminates.

THE CLIMBS are described from LEFT to RIGHT.

There are two subsidiary bays before the main crag. The first of these is just below the road. The left-hand side of the back wall of the first bay should be avoided lest the road itself falls into the quarry. The first climb starts two metres left of the right-hand corner of this bay.

1 Brain Attack   11m   HVS   5a   (1980)
Follow a peg-scarred crack to a ledge. Finish up parallel cracks to loose rock and the top. A poor start to the crag.

2 Itslide   11m   VS   4b   (1964)
The loose corner of the bay, with a shattered finish, is reached by a flaky pedestal. The corner direct is 5a, but both are poor routes.

3 Sunday   10m   HVS   5a   (1965- 1978)
Just right of the corner are twin cracks which join it at the bottom. This is the left-hand crack.

Bill and Dave Gregory enjoying the Pool Wall at Lawrencefield.
Photo: Dave Wilkinson.

4 Surprise, Surprise 9m VS 4b (1957-1965)
Ascend the groove six metres right of the corner to a grassy
ledge. Move left to climb steeply up the thin corner crack using
its companion a little to the right.

5 Friday 9m VD (1957-1965)
Start one metre right up cracks to the grassy ledge. Move right
on to a block then ascend direct via a thin flake.

6 Shallow Chimney 9m HD (1958)
Somehow ascend the obvious shallow, blocky chimney.

7 Split Second Timing 9m E1 5c (1981)
Climb the wall just to the right of Shallow Chimney.

† **8 Spec Arête** 9m E2 6a (1957-1965/1976)
The obvious, impending arête left of Frustration, using a
strategically placed runner in that route.

* **9 Frustration** 9m E1 5c (1958/1976)
The peg-scarred crack up the overhanging wall is started with
difficulty and is climbed direct.

10 Straight Crack 9m VD (1958)
Climb the broken cracks nearly two metres to the right. Some
suspect rock at the top.

11 The Last Wet Wednesday 9m VS 4b (1989)
Climb the crack, just right, past a small pinnacle and a tree.

12 Rocking Groove 11m HVS 5a (1958)
Start as for the previous route and climb the rightward-slanting
groove. An aptly named route with some loose rock and
vegetation.

13 Redbits 11m E2 5c (1978)
Strenuously climb the thin crack in the centre of the steep wall.

* **14 Slippery Wall** 12m HVS 5b (1957-1965)
Attain the widening crack in the upper wall either from the right,
the left, or direct (5c), and follow it to a difficult, sandy exit.

* **15 Quantum Crack** 9m HVS 5b (1957-1965)
Ascend the bulging crack just left of the big corner.

Billy Whiz , Lawrencefield.
Photo: Dave Wilkinson.

Frustration Area

16 Vaseline 9m HVD   (1957-1965)
The right-hand corner of the bay. Traverse right to finish.

17 Grass Groove 9m D   (1957-1965)
Climb the groove four metres right of the corner. Now,
thankfully, devoid of grass.

18 Seta 9m HS 4c   (1957-1965)
Tricky moves lead up the wall one metre right to a grassy ledge
and into a finishing corner.

19 Proud Crack 11m VD   (1957-1965)
Climb up to the claustrophobic chimney behind the monster
flake to the right.

20 Brain Cells in Collision 12m E3 5c   (1981-1983)
Follow Proud Crack to the grassy ledge then break out right
across the wall.

† **20a Last Day of Freedom** 11m E4 6a   (1991)
A serious line immediately left of the right arête of the wall.

*About 100m right is the main and extensive part of the quarry. The
only easy descents are at either end. At the extreme left-hand end*

and just right of the way down is a small but obvious slab halfway up the bank.

21 Gregory's Slab 9m S (1955)
Climb the slab, then a flake on the right to a broken finish past a small oak tree.

22 Summer Climb 12m HS 4b (1956)
Start just right and climb corners, to a mantelshelf, before easy blocks lead to a birch tree to finish.

Just right, and at a lower level, is a large sandy corner with a big angular block.

* **23 Three Tree Climb** 21m HS 4b (1952)
Start up either of two cracks about six metres left of the corner and follow these to a series of grooves. At the top of the cracks step right helped by a hidden crack round the arête on the right, if you can find it, then go up to a large ledge with a larch tree. Finish on the left or, harder, to the right.

* **24 Great Peter** 18m E2 5b (1956/1976)
Two metres left of the corner is a thin crack running straight up the wall. Climb it, crossing Pulpit Groove, and negotiating a loose block en route, to a large ledge. Finish direct, or abseil off the much-abused larch tree.

There is an iron stake belay, suitable for the next few routes, placed well back in one of the old fence-posts holes.

* **25 Pulpit Groove** 27m VD (1952)
Start with some difficulty, as for Three Tree Climb, then follow the right-leaning groove to the Pulpit stance. Good thread belay. Step right across the void then traverse right to a large shelf. Rowan tree belay. Friable rocks lead eventually to the top.

* **26 Great Harry** 21m HVS 4c (1953/1956)
The strenuous corner crack leads to the Pulpit, (good thread belay). Continue awkwardly to the larch tree on a ledge. Now take the corner direct to a friable finish or, safer and easier (VS), move diagonally up the left wall to the top. A sustained route.

27 Too Good to be True 21m E4 5c (1978)
Start in the centre of the wall right of Great Harry and climb direct up the wall to the ledge of Scoop Connection. Finish up a short corner.

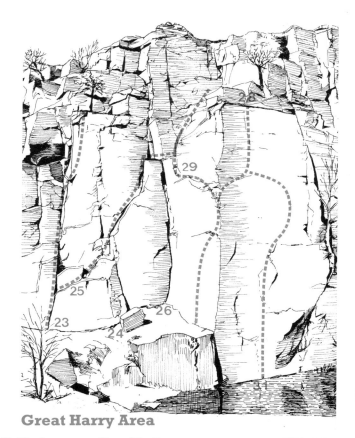

Great Harry Area

** **28 Suspense** 21m E2 5c   (1956/1975)
Start as for Too Good... but trend rightwards to a small ledge on
the arête. Move round the arête on to the steep wall and finish
past a (sometimes) in-situ peg.

* **29 Scoop Connection** 22m E3 5b   (1957-1965)
As for Suspense to the small ledge, then move left to follow a
very sloping ledge to the Pulpit stance. Definitely not a route for
the faint at heart!

† **30 Brainstorm** 21m E4 5c   (1981-1983)
Climb the left-hand side of the obvious arête rising from the
right-hand end of the ledge. From the 'shelf' move left and finish
as for Too Good to be True, or at the junction with Suspense
move on to the right-hand side of the arête and finish direct;
† **Brain Death**, E4 5c, (1989).

* **31 Pool Wall** 21m E4 6b   (1958/1981-1983)
Superb wall climbing. Start at low-water level and climb the wall
two metres right of the arête to a thin break. Move up right, crux,
then back left to finish up Suspense.

Mind over Watter, E2 5c, (1979), is a totally indirect eliminate
which pulls onto the front face as for Pool Wall, but then
continues traversing rightwards to the tree. It then swings back
on to the wall and follows Pool Wall into Suspense.

*The next climbs are reached by traversing behind the pool, from
its right-hand side, across a large ledge system known as The
Great Shelf. This can be tricky during winter floods. For the first
five routes climb the short corner, VD, at the left-hand end of The
Great Shelf. For Side Pocket and Cascara, traverse left to a thread
belay in the wide crack of Cascara behind the sycamore tree right
of Pool Wall. Above are four leftward-facing corners which get
bigger as one goes from left to right.*

32 Side Pocket 18m HVS 5a   (1990)
Climb the crack one metre left of the arête, using holds on the
arête, to an awkward mantelshelf and a large ledge. Take any of
the finishes above. Masochists can swim or abseil to the ledge at
water level and reach the sycamore by the broken crack below
it, **The Table Leg**, VS 4c, (1990).

33 Cascara Crack 18m HS 4a   (1953)
Climb the strenuous chimney-crack behind the sycamore to a
large ledge then move right for one metre into the second
corner crack to finish.

34 Mildly Laxative 18m VS 4c   (1990)
Start two metres right of Cascara Crack and climb the wide rusty
crack to an awkward landing on a large ledge. Climb the rising
steps and the easier third corner crack to finish.

* **35 Austin's Variation** 9m VS 4c   (1956)
The fourth corner, with the overhanging flake, gives an
alternative finish to the previous two routes. Take a Friend 4
along; you might find it useful.

* **36 Lawrencefield Ordinary** 22m VD   (1952)
Ascend the short corner just right of Mildly Laxative to its large
ledge at 10m. Move left across the rising steps and go up the first
short corner above Cascara Crack to the rowan tree of Pulpit
Groove. Various finishes can be used.

The next few routes lie on the impressive **GREAT WALL**.

37 S.A.E. 21m HVS 5b   (1956/1964)
Start up Lawrencefield Ordinary, but move right into the main
corner above the left-hand corner of The Great Wall. Finish
direct, or *'move right and climb a series of small steps on doubtful
rock to the top. This is exposed and trying.' – 1957.*

38 Crystal Clear 21m E1 5b   (1979)
Follow S.A.E. to a grassy ledge below its main corner ledge.
Move right and climb the broken corner and the crack above on
bad rock. A poor route.

*The next routes have a finishing belay on two iron stakes near the
decayed fence.*

* **39 High Plains' Drifter** 21m E4 6a   (1977)
Start at the left-hand end of the lowest large ledge below The
Great Wall. Move up and one and a half metres left, then climb a
crack and groove to a sapling. Ascend the wall, small wires, via a
short ramp to an old peg. Move left then go up to the large
ledge, crux. Move right to finish up the wall to the right of the
flake.

** **40 Boulevard** 18m E4 6a   (1956/1975)
Start as for the previous route and climb easy ledges then move
right to attack the thin peg-scarred crack in the upper wall with
conviction. Low in the grade and well-protected.

† **41 Von Ryan's Express** 19m E5 6b   (1985)
A serious route taking an unbelievable line up the centre of The
Great Wall. Start as for Boulevard, or more directly up the slab
on the right, to gain the break midway between Boulevard and
Billy Whiz. A difficult move up (side-runners in break) allows a
small, lonely ledge in the centre of the face to be gained.
Leaving this is both difficult and serious but the top, or a hospital,
can soon be reached.

* **42 Billy Whiz** 19m E2 5c   (1957-1965/1975)
Start up the slabby groove below the centre of The Great Wall to
the break. Move up the curving weakness on the left to reach a
thin slanting crack one metre right. Follow this to its end, slot in a
runner, anything from a medium-sized Hex. to a small Rock
should fit, then rush up the wall above on larger holds before
strength fades.

* **43 High Street** 20m E4 6a   (1956/1975)
Start as for Billy Whiz up the slab to the break. Above and on the
right is a peg-scarred crack. Climb it direct to the top after
difficult initial moves.

44 Holy Grail 22m E4 5c   (1977)
Start as for Excalibur, then move three metres left as soon as
possible after the steepening at the major horizontal break.
Climb the steep wall direct.

† **45 Heavy Plant Crossing** 40m E5 6b   (1986)
A high-level traverse of The Great Wall. Start up Excalibur and
traverse left with the feet just above the crux of High Street to
good protection on Billy Whiz. Continue to Boulevard (crux) and
thence to finish up High Plains' Drifter.

* **46 Excalibur** 21m VS 4c   (1955)
The corner crack at the right-hand end of Great Wall is reached
via the grassy groove below it and climbed in a superb position.

47 Great Wall Traverse 15m S   (1953)
Starting from the ledge ten metres up Lawrencefield Ordinary,
move right across a slab to a sloping ledge. Cross below Great
Wall at this level to Excalibur. Now climb the right wall to a
sandy bay, moving right to a large ledge. There are three exits:
Pimpernel, S, (1951-1957), the left-hand corner crack;
Guillotine, S, (1951-1957), the centre of the wall; **Reprieve**, D,
(1951-1957), the slabby rocks at the right-hand side of the ledge.

Great Wall

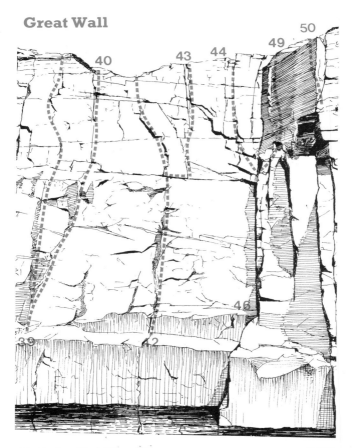

48 Jughandle 12m VD (1953)
Climb up to the final corner of Excalibur via giant steps on the
right of the main corner, then traverse the break rightwards to
the final large ledge of Great Wall Traverse.

49 J.J.2 21m E1 5b (1976)
Start up the red groove, previously taken by **Blood Red Sword**
(1979), to the right of Jughandle then layback the obvious crack
two metres right of Excalibur's first ledge.

50 The Gordons, The Gordons 5m E3 6a (1985)
An alternative finish to J.J.2. From the large ledge of Great Wall
Traverse, climb the right-hand side of the arête until a move can
be made leftwards round the arête to finish up the wall. Harder
for the short.

The next two routes are best ignored.

51 Louisette 20m S (1952)
From just right of the pool gain the slabby face right of Jughandle
and climb it diagonally right, then left to a groove in the top
left-hand corner leading to a large ledge. There is a choice of
exits.

52 Guillotine Groove 20m S (1952)
Ascend the vegetated corner just to the right past a sloping
ledge to a pillar belay. Climb the right-hand wall and a groove
on the left to the large ledge. A choice of finishes is possible.

*An abseil descent from rickety trees above Gingerbread is
possible for all the routes between Once-pegged Wall and Nova
but it is not recommended. It saves a trek but care should be taken
with dead wood!*

* **53 Once-pegged Wall**—9m VS 5a (1955/1957-1965)
Follow the obvious line of peg-pockets close to the arête then
move left round the arête at a foot-ledge high up.

54 Morning Glory 9m E2 5c (1983)
Climb the parallel line of peg-holes, just right again, taking care
not to use holds on adjacent routes.

* **55 Limpopo Groove** 9m VS 4b (1955)
The obvious corner crack is often greasy and sandy but can
always be well-protected.

*To the right is an attractive clean slab, **THE GINGERBREAD
SLAB**. It rises to ten metres in height and is climbable almost
anywhere. Only the most definite lines are recorded here.*

Gingerbread Slab Area

* **56 Gingerbread** 9m HVS 4c   (1952)
The obvious left-hand arête. *'Rubbers will preserve the delicate holds for future generations.'* – 1957. Poorly-protected and with the crux at the top.

57 Meringue 9m HVS 5a   (1953/1955)
The thin crack two metres right. Poor wires can be arranged but you would be well advised not to fall off!.

58 Eclair 10m E1 5b   (1957-1965)
Unprotected climbing up the slab one metre right of Meringue.

59 Vanilla Slice 10m E2 5c   (1965-1978)
Very delicate and un-protected slab climbing one metre left of
Snail Crack.

* **60 Snail Crack** 18m HVD   (1952)
The obvious crack on the right to the ledge.

61 Nailsbane 20m VD   (1952)
The cracked wall just right is followed leftwards to a mantelshelf
and an awkward exit on to a ledge on the left.

62 Tyron 18m VS 4c   (1957-1965)
Climb the cracked wall two metres right to a tricky landing on a
vegetated ledge. Finish up the short steep wall behind.

63 Nova 18m HS 4b   (1956)
Climb the right-hand side of the cracked wall to land awkwardly
on the ledge of Tyron. Finish up the steep wall behind.

*To the right is a horrible corner with a detached and
dangerously-leaning flake.*

64 Flake Climb 15m D   (1951-1957)
Climb the flake then step right to grass. Finish up the corner.

65 Grooved Arête 15m VS 4c   (1957-1965)
Climb a repulsive groove right of the flake, then the corner.

The scrappy, short arête to the right is **Elytrocele**, E1 6a, (1987).

66 The Ashes 15m S   (1955)
Start two metres right of Elytrocele. Ascend parallel cracks to a
ledge then go up the easy crack above.

67 Urn 15m HVD   (1965-1978)
Two metres right is a red crack leading to a ledge. Ascend this
then climb the crack in the slab above.

68 Scotia 15m VS 4b   (1957-1965)
Ascend the dusty, blocky, red cracks just right to finish either up
the cracks in the slab or the right-hand corner. Some suspect
rock.

The broken blocks and cracks to the right are **Fractus**, (the Latin
for broken), S (1957-1965). Those without a classical education
may still receive an English 'fracture'.

69 Howarth's Wait   12m   S   (1978)
Trend rightwards across the broken rocks to a large corner
containing a tree. Climb the corner.

*15m right the ground is hollowed into a stone-filled depression,
often with stagnant water.* **STONEMASON'S BUTTRESS** *rises
from this. It has a large grassy ledge at half-height. Above the
left-hand end of this ledge is a shattered wall broken by vertical
seams.*

70 Avalanche   9m   VD   (1956)
Wander up the shattered wall.

71 Tony's Chimney   6m   VD   (1955)
A surprising struggle up the shallow chimney below the
left-hand end of the large grassy ledge.

72 Callus   6m   VS   4c   (1978)
The arête and thin crack just to the right.

73 Verve   17m   VS   4c   (1964)
Start at the left-hand edge of the depression in the ground up a
thin corner crack past a vegetated ledge to the large grassy
ledge at half-height. Climb either a narrow corner in the same
line or the more difficult crack on the left.

74 Stonemason's Climb   21m   HVS   5a   (1952)
Ascend the obvious, ledgy left-hand arête of the buttress to
easier climbing. Move right to the steep finishing corner, or
climb the wall direct.

75 Going for the One   21m   E2   5b   (1981-1983)
Climb a thin crack one metre right, then move right onto a
sloping ledge (crux). Climb a short wall to the left to a large tree
(unprotected). Move right to a ledge and, from a good hold on
the arête above, lunge up and continue easily to the top. A
runner may be placed in Blacksmith's Climb to protect the
lunge. Despite this, the grade remains the same.

76 Blacksmith's Climb   21m   VS   4c   (1956/1957-1965)
The steep corner is climbed direct past a tree to a second tree.
Finish up the broken crack-line.

77 Tuesday's Child   21m   HVS   5a   (1964)
From a ledge slightly higher and to the right of the start of
Blacksmith's Climb follow a thin crack to a second ledge, then
climb the bulging, but tree-protected, arête above to the third

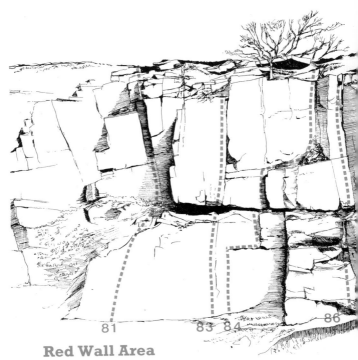

81   83 84   86

Red Wall Area

ledge. Finish up the awkward crack in the arête above, (crux), or escape up the corner crack on the right.

78 Vector 17m HS 4b   (1955)
Right and higher again is a prominent crack, reached via easy ledges. Follow it to a corner crack or curved flake just right.

79 Sinister Crack 19m VS 4c   (1964)
From six metres up Vector, move right to a large ledge then follow the leaning crack to a blasted oak.

Farther right is a steep wall with a shallow, sandy cave at half-height – **RED WALL**. *Starting at the far left end of the lower part of this wall is:*

80 Moss Corner 14m VD   (1957-1965)
Go round the lower wall on its left and climb the main angle on the right above.

81 Finale 15m VS 4c   (1956)
From below, and one metre right of an oak tree, climb the lower wall delicately. Finish up a steep corner left of Moss Corner.

† **82 Rattus Norvegicus** 15m E5 6b   (1981)
Start two metres left of the parallel cracks of Delectable Direct
and move up and right to a rock-over, crux, at two and a half
metres. Climb the upper wall past two tricky sections. Totally
unprotected. E3 with side-runners in Delectable Direct.
Originally graded as E2.

* **83 Delectable Direct** 15m HVS 5b   (1956/1964)
Follow the peg-scarred crack one metre left of Red Wall direct.

84 Red Wall 17m E1 5b   (1956)
Ascend the shallow corner below the centre of the upper wall,
then move right to a short corner which is followed to a ledge
(possible belay in the right-hand corner). Either finish up the
back right-hand corner at 4b, or climb the wall one metre left of
the corner with a long reach to a difficult mantelshelf (nearly
impossible unless the second has wide shoulders and you both
have good balance). The crack just left again can be climbed at a
hard 5b.

* **85 Delectable Variation** 22m VS 4c   (1957-1965)
As for Red Wall to the ledge (possible belay in the right-hand
corner) then traverse left, respecting the flakes, to finish up the
fine arête. The finishing arête can be gained from directly below,
Rockhopper, E1 5c, (1984).

* **86 Cordite Crack** 15m HS 4b   (1955)
Move up to the obvious steep corner-crack left of the
pock-marked wall. Climb up this to the top. Strenuous climbing,
but easy route finding!

*The wall to the right has seven definite crack features. They are all
reached from the right along a huge sloping ledge below the wall.*

† **87 Skyline** 12m E3 5b   (1957-1965/1981)
The arête on the left of the buttress is climbed using the
peg-scarred crack to better holds at nine metres. Very loose.

* **88 Block Wall** 12m E4 6b   (1965-1978/1981)
Reach and climb the obvious line of peg-holes up the centre of
the wall. Tough on the fingers. The best of the routes hereabouts,
which still isn't saying much!

Right: Pete 'POD' O'Donovan on the fifth ascent of London Wall, Millstone Edge.
Photo: Sharples collection.
Overleaf: Keith Sharples on Millstone Edge's most attempted arête, Technical Master.
Photo: Ian Smith.

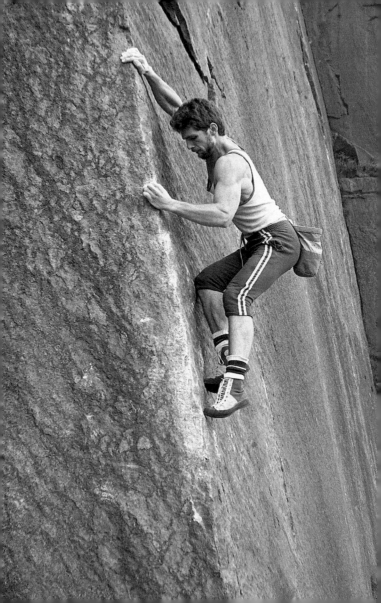

The dirty groove just right of a jutting flake leads to a grassy terrace. Finish up the third (and rotten) crack, **Varlet**, VS 4c, (1958).

89 Knave 15m HVS 5b   (1983)
To the right of Varlet the slab is cutaway. Climb the arête on the right of the cutaway and the dirty slab to the terrace. Finish up the fourth crack from the left.

90 Slab and Groove 15m HVS 5b   (1957-1965)
Gain the slab near the right-hand corner and move into the corner. Climb this to the terrace. Finish up the fifth crack from the left.

91 Formic Escape 6m HS   (1989)
The main corner on the right offers a finish for those defeated by the top cracks or who wish to flee the ants.

92 Lone Ridge 18m S   (1957-1965)
Go easily up the rock steps right of Slab and Groove to an arête which is started from the left.

93 Tricky Cracks 14m S   (1957-1965)
Starting up the broken cracks just right, climb the projecting buttress above by two parallel cracks.

The crag now deteriorates giving numerous problems and two further routes 100m to the right.

† **94 Middle-aged Spread** 12m E3 6a   (1989)
Start three metres left of the next route by a mantelshelf on to the obvious ledge on the arête at head-height. Move right and climb the slab direct to the top; side-runner in Howard's Slab if needed.

95 Howard's Slab 10m HVS 5a   (1957-1965)
A delicate climb up a scooped wall, with some suspect holds.

Although many sections of the crag can be girdled according to choice, there is a complete girdle which is recommended for anyone wishing to upset climbers on the fifty odd routes it crosses. Choose a sunny Bank Holiday for maximum aggravation.

Previous Page: Neil Foster on a rare ascent of Great Arête, Millstone Edge.
Photo: Ian Smith.
Left: Paul Carling on Supra Direct, Millstone Edge.
Photo: Ian Smith.

96 Playtex Very long   VS 4 (your enjoyment)   (1964)
There are some pleasant bits, some strolls along ledges, and a
little jungle bashing. Start up Cordite Crack and move across the
Delectable Variation. Keep left to climb Vector to a stance. Go
down an awkward corner then move diagonally across
Avalanche Wall to a short slab. Cross this (very problematical as
most of it has fallen down) and move six metres down to a tree.
Traverse the obvious ledge and pull round the arête to a terrace
and gaze out upon Nova. Go down two metres, across the top
section of Flake Climb and traverse at that level to the
Gingerbread arête. Swing left and climb up Limpopo Groove.
Go left again and down three metres to hand-traverse the
obvious break at the steepening of Great Wall to its centre.
Descend diagonally to the foot of Cascara Crack, then climb it to
a junction with Pulpit Groove which is reversed to the Pulpit. Go
up Great Harry then move left to finish down Summer Climb. Or,
if you can read backwards, do the whole lot the other way round!

*Some short climbs exist at the right-hand end of the quarry. These
have been left unrecorded for others to re-discover; please don't
send in details of their supposed first ascents as the first ascent lists
are already littered with routes that are no longer described.*

LAWRENCEFIELD LIST OF FIRST ASCENTS

1952 Aug.	**Three Tree Climb, Nailsbane, Pulpit Groove, Guillotine Groove, Gingerbread, Lawrencefield Ordinary** Albert (Bert) Shutt, Reg Pillinger.
1952 Oct.	**Stonemason's Climb** Peter Rickus, Reg Pillinger.
1953 Feb.	**Louisette, Snail Crack** Bert Shutt, Reg Pillinger.
1953 Feb.	**Cascara Crack, Great Wall Traverse** R A (Dick) Brown.
1953 Sept.	**Great Harry** Harry Hartley, Reg Pillinger.
1953 Sept.	**Jughandle, Meringue** (1pt) Bert Shutt, Reg Pillinger, Tony Davies. *First free ascent of Meringue was in 1955.* *An attempt was made at this time to force a direct route up the Great Wall, but in the event it was to prove abortive.*
1955 March	**The Ashes** John Henry Fearon, Bert Shutt (alternate leads).
1955 July	**Limpopo Groove** Dave Gregory (solo). *Named before it was done, after Kipling's great, grey, green greasy river.* *After his ascent, Gregory fell from the terrace into the pool to join a dead sheep. Evidently the sheep couldn't fly either! Strangely, the sheep did not complain.*

1955 July	**Meringue** John Fearon. *First free ascent.*
1955 July	**Gregory's Slab** Wilfred (Wilf) White, Reg Pillinger, D Bradley. *A large team from Sheffield and some lads from the Valkyrie were sheltering from the sun under the birches, Dave Gregory recalls that he kept protesting desultorily that somebody ought to do some climbing. Eventually Wilf did and passed the name of his tormentor down to posterity attached to this route.*
1955 Summer	**Cordite Crack, Excalibur** Peter Biven, Trevor Peck. *Cordite Crack needed considerable cleaning. It had previously been tried by John Fearon who had not thought the labour of removing an immense bird's nest worth the effort. The name, Cordite Crack, comes from the machine gun scars on the wall to the right. The gun, used in practice by the military, was placed on the stainless steel mounting still visible amongst the trees. Excalibur also needed a mammoth cleaning session. Two pegs runners were used to protect the ascent.*
1955	**Peg Wall** (A1) Don Morrison, Al Hall, Pete Marks. *First free ascent in 1957-1965.*
1955	**Tony's Chimney** Tony Davies.
1955	**Vector** Dave Gregory, Bert Shutt, Tom Collins.
1956 Summer	**Summer Climb** Bert Shutt, Dave Gregory, John Fearon.
1956 Summer	**Avalanche** Don Morrison, Reg Pillinger.
1956 Summer	**Piton Variation** (A1) Peter Biven, Trevor Peck. *First free ascent in 1964.*
1956 Summer	**High Street** (A1), **Boulevard** (A1), **Suspense** (A1 & VS), **Great Peter** (A1 & VS) Peter Biven, Trevor Peck. *First free ascents of most of these routes were in 1975. Great Peter was freed in 1976.*
1956	**Blacksmith's Climb** (2pts) Reg Pillinger, Bert Shutt, Alan Clarke. *First free ascent remains unknown.*
1956	**Nova, Red Wall** Don Morrison, John Fearon. *Morrison led the first pitch of Red Wall whilst Fearon led the corner. Rumour had it that the finish lay up the crack immediately left of the corner. This is ferocious. Failure on this led people to try the usual finish which goes up the crack just left again and contains a typical Morrison manoeuvre.*
1956	**S.A.E.** (1pt) Don Morrison, Al Hall, Pete Marks. *Earlier attempts by Wilf White, John Fearon and Dave Gregory had failed at the top at a broken band of rock. However, they left a peg which Morrison used for aid on his ascent. Morrison, at that time, was trying to arrange the 'Sheffield Andean Expedition'. It never left Sheffield! First free ascent in 1964.*
1956	**Finale** Don Morrison.
1956	**Great Harry – Direct Finish** Ernie Marshall, Alan Clarke, Reg Pillinger.

Publication of the 1957 Further Developments on Gritstone. Other routes whose first ascent details are unknown include:
Austin's Variation, Variations 1 and 2, Pimpernel, Guillotine, Reprieve, Flake Climb.

1958	**Shallow Chimney, Straight Crack** Eric Byne, Jean Turner.

Although this was Byne's first new route here, he had been instrumental in pointing out the possibilities to Biven and Peck.

1958   **Rocking Groove**   Fred Williams.

1958   **Frustration** (A1)   M A James.
First free ascent in 1976.

1958   **Suspense Direct** (A1)   Alan Clarke, Walt Hulka.
The pair did a pendulum from the big ledge on the left to just above the water level. Clarke hit the water but he recalls that 'Walt was always the smart one... he didn't hit the water'.
First free ascent in 1981-1983.

1958   **Varlet**   Don Morrison

1963   **Ledgeway**   Don Morrison, John Loy.
The route fell down in a rock-fall in 1981.

1964 June 3   **S.A.E., Delectable Direct**   Don Morrison, Les Gillott, Alan Clarke.
First free ascents, the latter of Piton Variation.

1964 June 10   **Playtex**   Don Morrison, Les Gillott.

1964   **Itslide, Sinister Crack**   John Loy (solo).

1964   **Verve**   Pete Crew, W Ward.

1964   **Tuesday's Child**   John Loy, Don Morrison, Pete Marks.

1957-1965   **Once-pegged Wall**   Anon.
First free ascent of Peg Wall.

1957-1965   **Howard's Slab**   Ted Howard.

1957-1965   **Blacksmith's Climb**   Anon.
First free ascent.

Publication of the 1965 Sheffield Froggatt Area guidebook. Other routes whose first ascent details are unknown include:
Friday, Slippery Wall, Quantum Crack, Vaseline, Grass Groove, Seta, Proud Crack, Suspense Variation (top-roped only; later recorded as Scoop Connection), **Eclair, Tyron, Grooved Arête, Scotia, Fractus, Moss Corner, Skyline** (A1), **Lone Ridge, Tricky Cracks, Delectable Variation, Slab and Groove.**

1975 Aug. 7   **Boulevard**   Ed Drummond, Jim Reading.
First free ascent.

1975 Aug. 14   **High Street**   Jim Reading.
His second, Clive Jones, failed to follow.
First free ascent.

1975   **Suspense**   John Allen, Nicky Stokes.
First free ascent.

1975   **Billy Whiz** (*née* Harlequin)   Geoff Birtles, Ernie Marshall, Tom Proctor, Giles Barker.
The first use of chalk by this group.

1976 Jan.   **Great Peter**   Clive Jones, Jim Reading.
First free ascent.

1976 Feb. 14   **Spec Arête** (*née* Jealous Jelly)   Nicky Stokes, John Allen, Steve Bancroft.

1976 March 6   **J.J.2.**   Nicky Stokes, John Allen.
Named after another climbing member of the Stokes family who was 'into' body-building.

1976   **Frustration**   John Allen, Steve Bancroft, Nicky Stokes.
First free ascent.

1977 Sept.   **High Plains Drifter**, **Holy Grail**   Jim Reading, Rob Malinson.
After the ascent of High Plains Drifter, Jim dropped Robbi's best Moac nuts into the pond. Pronouncing the pond too deep to retrieve the nuts, Jim led off to the pub. Robbi returned with his girlfriend and frogman's gear the next day only to find the water knee deep.
Jim Reading (with John Store) also climbed a variation on Billy Whiz up its left wall/flake at that time but details are vague.

1978 April 15   **Redbits**   Pete Blackburn, D Ferguson.

1978 Oct. 18   **The Bread Line**, **Balloon**   Gary Gibson.
No longer described in the current text as they are all on the shattered right-hand section.

1978 Oct. 21   **Too Good to be True**   Mark Walton, Phil Wilson, Paul Delaney.

1978 Oct. 22   **Callus**   Gary Gibson (solo).

1978 Oct. 22   **Steel**, **Pulse**   Gary Gibson.

1978 Oct. 22   **The Zygote**, **Outside Tokyo**   Gary Gibson, Ralph Hewitt, Derek Beetlestone.
Only Callus is now described, the rest have returned to nature.

1978   **Howarth's Wait**   Dave Gregory.
Named by Gregory to commemorate Paul Howarth's wait for a party to finish a 'normal' route so that he could continue with Playtex, the girdle.

1965-1978   **Scoop Connection**   Keith Myhill.

Publication of the 1978 Froggatt Area guidebook. Other routes whose first ascent details are unknown include:
Sunday, **Surprise Surprise**, **Vanilla Slice**, **Urn**, **Block Wall** (A1).

1979 April 16   **Mind over Watter**   Marcus Tierney, Steve Adcock.

1979 May 5   **Red Knuckle Arête**   Colin (Choe) Brooks, Chris Addy.
No longer described.

1979 July 23   **Crystal Clear**, **Blood Red Sword**   Gary Gibson, Ian Barker, Steve Keeling.
Blood Red Sword is not described in this guidebook but the corner that it followed is included in the current description of J.J.2.

1979 Oct. 11   **Terminator**   Loz Francomb.
No longer described.

1980	**Brain Attack** Martin Crook, Dave Farrant.
1981 Aug. 29	**Split Second Timing** Gary Gibson, Jon Walker.
1981 Oct. 31	**Rattus Norvegicus** Gary Gibson, Neil Harvey.
1981	**Skyline** Daniel Lee.
First free ascent.
1981	**Block Wall** Dominic Lee.
First free ascent.
Lee used two peg-runners on the first ascent although these were eliminated on the second ascent by Jerry Moffatt.
1981-1983	**Pool Wall** (*née* Suspense Direct) Roger Greatrick, Al Carn.
Climbed at the time with two peg runners, now led without, although the nut slots have been improved and a layaway is used where the second peg was.
First free ascent.
1981-1983	**Going for the One** Phil Barker, Adey Hubbard.
1981-1983	**Brain Cells in Collision**, **Brainstorm** Paul Mitchell (solo).
	Publication of the 1983 Stanage Millstone guidebook.
1983 Sept. 5	**Knave** Dave Gregory, Jim Rubery.
1983 Sept. 29	**Morning Glory** Dominic Staniforth (unseconded).
After top-roping.
1984 Oct. 14	**Rockhopper** B Davidson, S Biskill.
1985	**Von Ryan's Express** Tony Ryan, Mick Ryan.
1985	**The Gordons, The Gordons** Johnny Dawes, Paul Clark.
1986 Nov.	**Heavy Plant Crossing** Chris Plant, Mark Pretty.
1987 May 14	**Elytrocele** Pete Oxley (solo).
Probably done before.
1989 Sept. 20	**Middle-aged Spread** Al Evans.
Top-roped first.
1989 Oct. 15	**Formic Escape** Dave Gregory.
1989 Oct. 20	**The Last Wet Wednesday** Dave Gregory, Alastair Ferguson.
1989	**Brain Death** Anon
1990 April 21	**Mildy Laxative**, **Side Pocket** Dave Gregory, Alastair Ferguson.
1990 April 28	**The Table Leg** Dave Gregory, Bill Taylor.
1991 Oct. 20	**Last Day of Freedom** Bill Gregory.

YARNCLIFFE QUARRY

O.S. ref. SK 255794

by Jon Barton

> 'All the climbs in the quarry call for steady and skilful
> leadership, and that delicacy of touch so necessary when on
> rock whose soundness is not above suspicion. For this
> reason we do not give the name of any route on the quarry
> as being typical of its standard.'

Don Morrison and Pete Marks,
Sheffield – Froggatt Guidebook, 1965.

SITUATION and CHARACTER

The quarry lies just off the B6521, Fox House to Grindleford road.
It is a popular quarry with beginners and low-grade climbers
who find much to climb here, although it is worth noting that it
can be sandy after rain. Also heavy use by climbers is eroding
holds on the slabs and destroying vegetation. The quarry is very
sheltered and the left-hand slabs get the sun. However, the
right-hand walls are slow to dry but offer valuable shade in hot
weather. There is some poor rock in the quarry and care must be
taken when climbing in these sectors.

APPROACHES AND ACCESS

The SYT No. 240, will usually stop on request near the quarry.
Alternatively both the SYT No. 272 and the Trent No. 244 stop at
the Fox House. Walking from here to the quarry is unlikely to
take more than thirty minutes. Alternatively, take the rail link to
Grindleford, then walk up the hill. Again thirty minutes should
suffice.

The quarry is to the east of the B6521, just near a farm house. A
gated track leads into the quarry and although the numerous
trees hide all but the uppermost rock, the crag is easily spotted.

The quarry is owned by the National Trust which is willing to
allow it to be used for climbing provided that the common sense
by-laws are obeyed. NO CAMPING IS ALLOWED. The Trust is
increasingly worried about litter here and climbers are asked to
leave none and even take away that which they find there.

HISTORY

The quarry was discovered in 1950 by the Valkyrie Mountaineering Club. The principal explorers, Don Chapman, Nat Allen, Don Cowan and Joe Brown recorded several routes including *Cardinal's Crack* and *Trised Crack* and *Bow-Shaped Wall. Fall Pipe* by Ted Howard and *Latecomer* by Don Morrison were added about 1964. Sometime after the 1965 guidebook was published, J R Barker, W Phillips, P Brown and R Scott climbed *S.T.P., Inverted Jigsaw, Sulu* and *Zapple*, which had been a peg route. The lesser routes of *Hidden Crack, Capital Cracks* and some of the fillers-in on the slabs were added by Dave Gregory and Geoff Milburn. In 1977 Jonathan Lagoe climbed *Stormfactor* and Ron Fawcett forced the magnificent arête of *Crème de la Crème*. In 1978 Malcolm Salter led Bruce Barnes up *Soldier Ant*, John Middleton led *Chalked Up* and Steve Adcock had a *Non-stop Nightmare*. Pete Wilson climbed *Rhythm of Cruelty* in 1979. 1980 saw Gary Gibson doing *Five Minutes* and the crag then took a rest.

In 1985 a barrage (for Yarncliffe Quarry!) of new routes included *Flying Without Wings* by Nigel Slater and *Rubble Trouble* by Bill McKee. *Zappa* was contrived by Dave Candlin and the desperate *Hot Rats* by Paul Pepperday.

THE CLIMBS are described from LEFT to RIGHT and begin with the obvious arête at the left-hand end of the first sweep of slab.

* **1   Ant's Arête**   16m   HS   4a   (1950)
Fine, unprotected climbing on good holds at an amenable angle.

  2   Aphid's Wall   16m   VS   4c   (1972)
Take the easiest line up the slab just to the right.

* **3   Latecomer**   16m   VS   4b   (1964)
Start just right of, and move across to, the thin crack with a sentry-box. Just above this, move left and finish carefully.

  4   Soldier Ant   16m   HVS   5b   (1978)
Climb direct up the slab between Latecomer and Ant's Crack.

  5   Ant's Crack   17m   S   (1950)
The wide crack just to the right.

  6   Ant's Wall   17m   HS   4a   (1972)
Climb direct to, and finish up, the indefinite crack just right.

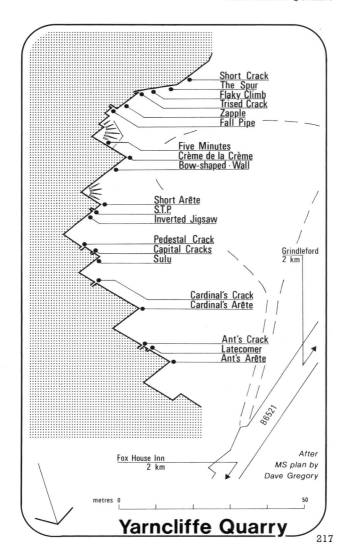

Short Crack
The Spur
Flaky Climb
Trised Crack
Zapple
Fall Pipe

Five Minutes
Crème de la Crème
Bow-shaped · Wall

Short Arête
S.T.P.
Inverted Jigsaw

Pedestal Crack
Capital Cracks
Sulu

Grindleford
2 km

Cardinal's Crack
Cardinal's Arête

Ant's Crack
Latecomer
Ant's Arête

B6521

Fox House Inn
2 km

*After
MS plan by
Dave Gregory*

metres 0   50

Yarncliffe Quarry

217

7 Formica Slab 17m VS 4b (1972)
Ascend the slab between Ant's Wall and Angular Climb.

8 Angular Climb 17m MS (1951-1957)
Follow the broken crack with a tree in it, six metres left of the corner.

9 Centipede 17m VD (1965-1978)
Two metres right is a dirty crack beside a small birch.

To the right is another crack, D, and the main corner, D; both routes are of little merit.

10 Hidden Crack 26m VS 5a (1971)
Climb a diagonal crack in the side wall to reach Cardinal's Arête at half-height. Traverse left and climb the crack direct, finishing over a small overhang.

† **11 Wake me if I Die** 20m E1 5b (1989)
Follow Hidden Crack to the ledge. Move one metre left to a small block, then follow the crack to finish.

12 Cardinal's Arête 20m VS 4c (1951)
Climb the front of the overhanging arête (or start up the side wall to the left and move rightwards on to the arête, 4b). Follow the arête direct, treating the rock with respect.

13 Cardinal's Slab 20m VS 4c (1972)
Climb the slab two metres right of the grassy break. Finish up a thin crack.

14 Threatened 20m HVS 5a (1978)
Ascend the slab between Cardinal's Slab and Cardinal's Crack.

* **15 Cardinal's Crack** 20m VS 4b (1950)
The fine wide crack to the right has a loose finish.

* **16 Chalked Up** 20m E1 5a (1978)
The unprotected slab two metres to the right, is climbed by some pleasant moves.

17 Griffin's Wall 20m HS 4a (1952)
Climb the slab to the right, finishing up a short crack.

Just right is the unpleasant **Caterpillar Corner**, S, (1951).

* **18 Sulu** 20m VS 4c (1971)
Climb the thin crack just left of the arête to a ledge. Finish up the arête above, moving on to the front face for the final moves.

* **19 Rhythm of Cruelty** 20m E3 5b (1979)
Start just round the arête to the right. Layback the arête to a
ledge and finish direct.

20 Pedestal Arête 22m VS 4b (1951)
Start five metres right of the arête and climb stepped rocks
leftwards to the top of the pedestal. Finish as for Sulu or straight
up.

21 Capital Cracks 20m VS 4c (1971)
Climb the front of the pedestal between Sulu and the start of
Pedestal Arête by a crack. From the ledge move right and climb
the thin cracks three metres right of the arête.

22 Pedestal Crack 20m VS 4b (1951)
Climb the wide crack just right to a bad landing. It is possible to
finish direct, but it is best to traverse off left. Not nice.

Ten metres right is a disgusting corner.

Swastika I, S, (1951), and **Swastika II**, VS, (1951), take the right
wall and are best forgotten. Slightly better is the next route.

23 Non-stop Nightmare 20m E1 5b (1978)
Start in the disgusting corner. Move left and go up strenuously to
finish left of the small oak. Finish as for Pedestal Crack.

† **24 Flying without Wings** 22m E5 6b (1985)
This serious route takes the wall and flake left of The Inverted
Jigsaw. The moves from the flake are difficult and bold,
particularly for the short. A tree provides an abseil descent.
Reputedly harder than Crème de la Crème.

25 The Inverted Jigsaw 23m E1 5b (1971)
Start at the lowest part of the wall on the right of the disgusting
corner. Follow the thin crack to finish. Poor rock and poor
protection.

* **26 S.T.P.** 13m VS 4c (1971)
The obvious jamming crack just left of the end of the wall.

27 Rubble Trouble 15m E3 5c (1985)
From S.T.P. swing left on good holds to follow a thin crack and
the left-hand tottering groove above, stepping right to finish.

28 Short Arête 8m S (1965-1978)
Climb just right of the arête.

The quarry deteriorates for a short way then 20m right of S.T.P., and three metres left of a fine, sharp arête, is:

29 Bow-Shaped Wall   16m   HVS   4c   (1952)
Climb a thin crack to a doubtful flake, avoiding the terminally loose block on the left. Climb the flake and the crack above to finish.

* **30 Crème de la Crème**   16m   E5   6b   (1977)
Climb the fine arête by laybacking facing right. Very hard to start but interest is maintained throughout. One peg runner at about mid-height.

31 Five Minutes   8m   E2   5b   (1980)
Start at the left-hand end of the large ledge of Fe Fand Corner and climb the wall to the right of Crème de la Crème trending left. Strenuous.

Fe Fand Corner, HVS 5a, (1952), takes the vegetated area just right. The route follows the grassy risers and finishes up some steep moves left of the corner. **Great Bay Escape**, VD, (1951), is the poor groove-line just right.

23 metres right is a fine groove and crack-line. Immediately left is the next route.

Christmas Grooves, S, (1951), follows a series of heather-covered grooves.

* **32 Fall Pipe**   16m   VS   4c   (1964)
The aforementioned groove and crack is well-protected but often greasy.

The wall to the right is split by twin curving cracks which merge about seven metres up. They give:

* **33 Zapple**   20m   HVS   5b   (1969/1971)
Climb the right-hand crack to the junction. Follow the crack above to the top, which is often sandy. Starting up the left-hand branch reduces the standard to 5a.

† **34 Zappa**   18m   E4   6a   (1985)
Start up Zapple but trend right to finish up Stormfactor. An independent start has been added using a nut for aid in the horizontal break, † **Hot Rats**, E5 6c, (1985). Both routes are now very dirty.

35 Trised Crack 15m VS 4c   (1951)
The flake crack five metres right of Zapple gives good
laybacking.

* **36 Stormfactor** 22m HVS 5b   (1977)
Climb Trised Crack to its top. Move left on to the wall along
diagonal cracks to a steep and often sandy finish.

37 Flaky Climb 8m HVD   (1952)
Climb the broken crack just right of Trised Crack.

38 The Spur 8m VS 4b   (1964)
The crack to the right is still rather dirty.

39 Short Crack 6m VS 4c   (1971)
Ascend the crack five metres right round the blunt arête.

The arête between the last two routes has also been climbed;
The Rowel, VS, (1972).

Contour, VS, (1964), is a girdle of the left-hand section of the
crag. The climbing is not very independent and the line is left to
individual choice.

YARNCLIFFE QUARRY LIST OF FIRST ASCENTS

1950 Dec.	**Cardinal's Crack** Don Chapman, J R (Nat) Allen.	
1950 Dec.	**Ant's Arête** Nat Allen, Don Chapman.	
1950 Dec.	**Ant's Crack** (*née* Ant's Wall) Nat Allen, R Kerry.	
1951 Jan.	**Cardinal Arête** Don Chapman, Nat Allen.	
1951 Jan.	**Christmas Grooves** Merrick (Slim) Sorrell, Nat Allen.	
1951 Feb.	**Caterpillar Corner** Nat Allen, Don Chapman.	
1951 March	**Pedestal Arête** Nat Allen, Don Chapman.	
1951 March	**Swastika II** Joe Brown, Slim Sorrell, Nat Allen.	
1951 May	**Swastika I** Nat Allen, Don Chapman.	
1951 May	**Great Bay Escape** Nat Allen, Slim Sorrell.	
1951 June	**Trised Crack** Don Cowan, Don Chapman, Nat Allen.	
1951 Oct.	**Pedestal Crack** Nat Allen, D Carnell.	
1952 March	**Bow-Shaped Wall**, **Flaky Climb** Don Chapman, Nat Allen.	
1952 May	**Fe Fand Corner** Nat Allen, J Willbourne.	
1952 May	**Griffin's Wall** J Willbourne, Nat Allen.	
Pre-1957	**Angular Climb** Anon.	

Publication of the 1957 Further Developments guidebook.

1964 June	**Contour** Don Morrison, Les Gillott.
1964	**The Spur** Anon.
1964	**Fall Pipe** Ted Howard.
1964	**Latecomer** Don Morrison.
	Publication of the 1965 Sheffield – Froggatt guidebook.
1967 May 7	**Waft** D Brady, P Craddock. *No longer described.*
1969 May	**Zapple** (Aid) J R Barker, W Phillips. *First free ascent in 1971.*
1971 April 21	**S.T.P.** W Phillips, J R Barker, P Brown, R I Scott.
1971 April 21	**The Inverted Jigsaw** J R Barker, P Brown, W Phillips.
1971 April 21	**Sulu** J R Barker, P Brown, R I Scott.
1971	**Zapple** P Brown, W Phillips, J R Barker, R I Scott. *First free ascent.*
1971	**Hidden Crack, Capital Cracks, Short Crack** Dave Gregory, Geoff Milburn.
1972 Aug. 29	**Aphid's Wall, Ant's Wall, Formica Slab, Cardinal's Slab** Dave Gregory, Dave Eyles.
1972 Sept. 3	**The Rowel** Dave Gregory, Geoff Milburn
1977 April 18	**Crème de la Crème** Ron Fawcett, Geoff Birtles. *The lower arête had been climbed previously by Nicky Stokes.*
1977	**Stormfactor** Jonathan Lagoe, Phil Smith, Alan Baker.
1978 Oct. 23	**Threatened** Gary Gibson, Derek Beetlestone.
1978	**Soldier Ant** Malcolm Salter, Bruce Barnes.
1978	**Chalked Up** Giles Barker.
1978 Nov.	**Non-stop Nightmare** Steve Adcock, Marcus Tierney, Brian Binton.
1965-1978	**Centipede** Anon.
	Publication of the 1978 Froggatt Area guidebook.
1979 May 6	**Rhythm of Cruelty** Phil Wilson, Gary Gibson, Paul Delaney, Paul Bird, Jon Walker, Mark Walton, Gary Welthall.
1980 Feb.26	**Five Minutes** Gary Gibson (solo). *Top-roped first.*
	Publication of the 1983 Stanage Millstone guidebook.
1985 May 8	**Rubble Trouble** Bill McKee, Dave Abbey.
1985 July 10	**Flying without Wings** Nigel Slater (unseconded).
1985	**Zappa** Dave Candlin, Paul Pepperday.
1985	**Hot Rats** (1pt) Paul Pepperday, Dave Candlin.
1989 May 9	**Wake me if I Die** Roy Bennett, Tim Rolfe.

YARNCLIFFE EDGE

O.S. ref. SK 256793

by Dave Gregory

'At Whitsuntide, 1956, Byne returned after an absence of 24 years, this time accompanied by Reg Pillinger of the Peak Climbing Club. The weather was almost too hot for climbing, but Pillinger, supported by Byne, spent several tense hungry hours in blazing sunshine, cleaning out and climbing the fine route now known as Yarn.'

Don Morrison and Pete Marks,
Sheffield – Froggatt Guidebook, 1965.

SITUATION and CHARACTER

Yarncliffe Edge lies slightly farther down the B6521 (the Fox House to Grindleford road) than Yarncliffe Quarry. The rock of the edge varies in character; some buttresses are natural gritstone with sound rock, other quarried sections are however somewhat friable. In summer, the edge is a Matto Grosso. In any season the routes dry out slowly after rain but in spring or autumn, though it is still heavily overgrown, the many insects and man-eating plants are less active. Many once traceable routes have been omitted and details of further apparent first ascents are not needed.

APPROACHES and ACCESS

Approach as for Yarncliffe Quarry, then walk downhill for 200m or so until a grassy drive, starting from a built-up gateway and stile, runs up to the edge. One can also follow the footpath from the top of the quarry along the top of the edge. The edge is the property of the National Trust which DOES NOT WISH THE EDGE TO BE USED FOR CLIMBING, intending it to act as a nature reserve. The edge is included in this guidebook for the sake of having a complete record and its INCLUSION IN NO WAY IMPLIES THAT CLIMBERS HAVE THE RIGHT TO CLIMB THERE. They do however have the right to consult a psychiatrist if they get the urge to explore this jungle.

HISTORY

In 1932 Clifford Moyer and Eric Byne started climbing here and thus they have a lot to answer for. 1956 saw the next visit. Byne returned with Reg Pillinger and cleaned and climbed *Yarn*. Byne and Charles Ashbury did the *Tall Story* start to *Yarn* and *Nightcap*. Alan Wright climbed *Crack O'Noon* in July and in August Don Morrison led *Misconception*, while Al Hall also did several routes. In September Pete Marks did some minor routes and seconded Morrison on *High Heaven*, then the best route on the edge. Len Millsom added *Dicrotic* and *High Hell* in the spring of 1960. In 1962 Tony Moulam climbed his route. Gabe Regan and Al Evans introduced modern standards in 1976 with *Crackline to Oblivion*. In March 1981 Paul Mitchell introduced modern names with *The Snail and the Goat Meet Mr Dali and His Amazing Performing Flapjacks*. Some other hard routes were added, in particular the desperate *Rock Lobster* by Mark Stokes, before the crag sank under the vegetation.

The CLIMBS are described from LEFT to RIGHT and are approached along a grassy drive which gradually becomes over-grown. One is forced leftwards towards the overgrown and unused rock-faces, just left of the big blunt arête of Yarn. Line Shooter is the shallow rhododendron-filled corner, six metres left of Yarn.

1   The Snail and the Goat Meet Mr Dali and His Amazing Performing Flapjacks   8m E3 6a   (1981)

Start four metres left of Line Shooter. Go up a short crack and move right to use another short crack to gain the rib. Climb this and go right to finish, wondering why and pondering the meaning of life.

2   Line Shooter   26m   VD   (1956)

Climb, if you must, the shallow rhododendron-filled corner/groove to the terrace. A ledgy rib leads up leftwards to a cave. Finish up the chimney, exiting right.

The next two routes take diagonal lines right where the crag is highest (but they are best left.)

Chris Craggs soloing Excalibur, Lawrencefield.
Photo: Craggs collection.

3 Thrid 30m HS (1964)
Take any start to the terrace, then go up a corner crack and move right to a ledge with a tree. Move up and left under the overhang till the nose can be climbed on poor holds.

4 Valhalla 33m HS (1956)
Take any start to the terrace. Traverse right to a big slab and climb the rightward-slanting crack to a ledge with a tree. Pull up to the overhang and traverse right on to the exposed face. Climb this direct to a hard finishing mantelshelf.

5 Yarn 33m S (1956)
Start a metre or so right of Line Shooter. Go up the wall to a ledge and traverse right across little ribs to a fir tree ledge. A short rib leads to the terrace. Traverse right and follow an exposed crack near the edge of the slab to a ledge. Avoid the final nose by going leftwards up an interesting mantelshelf.

The **Via Tall Story**, S, (1956), variation start takes the steep crack which leads direct to the conifer tree.

6 Short-arse Wall 8m E3 5c (1981)
The wall down left of Thread. Go up into a shallow niche and make hard moves left to finish just right of the arête. Unprotected.

7 Thread 23m VS 4c (1957-1966)
Start at a higher level and climb either side of the diamond-shaped flake into a niche. Move right and go up the groove; move leftwards to finish up a sentry-box chimney with suspect rock.

8 Dicrotic 21m VS 4c (1960)
Go up the steep wall just right on small holds to a ledge. A short wide crack leads to the chimney of Thread.

9 Crack O'Noon 15m HS (1956)
The obvious corner crack.

10 Night Cap 15m VD (1956)
Climb the giant staircase on the right of the corner, moving left, then back right to a niche. An arête leads to an oak tree.

On the right is a small detached buttress.
Dainty Thread, HD, (1956), takes this, finishing direct over the prominent nose.

Chris Craggs enjoying solitude on Zapple at Yarncliffe Quarry.
Photo: Craggs collection.

About 25m right of Night Cap *is* **SPIDER WALL** *which is bisected by a wide ledge.*
Spider Crawl, HD, (1951-1957), takes the lower buttress on its left corner, followed by the cracked slab and corner above, finishing rightwards. **Central Route**, VD, (1951-1957), takes the centre of the lower wall.

11 Phobia 16m HVS 5b   (1962)
Follow the previous route to the ledge. Climb the upper wall past a diagonal crack and trend leftwards on small holds.

12 Spider Crack 16m S   (1956)
Take a wide crack past trees to the left-hand end of the ledge and a small pinnacle. Follow the flaky crack above.

Just left of the main corner, sycamore and birch trees battle for ascendancy on a ledge at three metres.

13 Crackline to Oblivion 16m E1 5c   (1976)
Climb the awkward crack behind the trees, move right and climb the leftward-slanting crack to finish.

14 Misconception 21m VS 4b   (1956)
The main corner which has some loose rock.

The next three routes were once the pick of the edge but are now covered with black lichen and grosser vegetation.

15 High Hell 21m E1 5b   (1960)
Begin near the corner and move rightwards across the wall into an open groove. Go up this and move right to a gangway. Climb past a tree to a large ledge and finish up the short arête.

16 Rock Lobster 7m E4 6b   (1981)
Between High Hell and High Heaven is a faint line of flakes. Climb this and finish rightwards to the tree on High Heaven.

17 High Heaven 21m HVS 5b   (1956)
Climb the steep flake crack (*requires abundant energy – 1957*) to a beech tree. Go up the ramp to a peg. A long pull up the wall on the right leads to a large ledge. Move across to an overhang; go over this to finish.

Beyond the ledgy, grassy buttress to the right of High Heaven is a steep, leftward-facing wall. Hidden in amongst the grass are: **Limpet Slab**, HS, (1964), **Cob Web**, VD, (1956), **Spinner's Delight**, S, (1951-1957), and **Introvert**, VD, (1964).

18 Extrovert 15m S   (1964)
Climb the short ferny corner and the left-hand of the twin cracks
on the left side of the face.

19 Unity 1 15m VS 4b   (1964)
After hard moves up the short, steep wall climb the right twin
crack to a tree belay.

20 Pullover 15m HS   (1956)
Start below the prominent arête. Pull up into a niche and fight up
the chimney to a big ledge. Go up the corner and make an
exposed step left onto a ledge on the arête. Finish up the arête.

21 Formic Frenzy 7m E2 6a   (1982)
Climb the overhanging wall just right on jugs to a very hard
move to attain the rib. Use the rib to move left to finish. Short,
brutal and unprotected.

22 Moulam's Crack 9m VS 4c   (1962)
The obvious corner crack at a higher level behind the oak tree.

23 Staccato 9m HS   (1964)
Climb a thin crack three metres right to a small ledge. Finish
easily.

24 Integrity 9m D   (1964)
Just right again. Pleasant climbing up the wider crack.

25 Lichen Wall 9m D   (1956)
The bigger crack up the broken wall to the beech tree.

26 Ding Dong Corner 11m D   (1956)
Climb the crack in the right-hand arête of the bay to the tree.

27 Ding Dong Wall 8m S   (1956)
Any of three lines up the steep cracked wall to the right.

There are several small routes on the rocks to the right which,
because of their overgrown nature, have not been described in
detail. May they rest in peace. However for the history buff, and
to avoid any new wave of exploration, they include: **Bobbin**, D,
(pre-1933), **Monkey Corner**, D, (pre-1933), **Cordyalis Crack**,
HS, (1972), **Flying Ant Crack**, VS, (1972), **Dexterity**, HS, (1964),
Slantside Groove, S, (1956), **Siegfried**, HS, (1956), **Jim Jam
Arête**, D, (pre-1933), and **Pornography**, S, (1951-1957).

YARNCLIFFE EDGE LIST OF FIRST ASCENTS

Pre-1933	**Bobbin, Monkey Corner, Jim Jam Arête** Clifford Moyer, Eric Byne.	
1956 Whitsun.	**Yarn** Reg Pillinger, Eric Byne.	
1956 June	**Via Tall Story, Night Cap** Eric Byne, Charles Ashbury.	
1956 July	**Crack o' Noon** Al Wright.	
1956 Aug.	**Slantside Groove, Ding Dong Corner, Lichen Wall, Cob Web** A N Hall.	
1956 Aug.	**Misconception** Don Morrison, A N Other. *A cleaning epic: Morrison almost killed his second with a loose block.*	
1956 Sept.	**Spider Crack** Ernie Marshall.	
1956 Sept.	**Dainty Thread** Pete Marks.	
1956 Sept.	**Line Shooter, Valhalla, High Heaven** Don Morrison, Pete Marks.	
1956 Oct.	**Pullover, Siegfried** Don Morrison.	
	Publication of the 1957 Further Developments guidebook. Other routes whose first ascent details are unknown include: **Spider Crawl, Central Route, Spinner's Delight, Ding Dong Wall, Pornography.**	
1960 Spring	**Dicrotic, High Hell** Len Millsom.	
1962	**Phobia** (*née* Spider Wall Central) H Rainey.	
1962	**Moulam's Crack** Tony Moulam.	
1964 Spring	**Thrid** Don Morrison.	
1964	**Extrovert, Staccato, Dexterity, Limpet Slab, Introvert, Integrity** Don Morrison.	
1964	**Unity 1** Alan Maskery, Trevor Wright.	
	Publication of the 1965 Sheffield – Froggatt guidebook. First ascent details for **Thread** *are unknown.*	
1971 May 9	**W. Anchor** P Court, R Guthrie. *Not in the text.*	
1972 Sept. 17	**Corydalis Crack** Geoff Milburn, Dave Gregory, Dave Eyles, Hugh Dowding.	
1972 Sept. 17	**Flying Ant Crack** Dave Gregory, Dave Eyles, Geoff Milburn.	
1976 Nov.	**Crackline to Oblivion** Gabe Regan, Al Evans.	
	Publication of the 1978 Froggatt Area guidebook.	
1981 March	**The Snail and The Goat....** Paul Mitchell, Dave Greenald.	
1981 March	**Short-arse Wall** Paul Mitchell (solo). *Top-roped first.*	
1981 March	**Rock Lobster** Mark Stokes (solo). *Eventually soloed after many a lob.*	
1982 July 6	**Formic Frenzy** Paul Mitchell.	

PADLEY QUARRY

O.S. ref. SK 252784

by Bill Taylor

> *'The crag is now worthy of a full day's climbing, and at the time of writing it is obvious that there are still one or two cracks which can be made to yield in the future.'*

> Don Morrison and Pete Marks,
> Sheffield – Froggatt Area guidebook 1965.

SITUATION and CHARACTER

Padley Quarry, unmarked on the O.S. sheets, lies above and behind the Maynard Arms Hotel, just off the B6521 which is the Grindleford to Fox House road. It is not a nice place, being small and heavily wooded. Most of the routes contain vegetation and loose rock. It dries slowly after rain and, when dry and sunny, suffers from millions of ants which have established territorial rights. The quarry is rarely visited and the ants are almost certainly very hungry. They are unlikely to be pleased if one walks all over their empire. Best stay well away.

APPROACHES and ACCESS

The SYT No. 240 runs past the Maynard Arms. Uphill from the Arms, and just opposite a telephone box, is a private road marked 'TEDGNESS ROAD NO THROUGH ROAD'. Follow this road until, just past 'High Lodge' on the left, a track goes off left sign-posted to Haywood car park and Froggatt Edge. Thirty metres along this, at the end of a wire fence on the left, an entry can be made into the quarry on the left over grassy spoil heaps.

The quarry is owned by the National Trust which refers to it as Tegness Quarry and is willing to allow climbing provided that its common sense bye-laws are observed. Camping is not allowed.

HISTORY

Unfortunately, this quarry was discovered in 1956 by Don Morrison and friends from the Pennine Mountaineering Club. By the 1957 guidebook, ten routes had been established. Predictably the guidebook drew attention and further excavations by Len Millsom and Maurice Dunkley produced a few more routes, added to by Morrison and Pete Marks during work for the 1965 guidebook. Some aid pitches were added, to be later freed by Gary Gibson. Most of the possible pitches have been done even if many have been omitted from this text! R.I.P.

The shallow, smaller, left-hand bay contains poor quality overgrown rock. Only the desperate will climb here, but it is said to be good training for some of the gritstone quarries south of Matlock. The right-hand blunt arête of this bay, which has a small vertical slot one metre up, runs into easy-angled vegetated slabs, capped by a short, blocky section.

The CLIMBS are described from LEFT to RIGHT.

LOWER CRAG

1 Redant 14m HS (1956)
Climb the blunt arête to its pulpit top. Finish up the vegetated slabs.

2 Redant Castle 14m S (1956)
Gain the pulpit by the wide crack two metres right of the arête. Vegetate up the slabs to finish!

3 Insertion 15m VS 4b (1956)
Climb the shallow broken corner two metres right to a heathery ledge. This can also be reached by the flake two metres left and a traverse left, **Twilight**, HS 4a, (1965-1978/1978-1983). Gain and finish up the slab as for Redant.

4 M.G.C. 18m HVS 4c (1957-1965)
The right-angled grotty corner leads to an overhang then an arête on the right. Finish up the centre of the upper wall.

5 Rest Assured 9m E2 5c (1979)
The obvious peg-scarred crack five metres right of M.G.C. leads through a bulge to a birch belay. The wise abseil off.

Just right is a groove and corner, with grass and rhododendrons, **Dietrious**, *5a, (1957-1965). Use any finish on the upper wall, if you must.*

6 In the Shadow 9m HVS 5b (1979)
Climb twin cracks, one of which is heavily peg-scarred, in the slab on the right.

7 Whisky and Lemon 9m VS 4b (1956)
Right of In the Shadow is an obvious, square-cut channel containing a small tree. Climb the channel to a choice of finishes.

8 Millsom's Eliminate 9m E2 5c (1957-1965)
The mossy slab to the right has an obvious left arête. The grade depends on the quantity of moss which at present is copious.

In the centre of the slab is a hard mantelshelf leading up the slab leftwards to the terrace, **Briggs' Dilemma**, HVS 5b, (1957-1965). Two more difficult mantel moves into the groove on the right provide the substance of **Shepherd's Wall**, VS 5a, (1957-1965). The slab and cracked arête in the grassy recess to the right are D and HS respectively. A girdle traverse of the Lower Crag, **Foot and Mouth**, VD, has been climbed from right to left, involving much traversing of heathery ledges.

UPPER CRAG

Just right of the centre of the upper crag, above the grassy terrace, is a steep gully. Working leftwards from this are **Vertical V**, S, (1956), up the obvious incut cleft and **Ladder Chimney**, S, (1956), the obvious stepped chimney round to the left. Moving right out of Ladder Chimney and up the arête is **Curved Arête**, VS 4c, (1957-1965).
Just left of Ladder Chimney is a ramp leading up leftwards. It is HVS 4c, and is gained and finished direct.
Three routes; **Fern Cleft**, (1957-1965), **Twin Trees**, (1957-1965), and **Hall Mark**, (1956), all VD, have been made up the short wall to the right of the gully but they are loose and not recommended.

PADLEY QUARRY LIST OF FIRST ASCENTS

1956	**Lost Groove, Redant, Redant Castle, Insertion, Whiskey and Lemon, Original Route, Ladder Chimney, Vertical V, Hall Mark** Members of the Pennine Mountaineering Club.
	Publication of the 1957 Further Developments guidebook.
1957-1965	**Millsom's Eliminate** Len Millsom.
1957-1965	**Briggs' Dilemma, Shepherd's Wall** Maurice Dunkley.
1957-1965	**Dietrious** Alan Clarke.
1957-1965	**Twin Trees** Harry Wood.
1957-1965	**Corner Crack, M.G.C., Curved Arête, Mantelshelf Corner, Fern Cleft** Don Morrison, Pete Marks.
	Publication of the 1965 Sheffield – Froggatt guidebook.

PADLEY QUARRY

1965-1978	**Twilight** (A1 & S), **Uncle** (A1 & S) Brian C Benton. *First free ascent of the former 1978-1983. However, the latter was subsequently dropped from the 1983 Stanage Millstone guidebook, although it was mentioned in passing as an old pegged crack.*
1968 June	**Square One** Brian C Benton, J Eastwood, F Swift.
1973 Sept.	**Delilah** (A1 & VD) Brian C Benton, George Sampson *First free ascent of the initial crack as part of In The Shadow in 1979 by Gary Gibson.* *G Sampson is the son of Sampson of Goliath's Groove fame.*
1973 Dec. 26	**Boxing Day** (A1 & D) Brian C Benton, George Sampson, F Swift. *First free ascent of the initial crack as part of In the Shadow in 1979 by Gary Gibson.*
1974 Feb. 3	**Cripple Crack** (A1 & D)Brian C Benton, George Sampson, F Swift, J Eastwood. *First free ascent of the first pitch as Rest Assured in 1979 by Gary Gibson.* *Publication of the 1978 Froggatt Area guidebook.*
1978 Nov. 4	**The Ramp** Paul Cropper, Antony (Ant) Heavyside. *Not now described in the text.*
1978-1983	**Twilight** Anon. *First free ascent.*
1979 July 14	**In the Shadow** Gary Gibson, Ian Johnson. *First free ascent of both Delilah and Boxing Day.*
1979 July 15	**Rest Assured** Gary Gibson, Ian Johnson. *First free ascent of first pitch of Cripple Crack.* *Gibson was later to comment "....... hell, almost two days spent in this hole"!* *Publication of the 1983 Stanage Millstone guidebook.*

TEGNESS QUARRIES

O.S. ref. SK 254781

by Dave Gregory

'Fingers   *30 feet*   *VS*
The hardest climb in the quarry, requiring a determined
leader of skill. Take the left-hand one of the two thin cracks
just on the right of Corner Crack. Straightforward holds lead
to a slight overhang which is the crux. This is overcome on
painful finger jams and tiny footfolds, and is followed by
finishing gingerly with a mantelshelf over poor rock.

Len Millsom,
Sheffield – Froggatt Guidebook 1965.

SITUATION and CHARACTER

Tegness Quarries stand 100m apart at the southern end of the
Longshaw Estate and are a prominent feature of the skyline when
seen from Grindleford and the Derwent Valley. They combine an
attractive position with some unattractive rock. The rock in the
Pinnacle Quarry is better weathered, less loose and has a more
stable top. However, it can be greasy after bad weather,
particularly in the Ace and Joker bay. The North Quarry is less
enclosed and quicker to dry but is marred by its rock, which is
considerably more friable, especially at the top or the crag.
Belays at the tops of all the routes are difficult to find, often
requiring ingenuity or an extra rope.

APPROACHES and ACCESS

The easiest approach, if travelling by car, is from the National
Trust car park which is below the Grouse Inn on the B6054 Fox
House to Calver road. From the car park, a sign points to the
quarries on Jubilee Hill. The Trent bus No. 244 runs along the
B6054. The quarries can also be reached from Grindleford using
the footpath passing Padley Quarry, giving access from
Grindleford by rail or bus. The quarries are owned by the
National Trust which is willing to allow climbing provided that its
bye-laws are observed. No camping is allowed.

HISTORY

The Crazy Pinnacle was discovered and climbed by the ubiquitous James W Puttrell during the closing years of the Victorian era. His companion and rival, Ernest A. Baker, published an account of two visits and included a photograph of an ascent of the pinnacle in his book, 'Moors, Crags and Caves of the High Peak' of 1903. By the Thirties the Original Route up the longer arête of the Pinnacle had become well-used and it is said that the brave (or foolish?) would stand on their heads on the summit. Around this time the majority of routes in the Pinnacle Quarry were climbed by Sheffield teams formed from Frank Elliott, Harry Dover, Gilbert Ellis, Eric Byne and Rupert Brooks. In 1962 Eric Byne suggested to the Parnassus Climbing Club that possibilities remained and Len Millsom and Brian Shirley climbed *Pisa* and *Thin Crack* (with a point of aid) and added *Corner Crack, Fingers* and *Ace* to The Pinnacle Quarry. They, with others, then turned their attention to the less attractive, and more recently worked, North Quarry and climbed most of the present routes. By early 1978, Thin Crack had been freed and Mick Fowler and John Stevenson had added *Barrage* and *Silver Spoon* to the Pinnacle. In April 1988 S. Purdy and C. Bell squeezed *Rock the Casbah* onto the Pinnacle and in May, Roger Doherty and R. Brook added *The Main Attraction* to the North Quarry. During work for this guidebook, Bill Gregory climbed *The Ego and The Id*.

THE CLIMBS

The Crazy Pinnacle Quarry is described first since it is reached first when walking from the National Trust car-park.

TEGNESS CRAZY PINNACLE QUARRY

O.S. ref. SK 255780

The Crazy Pinnacle now has six routes which are described in a clockwise direction.

* **1 The Original Route (The Crazy Pinnacle)** 9m D (c.1890)
The longest, stepped, arête. Descend by reversing the route or by a careful abseil.

2 Pisa 9m HS 4a   (1962)
The cracked south face just left of The Original Route.

234

Crazy Pinnacle Quarry

3 Barrage 9m E2 5c   (1976)
Climb the unprotected arête left of Pisa.

4 Silver Spoon 9m E2 5c   (1976)
The square-cut arête left of Barrage.

5 Thin Crack 9m HVS 5b   (1962)
Climb the thin crack facing the left wall of the quarry, and just
left of Silver Spoon, using holds on either arête.

6 Rock the Casbah 9m E1 5b   (1988)
The blunt arête containing cracks just left of Thin Crack.

The remaining climbs in the quarry are described from LEFT to
RIGHT.

Opposite Silver Spoon is a broken wall with the **Four Cracks**, VD – S, (pre-1965).

7 Chass 8m D   (pre-1965)
The cracked right wall of the open groove just right.
The jutting arête just right has also been climbed.

8 Chasm 8m D   (1978-1983)
The obvious corner just right of the jutting arête.

9 The Bridge 8m S   (1965-1978)
Climb the delicate groove one metre right.

10 Splinter 8m HS 4a   (pre-1965)
The shallow corner, one metre right again.

11 Profanity 8m HS 4a   (1978-1983)
The steep corner just right, behind the tree.

There are no more routes until, past the dirty left-hand corner of this bay and a short vegetated wall, there is a short arête with a twisted beech tree.

The wide crack in the next acute corner is Goliath. *Just left of its left arête is:*

12 Big Flake 7m VS 4b   (1965-1978)
The cracks on the right of the short slab lead to the flake.

13 Goliath 9m HVD   (pre-1965)
Climb the steep wide crack to the small tree, finishing up another wide crack.

14 Loose Setting 9m HS 4b   (1978)
Climb the steep crack through the niche just right of the arête.

† **15 The Ego and The Id** 7m E3 6b   (1990)
Climb the slanting crack on the right to just before its end and reach up and left to climb the thin crack gymnastically. Finish rightwards, or more strenuously leftwards. In either case, have no recourse to the corner either for climbing or to find runners.

16 Corner Crack 10m HS 4b   (1962)
Climb the crack in the back left-hand corner of the bay.

* **17 Fingers** 10m VS 4c   (1962)
Start at the foot of Corner Crack and climb the left-hand of the two cracks in the back wall.

18 Fumbs 10m HVS 5b   (1965-1978)
The right-hand crack is climbed direct to a poor finish.

To the right is a slabby apron with cracks at each side.

19 Ace 10m HS 4a   (1962)
Climb the left-hand corner crack.

20 Joker 10m HS 4a   (pre-1965)
Follow the right-hand crack past a sapling to join Ace.

The path continues north from The Crazy Pinnacle Quarry to The North Quarry.

TEGNESS NORTH QUARRY   O.S. ref. SK 253782

This quarry is divided centrally by a short wall of rock. Beginning in the left half, at the extreme left end is a short, steep gully which can be used as a descent route.

The CLIMBS are described from LEFT to RIGHT.

21 Flaky Climb 8m VD   (pre-1965)
The obvious flake one metre right of the gully. Finish up the crack.

22 Inch Crack 9m S   (pre-1965)
Climb the thin crack two metres right, finishing direct.

23 Curving Crack 9m VD   (pre-1965)
Ascend the pleasant corner crack one metre right.

24 Wijit 11m HVS 4b   (pre-1965)
Four metres right is an unpleasantly loose groove in an arête.

25 Outram 11m VS 4b   (pre-1965)
Interesting moves up the right-hand side of the arête lead to a finish on poor rock.

The wall right again is taken by **Titanic**, VD, (pre-1965), and **Choss**, VD, (pre-1965), but loose rock means that they are best avoided. Over the short wall, which divides the quarry into two, is a square-cut block with a niche in its right-hand side.

26 The Niche 8m VS 4a   (pre-1965)
Climb into the niche and go out strenuously on loose rock.

27 Zig-Zag 7m S (pre-1965)
Eight metres right is a greasy corner. Climb the irregular flake
one metre right of the corner to a loose finish.

28 The Main Attraction 8m HVS 5b (1988)
The thin peg-scarred crack two metres left of the blunt arête.

29 Rainey's Delight 8m VS 4c (pre-1965)
Climb the delicate arête right of Zig-Zag via a ledge.

The overgrown slabby wall 30m right in a slight gully is taken by
Oak Tree Wall, D, (pre-1965), and **Sodd**, VD, (pre-1965), but
neither is worthwhile.

This is a somewhat dismal end to a dismal section of the
guidebook. It is probably best to rip these last few pages out of
your guidebook so that you aren't tempted to return once the
experience has faded from your memory. Do it now, you know it
makes sense!

The good news however, is that some of the best has yet to
come. Sprint across the road to a much better place altogether.

TEGNESS QUARRY LIST OF FIRST ASCENTS

c.1890	**The Crazy Pinnacle** James W Puttrell, Ernest A Baker. *Frank Elliott, Harry Dover, Gilbert Ellis, Eric Byne and Rupert Brooks all scratched about the area, though none of them had bothered to record his respective activities.*
1962	**Pisa, Diamond Crack, Corner Crack, Fingers, Ace, Thin Crack** Len Millsom, Brian Shirley. *Publication of the 1965 Sheffield Froggatt guidebook. Also contained were the following routes, which may well have been climbed by Elliott et al.* **Flaky Climb, Inch Crack, Curving Crack, Wijit, Outram, Titanic, Choss, The Niche, Zig Zag, Rainey's Delight, Oak Tree Wall, Sodd, Four Cracks, Chass, Splinter, Goliath, Joker.**
1973 March 11	**Rutter** Robert Dunn. *No longer described.*
1976 Nov. 21	**Barrage, Silver Spoon** Mick Fowler, John Stevenson. *Publication of the 1978 Froggatt Area guidebook.* *Other routes whose first ascent details are unknown, include:* **The Bridge, Big Flake, Fumbs, Loose Setting.** *Publication of the 1983 Stanage Millstone guidebook.* *Other routes whose first ascent details are unknown include:* **Chasm, Profanity.**
1988 April 2	**Rock the Casbah** S Purdy, C Bell.

| 1988 May 21 | **The Main Attraction** | Roger Doherty, R Brook. |
| 1990 | **The Ego and the Id** | Bill Gregory, Dave Gregory, William Taylor. |

FROGGATT EDGE

O.S. ref. SK 249770 to 252760

by Graham Hoey

> *'One raw, foggy day... Brown was persuaded to*
> *demonstrate this climb (Cave Crack) to some curious*
> *onlookers. Climbing in nailed boots he moved out under the*
> *overhang, grasped the knob, and pulled up into the*
> *jamming crack above. When he was belayed at the top,*
> *Sorrell, a heavily built policeman, began to follow him up.*
> *All went smoothly until he came to the pull-up on the knob,*
> *where his hand slipped off the wet rock and he fell*
> *backwards. The rope broke and the horrified onlookers saw*
> *him plunge head first among the sharp boulders below.*
> *Brown descended the crack with incredible speed and*
> *everybody ran to help what they assumed to be the injured*
> *climber, but Sorrell had fallen luckily and his main concern*
> *seemed to be the rope. He and Brown tested it with their*
> *hands, and once again it snapped. "My God", mumbled*
> *Sorrell, "to think we were using that rope on Cloggy last*
> *weekend."'*

Eric Byne, High Peak 1966.

SITUATION and CHARACTER

Starting life as a sandbank under the sea some 280 million years
ago, Froggatt Edge eventually became permanently exposed
around 180 million years later. In the years that followed, the
coarse gritstone stood up well to the destructive elements of
nature only to suffer markedly from quarrying activities in recent
times. The stone was used extensively for building and for
making grindstones which were used primarily for the grinding
of glass. Quarrying gradually came to an end towards the end of
the eighteenth century as cheaper imported stone arrived from
France, and except for the occasional rock-fall has remained
largely unaltered since then.

Despite its tribulations, Froggatt is a magnificent edge standing
proudly above the Derwent Valley, running roughly north to

Right: Mark Leach working towards The Crack, Froggatt Edge.
Photo: Neil Foster.
Overleaf: Hilary Lawrenson on Strapiombante, Froggatt Edge.
Photo: Tony Kartawick.

south and parallel to the B6504 Fox House to Calver road. At the northern end, the edge is very broken. Hidden Buttress is shrouded in trees, lichenous, often damp and the rock quite brittle. Nevertheless, those who wish for solitude and dislike chalked-up, off-the-peg routes will gain a certain satisfaction from Hidden Buttress and its neighbours. Brookside Buttress is slightly cleaner, being more open and of better quality rock. It is in a peaceful setting and is well worth a visit.

The main edge is a virtually continuous face of exceptionally clean and quick-drying rock of the highest quality. Its chequered history has left a variety of features ranging from the natural buttresses with their rounded breaks and holds to the steep, smooth quarried walls and slabs containing sharper, more positive holds. Many of the popular routes are quite polished, but clean sticky boots and careful footwork renders this little more than an inconvenience. Lacking the blocky structure of some gritstone edges, there are few overhangs, but the cracks, slabs and steep walls offer a huge variety of routes. Indeed, probably the finest slab climbing in the Peak District is to be found here. A full range of abilities is catered for, from protected Moderates to unprotected E6s, including some of the best routes in the country, and mostly at reasonable grades. Consequently, a sunny weekend in summer is not always the best time for a visit, particularly on the main edge, but with such a magnificent view who minds a bit of queueing? Owing to its sunny aspect it is possible to have an excellent day's climbing throughout the year.

APPROACHES and ACCESS

There are two main approaches to Froggatt Edge, both from the B6054 Fox House to Calver road. The most popular approach is along the wide path above the edge which starts from the White Gate (O.S. ref. SK 254776) about 500m south of The Grouse Inn. Limited (thoughtful!) parking is possible alongside the road just north of the gate (remember to keep the gate clear for access). Alternatively, a National Trust car park exists farther up the road towards the Inn. Seven hundred and fifty metres along the top of the edge the path crosses a small stream just before a gate.

Previous Page: Mark Leach on Beau Geste, Froggatt Edge.
Photo: Neil Foster.
Left: Chris Wright on Oedipus, Froggatt Edge.
Photo: Mike Lea/Wright collection.

Brookside Buttress lies alongside this some 75m downstream. The main edge starts 550m south of this, 140m after a left turn in the path, with an easy descent past Strapiombo Buttress. For those wishing to descend Pinnacle Gully, the top of the pinnacle can just be seen on the right just past a collection of large rounded boulders, some 235m after the bend in the path. An easier descent can be made at the southern end of the edge where a small path leads diagonally rightwards down the broad gap between the Froggatt and Curbar Edges. Chequers Buttress is the first obvious buttress reached from this path.

An alternative approach is via a footpath starting just below the Chequers Inn at O.S. ref. SK 247760. Very limited parking is available at a bend in the road some 75m farther south. Although this is a quicker approach, it is steeper and lacks the superb views of the top path.

Those who like a brisk walk to get going should note that it is possible to approach from the car park in the Baslow-Curbar gap and walk the entire length of Curbar Edge.

For those without private transport, the Trent bus No. 244 passes the edge and the driver can usually be enticed to stop at The Grouse Inn, the White Gate or at the Chequers Inn itself. The SYT 240 and 272 stop at the Fox House from which a pleasant walk through the Longshaw Estate brings one on to the road just above The Grouse Inn. Alternatively the train can be taken to Grindleford, which is also served by the SYT 240. From here a track leads up through woods to the White Gate. Also bus No. X67 runs through Calver and Baslow; alight at Calver and prepare for the up-hill flog.

The edge is the property of the Peak Park and as such there are no access problems.

HISTORY

When James (Jimmy) W. Puttrell and W. J. Watson first visited Froggatt Edge in 1890 they would have seen a very different cliff than the one climbers are familiar with today. The quarrymen had been gone over a hundred years and since their departure the flora had returned with a vengeance. Not surprisingly their explorations were limited and, after a night in the cave, they ascended *Solomon's Crack*, which they actually named Chequers Crack after the nearby hostelry. They were also drawn to

Froggatt Pinnacle, but failed to gain the summit. Undeterred, Puttrell returned later with friends from the Kyndwr Club and by 'unique tactics' managed to ascend the short side of the pinnacle. In the period before the First World War, Puttrell continued his visits, sometimes alone and at other times with Henry Bishop and Douglas Yeomans. They made a very able team. *Silver Crack* (originally named Chequers Fissure), *North Climb*, *Nursery Slab* and *Swimmers' Chimney* were climbed by Puttrell while Bishop made the first clean lead of the pinnacle by the route now known as *Route One*. In 1913, Bishop added the hardest route on the edge at the time with his steep *Diamond Crack* and climbed, but never reported, many other lines possibly including Heather Wall.

After the First World War strict 'keepering' made visits to the edge virtually impossible. Frank Elliott, Harry Dover and Gilbert Ellis managed the occasional climb, including a much sought after second ascent of Route One in 1933, but this necessitated starting at dawn and leaving by 8 a.m.! So strict was the keepering that a major challenge was to walk from The Grouse Inn across the Eastern Edges to the Robin Hood Inn below Birchen Edge at night without being caught. This entailed crawling along on hands and knees at various points. It was quite common for dogs to be set loose and guns to be fired in the air! During the Second World War, access was relaxed, prompting visits by Jack Macleod, one of Sheffield's top climbers, who ascended *Terrace Crack*, *Grey Slab* and one of the *Jankers* routes.

After the War, access was further relaxed and members of the Sheffield University Mountaineering Club, under the leadership of Dick Brown, cleaned out and led the very popular *Heather Wall* which was originally called Advent Slabs, *Sickle Buttress* and *Trapeze*. Shortly afterwards the Polaris Mountaineering Club began to take an interest, culminating in Len Chapman's discovery of *Sunset Crack* and another way up the Pinnacle; *Chapman's Crack*.

Word of this activity soon reached the Valkyrie Mountaineering Club and late in 1948 they began the first thorough exploration of the edge. The main activists were Nat Allen, Chuck Cook, Wilf White, Don Cowan, Don Chapman, Tony Hyde, Ken Brindley and Ray Kerry. In September they visited the edge and met up with a group of Manchester climbers, two of whom, Joe Brown and Slim Sorrell, they had previously met in Wales. On his very first visit to the edge, Brown outclassed and astonished everybody by soloing on-sight, and in pumps, the initial crack of what was later to become part of *Valkyrie*. He was only seventeen at the time and already perhaps the best climber in the country. In the good weather that remained that year, the Valkyrie transformed the edge, putting up over twenty routes including *Tody's Wall*, *Three Pebble Slab*, *Brown's Eliminate*, *Hawk's Nest Crack*, *Pedestal Crack*, *Sunset Slab*, *Green Gut*, *Holly Groove*, *Broken Crack* and the *Jankers* routes. In the spring of the following year Brown returned with Wilf White and completed his ascent of the pinnacle leaving the outstanding *Valkyrie*. He also added *Chequers Climb* and in 1950 the esoteric *Cave Crack*. At around the same time Chuck Cook, for a small bet, leapt from the summit of the pinnacle to the main edge. 1951 saw the arrival of a brilliant teenager who could match Brown, Don Whillans. Whillans quickly eyed up the remaining possibilities and forced *Beech Nut* and *Chequers Crack*, undoubtedly taking note of the impressive crackline farther left. Another obvious feature was *The Great Slab*. This was top-roped by Wilf White and then, despite being green and dusty, was soloed on-sight, in plimsolls, by Brown, who was obviously in superb form.

The next few years were very quiet, Peter Biven led the direct on *Valkyrie* and the first tentative explorations of the northern buttresses were made by Wilf White and Nat Allen. In 1955 Whillans returned to fight up *The Big Crack*, which even with one point of aid was an impressive feat. Over the years the vegetation has gone and the loss of small blocks from the crack has left some excellent finger-jamming slots. *Strapiombo*, also by Whillans, was added the following year.

1958 saw Whillans's last, and arguably best, route on the edge before he moved on to grander things. *Cave Wall* was a remarkable solo ascent, which, even with modern protection, rates E3 and receives very few ascents. He even jumped off from the lip on his first attempt, and apparently didn't find the route particularly difficult, repeating it on a number of occasions.

The 1960s were years of quality rather than quantity. *Strapiombante* fell to Dave Brearly and the much-fancied *Chequers Buttress* was led by John Gosling. With the remaining lines being too difficult and/or dangerous, and the realisation that aid routes on limestone were a dead end, frustration set in. Lacking direction, some climbers resorted to aid and chipping

holds. *The Method* and *March Hare* succumbed to aid, *Oedipus....*
to the hammer, and *Long John's Slab* to both. Such abuse went
largely unknown, the climbing press was in its infancy and ethics
were, if anything, less clear than today. Things improved
however with Al Rouse's free ascent of *Long John's Slab* in 1969
and in 1973, John Syrett made the first clean lead of *The Big
Crack*. At about the same time John Allen and Steve Bancroft
quickly set about tidying up with free ascents of *March Hare*, *The
Method*, which became known as *Avalanche* and the aid route on
Great Slab, *Synopsis*. Many of the remaining 'blank' lines were
proved possible with Allen climbing *The Gully Joke*, *Hairless
Heart*, and *Artless* and Bancroft, *Heartless Hare* and *Narcissus*.
Their domination of the Great Slab area was only broken when
Mick Fowler found his way up *Hairy Heart*. In 1976 Allen left for
New Zealand, but not before producing his finest route,
Strapadictomy, which, at the time, was one of the hardest routes
in the Peak District. Following Allen's departure, greed once
again reared its ugly head. Severe wire brushing revealed holds
right of Long John's Slab resulting in Pete Livesey's *Downhill
Racer*. *Long John's* was itself a scene of hold improvement, but
the worst act of vandalism occurred on the line now taken by
Jugged Hare. The chipped holds were quickly filled in with
mortar, but today this is slowly falling out.

On a better note, some worthwhile routes were done. Steve
Bancroft climbed *Indoor Fisherman*, *Romance* and *Cavatina*, while
Al Evans, also busy in this area, climbed a few routes including
the sadly neglected *Krypton Factor*. On the main edge, Tom
Proctor forced his way up *Hard Cheddar*, a route which sees very
few ascents today. Bancroft, having had a long enough rest
(three years!), climbed the second pitch to *Narcissus*, *Narcissus II*,
as the Seventies came to a close.

The early Eighties saw contributions from a variety of
individuals. Phil Burke climbed the imaginative *Brightside*. Ron
Fawcett paid a visit and left *Spock's Missing* while Daniel Lee and
Dominic Lee, fresh from the Sheffield Polytechnic gym and
Rubicon Wall, tested out their fingers on *Circus* and *Mean Streak*,
both hard and serious routes. They also reascended the aptly
named *Avalanche* after a rock-fall. Paul Mitchell was quick to take
advantage of the pile of rocks to produce *Greedy Pig*, although
as the name suggests the style of the ascent was tainted. A clean
ascent came three years later from Keith Sharples. Undoubtedly
the major route of 1982 was Jonny Woodward's *Beau Geste*.

Jonny had attempted to top-rope the line on many occasions but had failed at the crux. Deciding that he needed the adrenaline in order to succeed, he tried leading it. After seven ground-sweeping falls, he finally made the top of one of the finest routes in the area.

1983 saw some important gaps filled by desperate climbing. *Jugged Hare* was proved possible by Johnny Dawes. Ron Fawcett managed *Neon Dust* and *The Mint 400*. Of similar difficulty was Jerry Moffatt's 'boulder problem', *Sole Power*, which, eight years later, sees few successful attempts. The following year and harder still is Dawes' *Benign Lives*, which despite its moderate size was one of the most important new routes on gritstone in view of its technical difficulty and seriousness. After losing a pebble (please DO NOT top-rope this route!) it was reascended by John Dunne in 1986. Ron Fawcett returned to climb the remaining blank section on Great Slab and added a very difficult route, *Toy Boy*. He also soloed the alternative start to Long John's Slab.

Probably the shortest and by far the hardest *protected* route was finally solved in 1986. After 26 days' effort spread over nine months Mark Leach finally proved 'The Crack' possible, and left *The Screaming Dream*. Rumour has it that Mark was under pressure to complete the route since he had prematurely written up his ascent in an article for an American magazine!

Since then only a few routes of any importance have been done, although Nick Dixon's *Third Burglar* is a bold addition. Paul Mitchell also solved a last great problem with his difficult *Slide Show*, which without side-runners and linked with a solo ascent of Moffatt's desperate top-rope problem, *Slingshot*, could be gritstone's first E10. Makes you think doesn't it?

THE CLIMBS are described from LEFT to RIGHT.

HIDDEN BUTTRESS *is the most northerly section of the edge, and is situated just above the road about 650 metres beyond the White Gate. Surrounded by trees it is usually green, lichenous, sandy and probably best left hidden. However, if you can't resist a visit then by far the easiest approach is along the road rather than from the top path. The buttress has a green groove on its left-hand side which is capped by a roof.*

1 Gyron Groove 11m HVS 5a (1956)
Climb the groove moving right and go up large friable holds on
the arête to overcome the roof.

Behind the damp lichen on the wall to the right are three cracklines.

* **2 Hot Knives** 11m E4 6b (1984)
The cleanest route on the wall and the hardest. At the left-hand
end of the wall, a thin crack starts about four metres above the
ground. This is reached by a thoroughly desperate start and is
followed by a perplexing move on to a ledge. A filthy, though
easier, crack remains.

3 Romance 8m HVS 5b (1978)
The left-hand of the three crack-lines is filled with lichen and
offers little in an attempt to live up to its name.

4 Cavatina 8m E3 6a (1978)
The next crack is no less unpleasant, just meaner and with a
greater abundance of flora.

5 The Iliad 8m VS 4c (1968)
Last and by all means least, the greenest of all.

*After 140m of desperate scrambling at the same level as Hidden
Buttress, a slabby buttress split by two wide cracks is reached. At
the time of writing, the next six routes were covered in lichen, but
are very worthwhile when clean.*

6 Slope Crack 9m S (1954)
The right-hand crack is quite awkward at mid-height.

† **7 Mastermind** 12m E4 6a (1985)
The unprotected wall just right of Slope Crack.

* **8 Krypton Factor** 12m E4 5c (1977)
Just to the right climb the wall, moving onto the arête to finish. No
protection.

9 The Slab 5m VS 4c (1954)
The small slab below, and to the right, of the previous route is
climbed by its central scoop.

10 Brush Up 10m VS 4c (1984)
Just right of The Slab, follow the arête to a ledge. Continue up the
stepped arête above.

* **11 Two Pebble Slab** 7m HVS 5c (1977)
The arête and slab of a small buttress nine metres up the slope.

Up and right again is a black overhanging wall.

12 Black Wall 9m HVS 5a (1957)
Start up a thin crack in the wall and continue past a fern until
moves right lead to a long reach over the bulge to finish.

13 Slipper Slab 11m HVS 5a (1954)
The slabby right-hand rib of the buttress is presently covered by
a fallen tree. If this should go then the rib is gained from the left
and then followed direct. A direct start is 5c.

14 Morty's Corner 12m HVS 5a (1957)
To the right is a quarried bay, the left corner of which provides a
clean route at last!

* **15 Downes' Crack** 11m VS 4c (1957)
The small but beautifully proportioned flake in the wall to the
right should not be underestimated. Best climbed quickly.

The right-to-left grassy staircase just to the right is **Pillar Wall**,
HD, (1956).

*Down and right of Downes' Crack, the next buttress is split by two
parallel cracks at its left-hand end.*

16 Just Crack 7m S 4a (1953)
The left-hand crack is climbed on widening jams.

The next three routes may need a good brushing.

17 Jacob 7m HVS 5b (1966)
The thinner right-hand crack has some hard initial moves.

18 Hibernation 8m E2 5c (1982)
Climb directly up the wall between Jacob and the right arête,
protected by a runner in Jacob.

* **19 Esau** 9m E2 5c (1973)
The arête itself feels exposed and has a hard move at
mid-height. A runner in Jacob, however comforting, is of little
real benefit.

† **20 Backseat Nothing** 6m E1 5a (1989)
Up the hill, almost directly behind Esau, is this shallow, scooped
arête.

21 Vomer 9m E2 5c · (1966)
The isolated steep prow 50m farther right is gained from the left
by a problematic wall then climbed boldly above a nasty
landing. The upper arête can be reached direct and is known,
not unreasonably, as **Vomer Direct**, E2 6a, (1988).

*30m farther along, and 75m below the gate on the track, beside a
small stream lies* **BROOKSIDE BUTTRESS.**

* **22 Neb Crack** 9m VS 4b (1956)
The clean, steep crack in the north-facing wall of the buttress is
climbed direct.

* **23 Indoor Fisherman** 11m E3 5c (1977)
Starting from the tree, gain the fine arête to the right then follow
it direct to an awkward finish on rounded holds.

* **24 Tinsel's Tangle** 9m S (1956)
Climb the flake crack in the right rib before moving awkwardly
left into a shallow groove.

* **25 Crooked Start** 9m VS 4c (1956)
The face to the left of Tinsel's Tangle is scarred by a broken line
of cracks. Climb these bearing right to finish up the groove of
Tinsel's Tangle.

26 Piledriver 9m HVS 5b (1977)
Follow a thin crack just left of the more obvious crack in the right
wall, then move left and go up the centre. **Piledriver Direct
Start** is 6a, (1977).

27 Brookside Crack 6m D (1956)
The obvious spider-infested crack.

On the opposite side of the stream is **Ladies Buttress**, D, (1956).

*Returning to the top path, 85m past the gate above Brookside
Buttress a path bears down to the right and in 90m leads to a
massive boulder split down its valley face by a thin overhanging
crack.*

** **28 The Screaming Dream** 6m E7 7a (1986)
Crank out the crack, utterly desperate, but with a sound nut for
protection. Good value at over an E point per metre!

29 The Famous Chris Ellis 8m E3 6a (1984)
Climb the right-hand side of the boulder past a boss to make a
frightening mantelshelf onto a ramp.

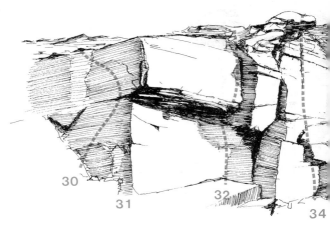

30
31
32
34

Strapiombo Buttress

100m farther along the top path, and to the left, is the Froggatt stone circle. Four hundred metres from the gate the path turns leftwards past a small boulder on the left containing a nasty finger slot and hence a chance to demonstrate one-arm pull-ups. Ninety metres past this boulder there is a small buttress on the right containing the following two routes:

Debut Wall, HVS 5b, (1973), follows the centre of the buttress, whilst **Debutante**, VS 4c, (1973), takes the right arête.

50m right is the start of the MAIN EDGE *which begins with a* buttress sporting the large rectangular roof of **STRAPIOMBO BUTTRESS**.

The left-hand face of the buttress starts with a shortish 5b problem up a wall and right-trending groove, **Strapathyroid**, an old problem.

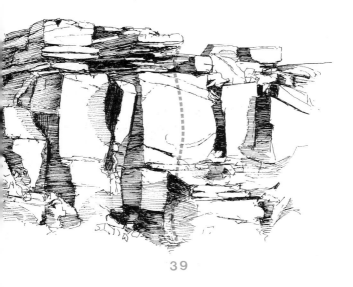

39

** **30 Strapiombante** 8m E1 5b (1962)
Fine, well-protected climbing makes this route a popular first
Extreme lead. Follow the zig-zag crackline on good holds and
with a little forethought avoid 'the long reach left' for the
rounded finishing ledge.

*** **31 Strapadictomy** 9m E5 6a (1976)
Simply one of the best routes in the area symbolising the great
gritstone renaissance of the 1970s. To fully appreciate the route's
ethos put on your rolled-up Levi's, grow your hair and leave the
Friends in the sack. The lower arête is a delightful aperitif before
strenuous moves out right gain the magnificent flake above the
lip of the overhang. Powerful, yet balancy, moves up this lead all
too quickly to the top.

† **Cockchafer**, E5 6b, (1988), traverses the lip of the overhang
from the bottom of the flakes on Strapadictomy, rightwards into

the next route (feet underneath, hands above!). Side-runners were used on the first ascent but a cricketer's box is bad form.

* 32 Strapiombo 9m E1 5b   (1956)
The roof crack round to the right provides a classic fight, easing only in the finishing groove. Knee-pads are frowned upon thus allowing maximum pain.

33 English Overhang 9m VS 4c   (1978)
Pull up to the flared crack just to the right using a friable flake in the roof and climb it more easily.

34 Scarper's Triangle 9m VS 5a   (1957)
Climb a groove in the middle of the outside face, then direct to a crack. Alternatively, easier starts can be made up the arête on either side. **Broken Heart**, E1 5c, (1985), starts up the left arête then moves right to climb the slab right of the crack.

Eight metres right the next buttress has a smooth arête at its left-hand end.

35 Oss Nob 8m E4 6a   (1978)
Follow the arête of the concave slab using a thin crack in its upper reaches.

36 Left Flake Crack 7m S   (1965-1978)
The corner crack to the right.

37 Right Flake Crack 7m S   (1949)
The crack right of the hanging block.

38 Parallel Piped 6m E4 5c   (1986)
The left arête of the slab right of the two flake cracks has a couple of thin moves above a nasty landing. Harder for the short.

* 39 Benign Lives 7m E6 6b   (1984/1986)
Having had few solo ascents, and none on-sight, this Dawes offering of the mid-Eighties still commands great respect. From the easily-gained half-way ledge climb the centre of the slab direct. The top appears tantalisingly close, but clean technique, commitment and a dedication to Carling Black Label may just be enough to avoid the bone-crunching splat.
The right arête of the slab gives a good 5b problem climbed on its right-hand side.

The next buttress is 25m to the right.

† **40 Gentlefish** 8m E4 6a (1980s)
Climb the centre of the wall left of Chockstone Crack with a
runner in the latter route.

41 Chockstone Crack 8m HS 4b (1948-1949)
The wide crack in the steep wall provides a pleasant route.

42 C.H.M.S. 1 8m VS 4b (1977)
Climb out of the pit below and right to finish via a flaky crack in
the upper wall.

The thin crack in the centre of the lower wall to the right is
Leggit, 6a, (1978-1985). The wall left of Leggit is **Cast Off**, 6a,
(1978-1985).

*Right again is a large slab bounded on its left by a straight wide
crack which is taken by* North Climb.

*† **43 Science Friction** 11m E5 6a (1980)
The left arête of the slab leads easily on its right-hand side to a
thin crux section demanding careful footwork. A bulge near the
top forces a finish to the right. Originally protected by
side-runners on a chockstone in North Climb but has since been
soloed. Unfortunately the chockstone has now gone and the
crack is too big for Friends.

* **44 North Climb** 12m HVD (1906)
Indulge in some awkward jamming with a sense of history.

† **45 What's Up Doc?** 12m E2 5b (1990)
An eliminate, up the slab about one metre right of North Climb.
A pocket affords large Friend protection.

** **46 Sunset Slab** 12m HVS 4b (1948)
Smooth, delicate and exposed. Medical students should note that
this classic route has been the cause of some marvellous
textbook examples of fractures. Climb into the slab's scooped
centre from a crack on the right, then move delicately left to
finish up an unprotected blind flake. The **Direct** goes straight up
to join the flake but doesn't avoid the crux.

47 Sundowner 11m E2 5a (1972)
From the initial crack of Sunset Slab continue direct up the centre
of slab. With a side-runner award yourself a HVS.

** **48 Sunset Crack** 10m VS 4b (1948)
The thin crack to the right provides well-protected climbing with
good rests. A slight bulge provides the technical interest.

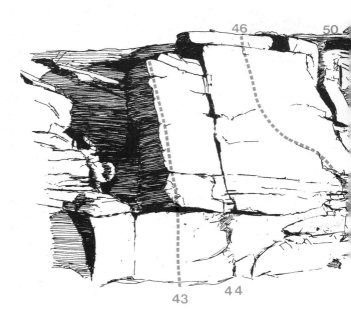

*About 100m below Sunset Slab and hidden from above is a large
boulder,* **SUNSET BOULDER***, which contains some worthwhile
extended boulder problems above a good landing.*
The left-hand line using a small layback flake is E1 6a, the crack
to the right is gained with difficulty at HVS 5c. Right again,
climbing to a pocket in the break and finishing direct, is E1 5c,
and two metres to the right, the steep slab is E2 6b, (all 1990).
The right arête is a 'traditional' Severe.

Immediately right of Sunset Crack is **NORTH GULLY** *which
provides a reasonably easy way down, with just a slightly awkward
move to start the descent.*

Sunset Slab Area

49 Turret Crack 9m S (1948)
The steep crack in the left wall of the gully.

* **50 Slab and Crack** 8m D (1948)
In the right corner of the gully lies this polished route, not to be confused with the E7 on Curbar Edge with the same name. (That one's not as polished.)

† **51 Ramp-art** 12m E5 6b (1986)
The crack and ramp in the steep wall to the right finishing in the gully after a crucial stretch for the final hold. Rumoured to be protectable by a hand-placed peg runner but really needs a direct finish.

·* **52 Beau Geste**   12m   E6   6c   (1982)
An outstanding route, possibly *the* gritstone route of the early
1980s, taking an awe-inspiring line up the right arête of the wall.
Possessing the bare minimum of holds, spaced protection that is
difficult to place and a desperate crux amongst continuously
hard climbing; it's gripping enough just reading about it. The
groove in the arête is climbed past small nut placements to the
break (Two 2½ Friends on the right). Moves leftwards lead to the
crux sequence and a still difficult finish past a crucial nut
placement (Rock 1 or RP3).

† **53 Epiphany**   12m   E4   6a   (1980)
Unprotected climbing up the arête to the right. Start up the crack
right of Beau Geste, then traverse right to the arête. This is
ascended direct but it is unfortunately (or fortunately!) possible
to escape rightwards at any point.

* **54 Holly Groove**   9m   VS   4c   (1948)
Climb the Holly-less twin-cracked corner that runs up from the
ledge.

* **55 Hawk's Nest Crack**   9m   VS   4c   (1948)
A good first VS lead. The crack just left of the cave is a
well-protected test of jamming technique. Finishing from the
large ledge up the exposed flake on the left may prove too much
for 'first-timers'.

To the right is **FROGGATT CAVE**, *scene of numerous bivouacs.*

The wall left **of** the cave provides a hard boulder-problem
requiring a fine balance of power and technique, **Rambeau**, 6c,
(1986). If successful head for Cave Crack or the gym.

* **56 Cave Crack**   11m   E2   5c   (1950)
Easy if you can do it, desperate if you can't. This strenuous route
is a thuggish way up the archetypal gritstone roof-crack leaving
the left side of the cave. Grunting, swearing and thrashing
around are par for the course.

57 Cave Crawl   10m   S   5a   (1948-1949)
A must for the Jung at heart but with Freudian desires to re-enter
the womb. Starting from the back left-hand corner of the cave,
layback quickly up past pigeon's droppings to gain a 'Journey to
the centre of the Earth' type passage leading into Swimmers'

Ron Fawcett on Artless, Froggatt Edge.
Photo: Keith Sharples.

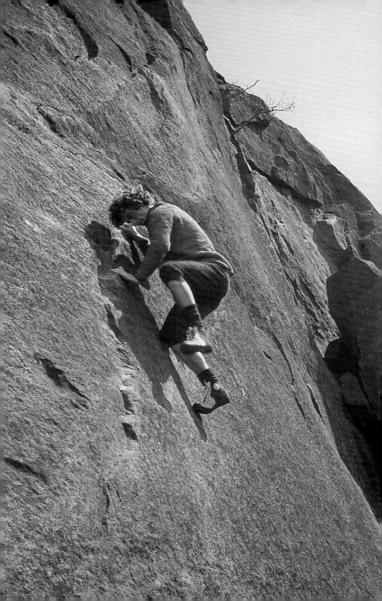

Chimney. From just below the top of this squeeze back leftwards to finish up the flake of Hawk's Nest Crack.

*** **58 Cave Wall**   11m   E3   5c   (1958)

An extremely bold climb even with the benefit of modern Friend protection. From the right-hand side of the cave, climb over the bulge to a small 'rescue ledge'. A very hard leg-press move, especially extending for the short, allows good holds to be gained in the wall above and an irreversible position. Press on with determination until it is possible to traverse off right at the wide break.

59 Beau Brummell   10m   E4   6b   (1982)

The arête immediately to the right yields most easily to a sequence of completely out of control drowning-man-type gestures. At the large ledge move left to cross the delightful rounded bulges above.

* **60 Swimmers' Chimney**   11m   HVD   (1890-1902)

An ideal route for the more experienced climber (old fogey) to demonstrate long-lost techniques to the young rock-jock (poser).

** **61 Brightside**   11m   E2   5c   (1980)

A fine, well-protected climb up the seemingly blank wall right of Swimmers' Chimney. From three metres up the chimney swing right and slightly downwards to a small foothold just above the lip then climb direct via long stretches between good holds up the faint scoop.

** **62 Greedy Pig**   12m   E5   6b   (1981/1985)

This short but very demanding direct start to Brightside follows the steep thin crack to the right, moving into Brightside as soon as possible. The small nut protection is good but difficult to place.

63 Avalanche   11m   E2   6a   (1967/1975/1981)

A deceptively difficult route. From the remains of its innards climb the steep groove to a stopping move at the lip.

Eight metres right, across broken rocks (an easy way down) is a steep wall crossed by a sandy cave. From its left-hand end sprouts a birch tree and:

Graham Parkes on the Big Crack, Froggatt Edge.
Photo: Craggs collection.

257

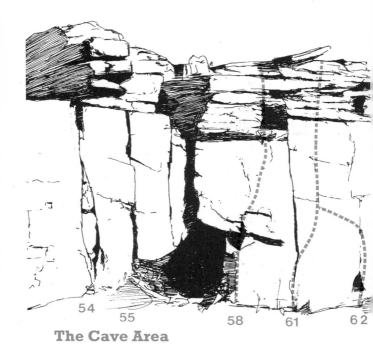

54
55
58
61
62

The Cave Area

64 Skogul 12m VD   (1951)
The crack containing the birch tree leads to a large ledge. Better
climbing follows up the blunt arête.

* **65 Mean Streak** 12m E6 6b   (1981)
Although recently vandalised the wall just right of Skogul still
presents a serious outing. Small nut protection exists for the
initial reachy moves past a small flake but after that you're on
your own as the holds gradually improve.

* **66 The Gully Joke** 15m E2 5c   (1975)
A fine climb taking a line up the wall left of the right-bounding
crack. From the right-hand end of the cave make long stretches

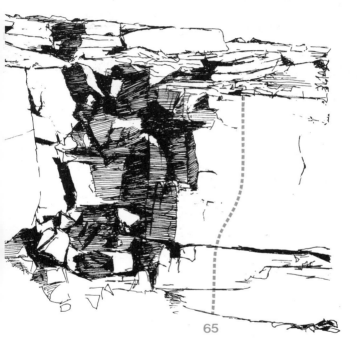

65

to gain and climb a groove left of the crack leading to a ledge (runners on the right in the crack). Move left and climb the wall on surprisingly good holds, taking care near the faint break shortly before the finish (crux).

* **67 Terrace Crack** 12m VS 4b   (1939-1945)
The right-bounding crack provides good climbing spoilt only slightly by its sandy nature.

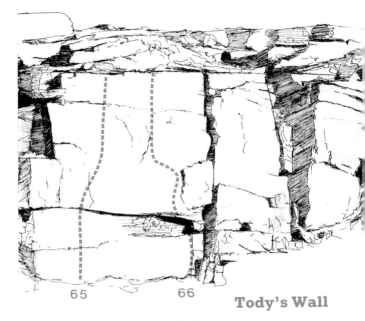

65   66   **Tody's Wall**

To the right is **Sandy Gully**, D, (1948).

Right again, the roofed-in **CENTRAL GULLY** *provides an easy way down.*

68 March Hare 9m E1 6a   (1968/1974)
The shallow groove in the left wall of the gully gives precarious bridging until better holds lead out left and up.

The wall right of the gully is split by a steep, bottomless crack gained either by a traverse from Heather Wall, **Heather Wall Variant**, HVS 5a, (1949), or via the starting moves of Nightshade. The crack provides steep, strenuous jamming.

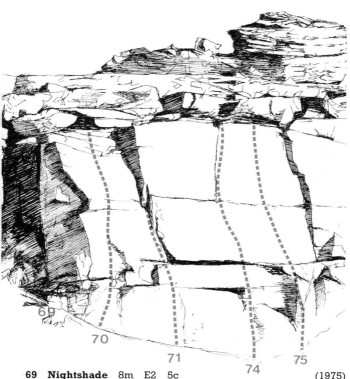

69 Nightshade 8m E2 5c (1975)
Hard moves on large pebbles enable a traverse line right of the crack to be gained. This is followed to the arête which is climbed on its right-hand side.

Starting down and right is Heather Wall, one of the most popular routes on the edge.

70 C.M.C. Slab 12m HVS 5a (1965/1978)
Follow the slab just left of Heather Wall, arranging protection in that route.

* **71 Heather Wall** 17m S   (1945-1948)
A fine route for beginners who might however need just a slight
tug on the start and on leaving the middle ledge. Climb a thin
crack in the lower section of the buttress to the ledge then
continue up the superb wider crack in the slabby corner above.
An inferior start may be made up the corner on the right.

† **72 Grip** 17m E2 5b   (1978)
Starting from the ledge of Heather Wall climb the arête on the
right.

73 Ratbag 8m E2 5b   (1974)
Starting from the ledge on Heather Wall, move out right to climb
the slab right of Grip. Only HVS with side-runners.

* **74 Tody's Wall** 18m HVS 5a   (1948)
A most entertaining climb, although the leader might not agree.
The crux move has been the scene of some of the worst
examples of climbing technique ever displayed, normally
followed by an embarrassing slither. From the centre of the bay
right of Heather Wall climb to a projecting block. Somehow gain
the top slab and finish with whatever dignity remains up the fine
crack above.

From the block on Tody's Wall, it is possible, though not
necessarily desirable, to traverse the slab rightwards for five
metres until a jump over the bulge leads to Silver Crack. This is
called † **Mushroom Black and White**, E3 6b, (1990).

75 Motorcade 9m E1 5a   (1969)
Start in the filthy corner to the right and follow this to climb the
centre of the slab right of Tody's Wall.

* **76 Silver Crack** 9m S 4b   (1890-1902)
From just right again, climb easy rock to reach this classic wide
crack.

† **77 Silver Lining** 9m E5 6a   (1986)
With low runners in the previous route wobble up its right arête.

78 Silver Traverse 9m VD   (1948)
Traverse the oblique crack and slab right of Silver Crack.

79 Origin of Species 8m E5 6a   (1978)
The slab right of Silver Lining is both precarious and bold. From
the break finish direct. Serious.

80 Bollard Crack 8m VS 4c (1948)
A short but awkward route taking the dog-leg crack to the right.

81 Heather Groove 6m HS 4b (1965-1977)
Right again, and at a higher level, the groove lies just right of a
rib and chimney.

*Just below the path at this point is a steep little face which offers
some good, secluded problems above good landings. The next
feature right of the bay containing Tody's Wall is a smooth slab.
The slab ends at a short steep wall which contains the following
route towards its left-hand end.*

82 Stealing the Misanthrope's Purse 7m HVS 5a (1974)
Climb the smooth wall past a pocket to gain a crack at the top.

The narrow prow farther left (just to the left of a small tree) has
been climbed, **Roman Orgy**, E4 6b, (1988).

The slab itself has several lines of ascent.

83 Soft Option 12m HD (1965-1977)
Climb the extreme left-hand side of the slab and the upper wall.

84 Two-sided Triangle 12m E1 5b (1978)
Ascend the slab to the left of Three Pebble Slab, just right of a
cutaway, via small pockets.

*** **85 Three Pebble Slab** 12m E1 5a (1948)
One of *the* classic gritstone slabs which has lost none of its sting
over the years. The pocket at mid-height happily swallows small
nuts and large Friends but just as happily spits them out if you
fall off. Start below the pocket and ascend to this by a series of
interesting mantelshelves. Move delicately right (crux) and
finish carefully up the long-pebbleless slab.

86 Four Pebble Slab 8m E3 5c (1972/1977)
A much thinner slab right of the original route starting from the
crack on Grey Slab. Hard once committed. A direct start is
rumoured at E4 6a.

* **87 Grey Slab** 12m S (1903-1904/1939-1945)
Some steep moves on good holds lead up the right side of the
slab and wall to a ledge. The wide crack above is just plain
awkward.

Pinnacle Area

† **88 Nanoq Slab** 12m E1 5b   (1990)
The slab right of Grey Slab is climbed direct and proves delicate
at the top.

The next prominent feature is the square block of **FROGGATT
PINNACLE**. *30m below this is a large split boulder:*

† **89   Third Burglar**   9m   E6   6c   (1987)
On the upper half of the boulder facing away from the edge is an obvious slab leading to a roof. Follow the slab, serious, then pass the roof by traversing left.

FROGGATT PINNACLE *is perhaps the edge's finest feature and there is little doubt that in terms of route quality it is one of the best inland pinnacles in the country. Its lower, quarried walls, are steep with square-cut holds, in contrast to the slabby, rounded features of its natural upper section. Its summit may be reached by a variety of climbs, some of which are outstanding. Descent is best made by abseil down the short north side from a ring bolt or by reversing one of the short routes, although Narcissus is not to be recommended! Wazzocks considering the infamous Cook's Leap across the gully to the edge should note that the landing was originally some two metres higher and consisted of soft peat and heather!*

***   **90   Valkyrie**   20m   HVS   5a,5a   (1949)
'The west side clearly interested Joe, and later, after patiently watching the abortive efforts of our best men, he amazed the gathering by pulverising the oblique crack that splits the lower wall of the pinnacle, finally reaching the ledge in what we have all come to accept as the Joe Brown style.' – Nat Allen, Hard Rock.
Not the original, but certainly the best route to the summit.
1. 10m. The steep oblique crack on the outside face leads strenuously to a break which is hand-traversed rightwards to gain a fine stance on the nose of the pinnacle. Keep the belay short if you wish to avoid being dragged half-way down Neon Dust when your second lobs off the hand-traverse!
2. 10m. Step right and go up to a short crack, then move left on to the nose passing a no-hands rest. The easier-angled but delightfully exposed rib leads to the summit.
It is possible to approach the ledge on the nose by going straight over the bulge slightly left of the belay **Valkyrie Direct**, HVS 5a, (1954).

91   Neon Dust   9m   E5   7a   (1983/1986)
Yet to have a second ascent, this bold and fingery climb follows the wall just right of Valkyrie's first pitch. An easier start, 6b, can be made by traversing in from the arête on the right.

***   **92   Narcissus**   9m   E6   6b   (1976)
Hard moves a long way above an even harder landing makes the prominent arête of the pinnacle a very serious proposition. One

of the hardest routes to have been on-sight soloed in the Peak District. If you make it to the ledge it's probably better to grovel off leftwards than to blow it on Valkyrie! Alternatively you could grab some gear and do:

† **93 Narcissus II** 9m E5 6b (1979)
From the top of Valkyrie's first crack make a long reach over the bulge to gain a short wide crack which soon eases.

The next two routes take the south face of the pinnacle.

* **94 Oedipus! Ring Your Mother** 9m E4 6b (1968)
Starting from the right-hand side of the face make a strenuous finger-traverse left to gain large holds below the obvious weakness right of the arête. You have now done the technical crux but are probably too tired to carry on – such is life. The rest of the route follows a line of worsening holds to a stretch or a worrying jump (!) for a good hold just below the ledge.
A direct start is possible at 6aish.

95 The Mint 400 9m E6 6b (1983)
Follow Oedipus until half-way along the traverse then launch upwards on small, distant holds to the break. Finish as you wish.

96 Pinnacle Arête 15m E2 5b (1948)
From a little way up Pinnacle Gully, make a rising traverse left round the arête to reach a ledge on the exposed south face. Step delicately right to the arête and climb this to the top.

97 Reverse Disco 12m E2 5c (1984)
Start immediately right of Pinnacle Arête. Climb straight up the black wall (wire runner in pocket), to join and finish up Pinnacle Arête.

98 Fame at Last 10m HVS 5b (1984)
Start farther up the gully and climb directly up the wall to the end of the traverse of Chapman's Crack (runner). Step right and climb a slight weakness to finish.

* **99 Chapman's Crack** 9m VS 4c (1948)
A surprisingly exposed route considering its position. Traverse left from the top of the gully to a mantelshelf and an interesting finishing crack.

100 Route One 6m VS 5a (1912)
Henry Bishop's original route up the pinnacle follows the short left arête of the north face.

101 Pinnacle Face 6m VS 5b (1947)
Ascend the wall to the right via a delicate rightwards traverse to finish past an unusual drilled hole.

The next routes are on the back wall of the bay to the right of the pinnacle, the first starting just right of Pinnacle Gully.

102 Truly Pathetic 6m HVS 5c (1976)
Better than the name suggests – a thin rightward-slanting crack.

** **103 Diamond Crack** 8m HS 4b (1913)
Originally graded as Very Difficult, this popular route has produced some pretty spectacular falls from the finishing crack so beware! Climb the polished cracks in the middle of the wall by some fierce jamming.

104 Corner Crack 8m D (1948-1949)

*The next buttress 15m right is **SICKLE BUTTRESS**.*

105 Left Broken 9m VS 5a (1953)
Short, but frustrating. The groove on the left yields quite easily, with thought, to much easier climbing.

* **106 Broken Crack** 10m VS 4c (1948)
Best experienced in a single push. This fine crack is a good test of laybacking and jamming techniques.

* **107 Sickle Buttress** 10m VD (1945)
A steep climb for the grade, so warn your arms in advance. Gain a ledge halfway along the buttress then move right across a scoop to finish in a groove on the arête.

108 Sickle Buttress Direct 9m VS 4c (1948)
Continue straight up the wall from the start of the scoop.

Alas, Sickle Buttress Arête has fallen from grace and it lives at the foot of the crag. In its place stands:

109 Performing Flea 9m HVS 5a (1985)
Climb the arête and the front face on the right of the buttress.

110 Flake Climb 11m VS 4b (1985)
Although the flake has gone, the name remains. Climb the dirty corner until technical difficulty precipitates moves out left.

111 Tree Survivor 10m E3 6a (1981)
The unremarkable chipped right wall of the recess gives an intricate problem with small holds and use of the right arête.

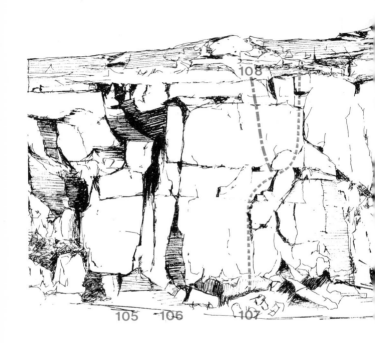

112 Sorrallion 10m VD   (1948)
Go up the 'staircase' until an awkward overhang up and right
gives a bit of substance to the route.

113 Congestion Crack 10m HS 4b   (1948)
Ascend the slim groove bounding the steep slab on its left.

*'To the left of Slab Recess is a steep smooth lichen-covered slab
which has so far resisted the Rock and Ice advances.' – 1961.*

* **114 Long John's Slab** 14m E3-ish 5c   (1968/1969)
A good introduction to the harder slab climbs at Froggatt, with
the crux moves relatively low down but unfortunately above a

Sickle Buttress Area

rather nasty boulder. Well what do you expect for E3 on gritstone? From the boulder a warm-up mantel gains the obvious ledge from which a very thin move, or if you're lucky a long stretch, enables good holds to be grasped. Continue more easily to the top. The † **Left-hand Start**, E6 6b, (1986), takes a curving line joining the parent route at the easy groove.

*** **115 Downhill Racer** 17m E4 6a   (1977)
Found Long John's alright? If so then this is number four in a selection making up a slab climber's apprenticeship (Sunset Slab is first, then Three Pebble Slab). Starting left of the shallow corner, climb the slab until moves left gain a thin break. A hard

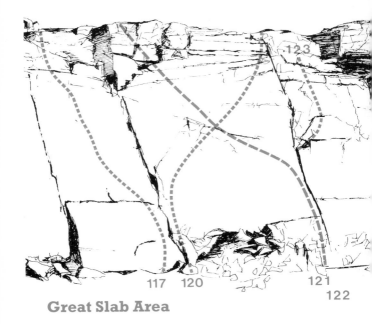

117 120   121
                                      122

Great Slab Area

move up is quickly followed by another to gain better holds and
a leftward-trending ramp. Finish with a stiff pull right of the easy
finishing corner of Long John's. Side-runners in the boulder of
Long John's and the corner to the right reduce the grade to E3
and remove all credibility in the pub. A direct start is 6c and
does not need any more wire brushing.

Uphill Driver, El 5b, (1977), takes the arête right of Downhill
Racer on its left-hand side, but it scarcely merits description.

116 Slab Recess Direct 15m HS 4b   (1948)
Usually identified by a foot-scraping and rope-dangling novice,
the shallow corner has some hard moves on good slots before
the easier steep final section.

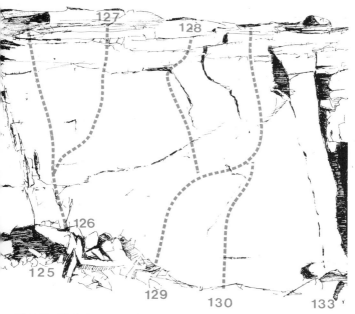

** **117 Slab Recess** 18m D   (1948)
A very good route for beginners to second on big, but polished
holds and with good rests, wandering up the recessed slab to the
right. Start up a broken crack on the right (Gamma) until a gentle
stroll leftwards allows the large flake to be climbed to the top.

Joe's Direct Slab. The area of rock between the two previous
routes contains a number of problems. The left arête is 6a, the
wall just right is 7a, the one-finger pockets in the centre 6a and
the original problem just right of centre via two finger ledges is
5c. Finally a delicate 6b traverse exists at about head-height.

118 Gamma 12m VD   (1951)
The broken crack used by Slab Recess is followed direct.

† **119 Polyp Piece** 10m E5 6c   (1987)
The extremely thin slab right of Gamma is climbed past small
undercuts to easier ground. A side-runner, a Rock 1, was used on
the first ascent just above the start of the diagonal break of
Allen's Slab.

* **120 Allen's Slab** 15m S   (1951)
A marvellous outing needing good footwork and balance. Start
up Gamma then follow the diagonal break to a ledge. Continue
delicately right to finish on good holds just left of a steep crack
(Trapeze Direct).

121 Swing 15m HVS 5a   (1967)
Not much to write home about. Climb delicately up the slab just
left of Trapeze Direct to a break. Hand-traverse leftwards along
this to a ledge and a direct finish.

* **122 Trapeze Direct** 12m VS 4c   (1948)
Fairly straightforward climbing up the crack to the right leads to
the only source of difficulty, the bulge. Outwit this then plod on
to the top.

* **123 Trapeze** 14m VD   (1945)
Good steep climbing on more than adequate holds. Follow
Trapeze Direct to the bulge, then traverse right to a left-trending
groove.

124 Alpha 12m HVS 5b   (1967)
A poor eliminate taking a direct line between Trapeze Direct and
Nursery Slab, hardly achieving independence.

125 Nursery Slab 9m M   (1906)
Broken rocks at the left side of the large expanse of slabs are
useful for ascent, descent, or side-runners.

To the right a remarkably fortuitous piece of quarrying has left
possibly the finest gritstone slab in the Peak. **GREAT SLAB** is
home to a superb collection of climbs spanning over thirty years
of climbing history. *Toy Boy* is by far the hardest route on the
slab but, for mere mortals, of the others, *Artless* is probably the
most technical, and *Jugged Hare* the most serious. *The Great Slab*

Right: Ed Wood on Saville Street, Millstone Edge.
Photo: Keith Sharples.
Overleaf: Bob Bradley on High Plains' Drifter, Lawrencefield.
Photo: Ian Smith.

itself is not to be underestimated, as the crux traverse has been the launching pad for many bruised kidneys and fractured bones!

*** **126 Heartless Hare** 11m E5 6a   (1975)
Number five on the syllabus. Just right of Nursery Slab is a faint weakness. Careful footwork soon brings small, but good edges to hand and slightly easier climbing. A side-runner in the obvious slot in Nursery Slab reduces the grade to E3.

 ** **127 Jugged Hare** 13m E6 6a   (1983)
The final exam! Right again is another, faint weakness, sadly containing some chipped holds. Climb this delicately to an uncomfortable position at the break. A very worrying move allows better holds on the steep headwall to be gained. Hesitate here and there won't be a re-take. The same side-runner as for Heartless Hare removes an E point.

*** **128 Hairless Heart** 15m E5 5c   (1975)
Simply superb, number six on the course. From the small ledge of The Great Slab make courageous friction moves up and right to reach the 'flake'. Keep cool up this until it is possible to make a final awkward swing right on to a loose jug. Sorry, perhaps you shouldn't have been told that! Recent chippings have been filled in but unfortunately unsightly scars still remain.

*** **129 The Great Slab** 18m E3 5b   (1951)
'A superb but serious route that blends all that is delicate and strenuous in slab climbing.' – 1957. The vintage line of the slab. Starting just left of centre follow a slight groove awkwardly to reach a small 'rescue' ledge. Now look down at the landing; horrible isn't it. Take a deep breath, then traverse delicately right on *'almost non-existent finger-and-toe holds until a good ledge is reached.' – 1957.* Good, but awkwardly-placed, holds lead to the top.

 ** **130 Artless** 15m E5 6b   (1976)
Starting right of The Great Slab, gain the small ledge at 2m. A long reach or a totally committing slap starts a hard sequence which culminates in a final hard move to reach holds on The Great Slab. Finish up this or, even better, the next route.

Previous Page: Inverted Jigsaw, Yarncliffe Quarry.
Photo: Ian Smith.
Left: Craig Smith on Cave Crack, Froggatt Edge.
Photo: Ian Smith.

* **131 Hairy Heart** 15m E6 6a (1975)
Low in the grade and the mock exam. Another excellent route.
From the big ledge past the crux of The Great Slab make some
thin, intricate moves up the shallow groove to reach a good
pocket. Carefully now, just one more awkward move, then the
top is reached.

† **132 Toy Boy** 15m E6 6c (1986)
Put your ski boots on for the start of this one! Starting from a
small boulder close to the once-pegged crack-line to the right
(Synopsis), climb the blank slab right of Artless by long reaches
and/or jumps on nothings. Hard to find the holds and harder still
to climb. For those who can do everything.

* **133 Synopsis** 12m E2 5c (1952/1974)
*'It has not been climbed "clean". It has however been beaten into
submission with the use of four pitons (one still remains near the
top) and a jammed piton hammer. It has nothing to commend it,
except possibly the perverted pleasure of swinging on loose
pitons.' – 1957.* On permanent loan from Millstone Edge, with
some interesting moves, particularly on the mid-height crux.
Protection is adequate given sufficient discipline to stop and
place it.

* **134 Parting Hare** 12m E3 5c (1983)
The inevitable traverse of Great Slab along the thin break where
the slab meets the headwall is climbed from left to right – if at all.

135 Beta 12m VD (1951)
The obvious broken corner to the right.

*To the right is a huge flake with a cave at its left-hand end. A
superb problem starts from inside the cave (feet off the ground
please!) then pull out to follow the shallow slanting crack, 6b.*

136 Spine Chiller 15m E4 5c (1984)
The left arête of the flake proves to be both scary and awkward
and the landing isn't the best.

137 Nutty Land 15m E1 5c (1976)
A contrived route up the centre of the flake.

* **138 Flake Gully** 12m D (1939-1945)
Worth doing for the finishing moves. Scramble up the gully
behind the flake then go up the wall above on monster holds.

To the right the edge falls back to form a long steep wall with a prominent right-angled corner on its left.

*** **139 Brown's Eliminate** 14m E2 5b   (1948)
A fine route on generally good holds where good balance pays dividends. Protection is distant when on the crux and it's not a good idea to throw a wobbler towards the top. From a few metres up the corner, traverse left to gain a big ledge (Friend in break at foot level on the left arête). Awkward, reachy moves allow the wall right of the arête to be climbed on slowly improving holds. Those liking 'barn door' laybacks will thoroughly enjoy the direct start up the arête to finish up the original route; **Straight and Narrow**, E2 5c, (1965-1978).

140 Armageddon 14m E3 5c   (1977)
A problem start left of the corner leads to the large ledge of Brown's Eliminate. Continue in a direct line on reasonably good holds. Side-runners to the right reduce the grade to E2.

*** **141 Green Gut** 14m S 4a   (1948)
The classic, and consequently polished, corner provides a steep, well-protected climb.

* **142 Pedestal Crack** 14m HVS 5a   (1948)
The steep crack just to the right is harder than it appears, particularly at the roof.

† **143 Slide Show** 15m E5 6c   (1988)
The roof right of the upper section of Pedestal Crack is protected by high side-runners in that route.

Slingshot, 7b, (1988), is so far only a top-rope problem, albeit one of the utmost difficulty. It takes the bulging wall right of Pedestal Crack to the ledge.

** **144 The Big Crack** 15m E2 5b   (1955/1973)
The steep crack-line in the middle of the long wall gives an excellent route, with good protection. The lower section is sustained on good finger-jamming slots with an awkward move to gain the wider crack. This succumbs to a different approach altogether.

145 Paranoid Android 15m E3 5c   (1981)
A harder and more serious variation is up the wall just to the left of the upper crack. Protected with low side-runners in The Big Crack.

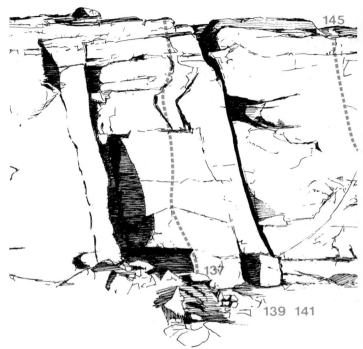

Below the edge at this point is a millstone. A good problem is to mantel onto the millstone without touching the ground.

† **146 Hard Cheddar/Circus** 16m E6 6b   (1977/1982)
In the right half of the wall are four thin steep cracks. The leftmost is a fierce hair-line crack and it requires a positive approach. From the halfway ledge continue boldly up the upper wall moving first rightwards to a thin break, then direct. Side-runners, to the right, are used on Circus.

* **147 Stiff Cheese** 12m E2 5c   (1974)
The second crack is short, but definitely stiff, with crux finishing moves above a hard landing.

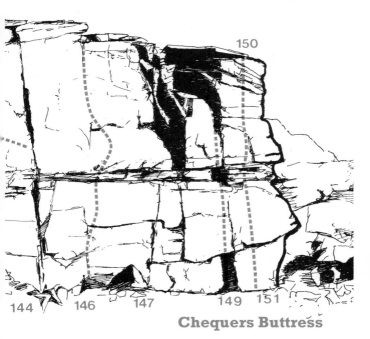

Chequers Buttress

148 Beech Nut 12m E1 5c   (1951)
The third crack proves awkward, particularly at the top.

*** **149 Chequers Crack** 14m HVS 5b   (1951)
The rightmost crack provides a steep but well-protected fight via
a combination of slippery laybacks and unfriendly jams. Getting
established on the midway ledge can be easy with a little
thought. The easier continuation crack is climbed on excellent
jams.

† **150 Spock's Missing** 14m E5 6b   (1981)
From the midway ledge of Chequers Crack, move right and
climb the centre of the fine face direct. Runners in the upper

crack of Chequers (and on the flake of Chequers Buttress if you can reach it!) help curtail a nasty crash.

† **151 Business Lunch** 6m E4 6c (1984)
The wall between Chequers Crack and Soul Power gives a direct start to Spock's Missing.

† **152 Sole Power** 6m E5 6c (1983)
The undercut lower arête of the buttress gives a desperate problem.

∗ **153 Chequers Buttress** 14m HVS 5b (1962)
A superb well-protected route in a fine position starting up the easy ramp right of the arête. From the break, traverse the wall above diagonally leftwards until a difficult move brings a monster biffo-jug on the arête into reach. Progress more easily up this, as down below the shutters click furiously.

∗ **154 Chequers Climb** 14m VS 4c (1949)
Worth doing for the final crack. From the break on Chequers Buttress traverse at a lower level to gain the finish of Chequers Crack.

155 Solomon's Crack 12m VD (1890)
Pleasant enough climbing up the starting ramp of Chequers Buttress followed by the corner above. A harder variation is the wide 'Victorian' crack in the left wall at Severe.

∗ **156 Bacteria Cafeteria** 12m HVS 5b (1979)
An eliminate line from the foot of the ramp via a tiny groove to finish up cracks right of the arête. Nothing to get lysterical about.

Right of the corner, the upper part of the face is split by two grooves.

∗ **157 Jankers Crack** 9m HS 4b (1948)
The left-hand crack is climbed direct.

∗ **158 Jankers Groove** 10m VS 4c (1948)
The right-hand groove is reached by traversing in from the previous route and begins with the crux move. The Whillans direct start needs a vicious fist jam in a slot at a strenuous 6a.

159 Jankers End 13m VS 4b (1948)
Continue the traverse of Jankers Groove until once round the arête a shallow groove can be climbed to a step left on to the slab to finish. It can also be approached from directly below.

278

Last and probably least there are the ubiquitous girdle traverses.

160   The Valkyrie Girdle Traverse   184m   HVS   5b   (1951)
A contrived girdle exists from North Climb to the pinnacle and consists mainly of stomach-traverses just below the top of the crag.

161   The System   134m   E3   5b   (1953/1967)
A girdle of the southern end of the crag from Jankers End to Broken Crack reversing the crux of The Great Slab *en route*. Usually soloed if done at all.

Thus endeth Froggatt Edge. Two hundred metres to the south lies **BEECH BUTTRESS** which contains the first routes on the magnificent **CURBAR EDGE**.

FROGGATT EDGE LIST OF FIRST ASCENTS

1890	**Solomon's Crack** (*née* Chequers Crack) James W Puttrell, W J Watson. *Climbed after bivouacking in the cave.*
1890	James W Puttrell, W J Watson, Ernest A Baker ascended the Pinnacle by some tricky tactics in the line of Route 1.
1890-1902	**Silver Crack, Swimmer's Chimney** James W Puttrell. *Silver Crack was originally called Chequers Fissure.*
1903-1904	**Grey Slab** Rucksack Club members. *The upper part only.*
1906	**North Climb, Nursery Slab** James W Puttrell, Henry Bishop, C Douglas Yeomans. *North Climb had previously been top-roped.*
1912	**Route One** Henry Bishop, C Douglas Yeomans. *First free ascent of James W Puttrell's 'route' of the same name.*
1913	**Diamond Crack** Henry Bishop, C Douglas Yeomans, F C Aldous, Claude Worthington. *Given Very Difficult at the time!* *Also at this time Bishop climbed many other routes on the edge which he unfortunately failed to record.* *The 1914-1918 war intervened then strict 'gamekeeping' held climbers at bay until 1933 when Harry Dover, Gilbert Ellis and Frank Elliott visited Froggatt and repeated Route One.*
1939-1945	**Flake Gully** Ivy Byne, Eric Byne. *"So obvious a route that it must have been climbed before"... wrote Byne.*
1939-1945	**Terrace Crack** Freda Rylett, Jack Macleod.
1939-1945	**Grey Slab** Jack Macleod, Freda Rylett. *Also at this time Macleod climbed one of the 'Jankers' routes.*

1945 Dec.	**Sickle Buttress, Trapeze**	R E Davies, R A (Dick) Brown.
1947	**Pinnacle Face**	Gilbert Ellis, Harry Dover.
1945-1948	**Heather Wall**	Dick Brown.

Originally called Advent Slab and later suggested by Lawrence Travis to be a Bishop route.

1948 Spring	**Sunset Crack, Chapman's Crack**	Len Chapman, Bob Tomsett.
1948 Autumn	**Slab Recess**	Sandy Alton, J Morgan.
1948 Autumn	**Tody's Wall**	Joe Brown, Merrick (Slim) Sorrell.

J R (Nat) Allen, arriving late that day, "saw Joe coming over the top as we got off the bus at Stoke Bar".
The top section had previously been climbed by Dick Brown and B Kay who traversed in from Silver Crack.
At one time the route was known as 'Puff's Paradise' because of the postures adopted by many leaders on the crux.

1948 Autumn	**Three Pebble Slab**	Joe Brown, Wilfred (Wilf) White, Tony Hyde.

Originally graded Very Severe (rubbers).

1948 Autumn	**Brown's Eliminate**	Joe Brown, Slim Sorrell, Wilf White.

"Some of the routes were extremely hard, such as Brown's Eliminate. The rock was friable and I top-roped the face three times before leading it. The holds were microscopic and the climb was only possible in nails which could be hooked perfectly on to tapering flakes that were uniformly about one eighth of an inch wide. These flakes broke off in time, leaving a larger gripping edge and the route has generally become easier". – Joe Brown. The Hard Years.
Originally given Very Severe, so it should really be about Severe by now!

1948 Autumn	**Pinnacle Arête**	Slim Sorrell, Nat Allen, Don Chapman.
1948 Autumn	**Green Gut**	Nat Allen, Wilf White.
1948 Autumn	**Slab Recess Direct**	Joe Brown.
1948 Autumn	**Trapeze Direct**	Wilf White, C (Chuck) Cook.
1948 Autumn	**Sandy Gully**	Nat Allen, Sandy Alton.
1948 Autumn	**Hawk's Nest Crack**	Joe Brown, Slim Sorrell.
1948 Autumn	**Holly Groove**	Slim Sorrell, Nat Allen.
1948 Autumn	**Sunset Slab**	Joe Brown, Tony Hyde, Wilf White.
1948 Autumn	**Turret Crack**	Don Chapman, Nat Allen.
1948 Autumn	**Slab and Crack**	Nat Allen, Don Chapman.
1948 Autumn	**Sorrallion** (*née* Flake Climb)	Nat Allen, Slim Sorrell.
1948 Autumn	**Congestion Crack**	Nat Allen, Slim Sorrell, Wilf White, J Morgan.
1948 Autumn	**Pedestal Crack**	Joe Brown, Nat Allen.
1948 Autumn	**Sickle Buttress Direct**	Nat Allen, Don Chapman.
1948 Autumn	**Broken Crack**	Joe Brown, Wilf White, Slim Sorrell.
1948 Autumn	**Silver Traverse**	Wilf White, Tony Hyde, Nat Allen.
1948 Autumn	**Bollard Crack** (*née* Chockstone Crack)	Slim Sorrell, Wilf White.

1948 Autumn	**Jankers End** Slim Sorrell, Nat Allen.

1948 Autumn   **Jankers Crack, Jankers Groove**   Joe Brown, Don Chapman.
Brown, serving his National Service at the time, was late back from leave and was put on 'jankers'. He was about 17 at the time.
The other active members of The Valkyrie Mountaineering Club at that time were; Chuck Cook, Don Cowan, K Brindley, Ray Kerry. Tony Hyde was a Sheffield University Mountaineering Club member who was friendly with the Valkyrie lads.

1949   **Chequers Climb**   Joe Brown, Wilf White, Nat Allen, Don Chapman.

1949   **Valkyrie**   Joe Brown, Wilf White.
A route destined for classic status. Brown had climbed the first pitch in September 1948, but his seconds on that occasion had been unable to follow and so the attempt was abandoned.

1949   **Heather Wall Variant**   Joe Brown, Nat Allen.

1949   **Right Flake Crack**   Wilf White, Slim Sorrell.

1950   **The Cave Crack**   Joe Brown, Slim Sorrell.
Originally graded as VS!

1951   **Allen's Slab**   Nat Allen, Wilf White.

1951   **Valkyrie Girdle Traverse**   Nat Allen, Don Chapman, Wilf White.

Publication of the 1951 Climbs on Gritstone guidebook.
Other routes whose first ascent details are unknown include:
Chockstone Crack, Cave Crawl, Corner Crack.

1951   **The Great Slab**   Joe Brown, Wilf White.
The belay was so far off-line that Wilf had to have a back-rope to prevent a huge swing. This represented another breakthrough in slab climbing; a very impressive achievement considering it was led on-sight in plimsolls!

1951   **Beech Nut**   Don Whillans, Nat Allen.

1951   **Chequers Crack**   Don Whillans, Joe Brown.

1951   **Skogul**   Joe Brown, Don Chapman, Nat Allen.

1951   **Gamma, Beta**   Nat Allen, Wilf White.
Gamma was originally called 'Grass Seed Saunter' by Nat but for some reason it appeared as 'Gamma' in the 1965 guidebook.

1952   **Piton Route** (5 pts)   Nat Allen, D Carnell, R Handley.
First free ascent in 1974 as Synopsis.

1953 May   **Oread's Girdle**   Dave Penlington, Dick Brown, Ernie Marshall (alternate leads).
Girdled the crag from Sickle Buttress to Jankers Crack.

1953   **Just Crack, Left Broken**   Slim Sorrell, Nat Allen.

1954 Nov. 7   **Valkyrie Direct**   Peter Biven, Barry Biven.

1954   **Slope Crack, The Slab, Slipper Slab**   Wilf White, Nat Allen.

1955 May 14   **The Big Crack** (1pt)   Don Whillans, Eric Price, Nat Allen.
Whillans used aid from an inserted chockstone to place another chockstone which was then used as a runner only.
First free ascent in 1973.

1956	**Strapiombo** Don Whillans, Joe Brown.
1956	**Neb Crack** Nat Allen, Wilf White.
1956	**Tinsel's Tangle** Wilf White, Tinsel Allen, Nat Allen.
1956	**Crooked Start** Wilf White, Nat Allen.
1956	**Brookside Crack** Wilf White.
1956	**Ladies Buttress** Dorothy Sorrell, Pat Allen, Mavis White.
1956	**Pillar Wall** Wilf White, Slim Sorrell.
1956	**Gyron Groove** Bob Brayshaw.
1951-1956	**Brookside Gully** Anon.

Publication of the 1957 Further Developments guidebook.

| 1957 May 25 | **Downes' Crack** Geoff Sutton, A J Maxfield. |

Named in Downes' memory. He had just died on Gasherbrum IV.
The route is just above the Bob Downes' Memorial Hut.

1957	**Black Wall** Wilf White, Nat Allen.
1957	**Morty's Corner** Joe (Morty) Smith, Nat Allen.
1957	**Scarper's Triangle** John Fearon, Dave Gregory.
1958	**Cave Wall** Don Whillans.

The most significant route since Great Slab and still worth E3 today. On the first ascent Whillans jumped off from the lip.

| 1962 Feb. | **Strapiombante** Dave Brearly, Paul Nunn. |
| 1962 | **Chequers Buttress** John Gosling, Mike Simpkins. |

Joe Brown had previously got out to the arête using a threaded stone for a runner. He was too short to reach the jug and when the stone fell out he decided to retreat!

| 1957-1965 | **North Gully** Anon. |

Publication of the 1965 Sheffield – Froggatt Area guidebook.

| 1964 | **Sandy Crack** Nat Allen, Derek Burgess. |

Its whereabouts remains a mystery.

| 1966 Oct. | **Vomer** John Gosling. |

Vomer is a thin wedge-shaped bone forming the middle part of a human nose.

1966 Oct.	**Jacob** Anthony Nicholls.
1967 Jan. 31	**Swing** Jim Perrin.
1967 April 24	**The Method** (1pt) E Emery, Eddie Thurrell, Bill Birch.

Now known as Avalanche.
First free ascent in 1975.

| 1967 April 29 | **The System** Bill Birch, Eddie Thurrell. |

The first complete ascent. All the climbing had previously been worked out by Dick Brown, David Penlington and others in 1953 as part of the Oread's Girdle.

| 1967 | **Alpha** The Alpha Mountaineering Club. |

(though not ALL did it!).

1968 Easter   **The Iliad**   Arthur Robinson, Bill Birch.

1968 June 16   **The March Hare** (1pt)   Bill Birch, A N Other.
First free ascent in 1974.

1968 Aug. 23   **Long John's Slab** (1pt)   Paul Gray.
A peg was used in the pocket to stand on.
First free ascent in 1969.

1968   **Oedipus! Ring Your Mother**   Tom Proctor (solo).
'Presumably with a prayer to that lady'. Heavily chipped by the first ascensionist. Named after some graffiti in the toilet at Stoney Cafe.

1969   **Long John's Slab**   Al Rouse (solo).
First free ascent.

1969   **Motorcade**   D Warriner, G Johnson.
Later named by Gary Gibson.

1972   **Four Pebble Slab, Sundowner**   John Allen, Neil Stokes.
Later claimed by Gary Gibson, the names are in fact Gary's.

1973   **Esau**   John Allen, Neil Stokes.

1973   **The Big Crack**   John Syrett, Tim Jepson, Al Manson.
First free ascent.

1973   **Debut Wall, Debutante**   John Allen (solo).

1974 July 6   **Ratbag**   John Allen, Steve Donnelly, Steve Bancroft.

1974 Aug. 13   **Synopsis**   Steve Bancroft, John Allen.
First free ascent of Piton Route.

1974 Nov. 20   **Stiff Cheese**   Steve Bancroft (solo).

1974   **March Hare**   John Allen.
First free ascent.

1974   **Stealing the Misanthrope's Purse**   John Allen (solo).

1975 Jan. 11   **Nightshade**   John Allen, Steve Bancroft, Neil Stokes.

1975 July 17   **Hairless Heart**   John Allen (solo)
Allen was spurred into action on a hot summer's day after Drummond top-roped the line in front of Allen but then left to go to work intending to solo it on his return. Bancroft later saw fit to record 'top-rope inspection probably advised'.

1975 July 25   **The Gully Joke**   John Allen, Steve Bancroft, Mark Stokes.

1975 Nov. 29   **Heartless Hare**   Steve Bancroft, John Allen.
Originally climbed with side-runners.

1975   **Avalanche**   John Allen, Steve Bancroft, Chris Addy.
First free ascent.
Re-climbed after a rock-fall in 1981.

1975   **Hairy Heart**   Mick Fowler, John Stevenson, Mike Morrison.
Side-runners were used on the first ascent. Has been on-sight soloed since, but it is still rarely repeated at the time of writing.

1976 April 12   **Artless**   John Allen (solo).
Originally called 'Artless Fart' (the route name that is!).

1976 May 6	**Narcissus** Steve Bancroft (solo).	

An all-day jumar inspection prior to the first ascent.
Both Artless and Narcissus were under-rated at the time and are rarely climbed even today.

1976 May 9	**Truly Pathetic** John Allen, Steve Bancroft.

1976 May 16	**Strapadictomy** John Allen, Steve Bancroft.

A major ascent which was originally graded 5c+ in Bancroft's Recent Developments.

1976	**Nutty Land** John Allen, Steve Bancroft.

1977 March 13	**Downhill Racer** Pete Livesey, Alex Livesey.

A very controversial ascent and well documented ("yes and well-chipped") in the climbing press. First on-sight solo by Bernard Newman, egged on by a group of 'friends'!

1977 May 1-3	**Krypton Factor**, **Two Pebble Slab**, **Piledriver** Al Evans

Two Pebble Slab was originally soloed next to a hanging rope, the first 'real' solo was by Graham Hoey the next day. Krypton Factor and Piledriver were climbed solo after top roping.

1977 Sept. 3	**Uphill Driver** Jim Burton.

Probably the first ascent of a line that has seen more than its fair share of 'first ascents'.

1977 Oct.	**Hard Cheddar** Tom Proctor, Al Evans, Ernie Marshall.

A horror; the 'seconds failed ignominiously' and the route has probably still had less than half a dozen ascents! To make matters worse a runner slot has apparently gone AWOL!

1977 Nov.	**Armageddon** Alec Burns, Andy Brown, T Wilkinson.

1977	**Piledriver – Direct Start** Steve Bancroft (solo).

1977	**Indoor Fisherman** Steve Bancroft, Neil Stokes.

1965-1977	**C.H.M.S.1** Chris Hale, Mark Shaw.

1965-1977	**C.M.C. Slab** Castle Mountaineering Club.

Publication of the 1977 Recent Developments supplement by Bancroft and the 1978 Froggatt Area guidebook.
Other routes whose first ascent details are unknown include:
Left Flake Crack, Heather Groove, Soft Option, Straight and Narrow.

1978 March 4	**English Overhang** Dave Gregory, Charles Darley.

Possibly climbed in the mid-1950s at the same time as Strapiombo by Don Whillans.

1978 April 23	**Cavatina**, **Romance** Steve Bancroft, Ian Hibbert, Phil Thorpe.

1978 Oct. 18	**Two-sided Triangle**, **Four Pebble Slab: Direct Start** Gary Gibson (solo)

The direct start to Four Pebble Slab was top-roped first. (It's about Diff!)

1978 Oct. 18	**Grip** Gary Gibson (unseconded).

1978 Oct. 18	**Origin of Species** Gary Gibson, Mark Hewitt.

Intense activity from Gibson. Side runners used.

1978   **Oss Nob**   Colin Banton (solo).
The first of many doubtful claims by Banton whose routes have been found to be very much harder than he graded them. This route was graded E1 5c and is actually E4 6a.

1979 June   **Narcissus II**   Steve Bancroft, Nicky Stokes.

1979 May 6   **Bacteria Cafeteria**   Gary Gibson, Jon Walker, Paul Bird.
Almost certainly done before and subsequently claimed by Colin Banton and Phil Burke.

1980 June   **Science Friction**   Mark Miller, Bill McKee.
First top-roped in 1979. A five metre long sling was used round a chockstone in North Climb as a side-runner! Mark later returned to solo the route. Rumoured to have been done by Chris Gore in 1979.

1980   **Brightside**   Phil Burke, Paul Nunn, John Sheard.
A good find snatched from underneath Paul Mitchell's nose and climbed after work one night. Burke recalls, "I press-ganged Paul and John, borrowed their gear, and did it".

1980   **Epiphany**   Phil Burke (unseconded).
Although Burke climbed this route first he didn't actually claim it, nor did he name it.
Subsequently, Jim Perrin climbed the line with John Redhead.

1980   **Gentlefish**   Anon.
Previously claimed by Colin Banton at E2 5b!

1981   **Spock's Missing**   Ron Fawcett (unseconded).
Ron turned up on the crag with a rope and just a few nuts – severely limiting his protection.

1981   **Mean Streak**   Dominic Lee (unseconded).
"Top-roped?" "Goes without saying", replied Dominic.
First on-sight solo John Dunne 1985-6.
Badly chipped in 1989-1990.

1981   **Greedy Pig**   Paul Mitchell (unseconded).
Using pre-placed and pre-clipped gear. Later that same year Mitchell and Barker returned to climb the route by placing the good gear with a long stick instead of by abseil.
First proper ascent in 1985.

1981   **Tree Survivor**   Jim Perrin.
Later claimed by John Redhead.

1981   **Avalanche**   Daniel Lee, Dominic Lee.
Re-ascended after a rock-fall; considerably harder.

1981   **Paranoid Android**   John Hart, John Stanger.
Previously attempted by Tom Proctor.

1982 Feb. 14   **Beau Geste**   Jonny Woodward.
THE *major route of the post Allen/Bancroft era. It went unrepeated until April 1986.*
"Must have been hard before Firés" – to quote the second ascensionist, Johnny Dawes.

1982 June 11   **Beau Brummel**   Martin Veale, Chris Craggs.
Martin in desperation on the lip during the first ascent.... "Chris is that a good hold up there?"..."Aye lad." It wasn't, but Martin did it anyway.

1982	**Circus**	Daniel Lee, Dominic Lee.

Top-roped, then led with increasingly lower side-runners – seldom repeated.

1982	**Hibernation**	David Liversidge.

1983 June 2	**Sole Power**	Jerry Moffatt (solo).

Jerry had just taken delivery of new Firés and felt that these gave him the advantage: hence the name. At that time it was a big project of Fawcett and the Lee brothers, who were all trying very hard to get the first ascent. Moffatt's ascent came after having practised individual moves and on his second attempt late one evening.

1983 Autumn	**The Mint 400**	Ron Fawcett (solo).

1983 Autumn	**Neon Dust**	Ron Fawcett (solo).

Direct start added in 1986 by Ron Fawcett.

1983	**Jugged Hare**	Johnny Dawes.

J.D.'s second appearance at Froggatt, having previously claimed a direct start to Downhill Racer. Originally called 'Attireless Tart' because of its naked lower half and an exhausting upper section. Side-runners were used on the first ascent.
Subsequently soloed on-sight in 1986 by Ben Masterson.

1983	**Parting Hare**	Nick Dixon.

1984 April 17	**Brush Up**	Bill Wintrip, Ian Smith.

1984 April	**Hot Knives**	Jerry Moffatt (unseconded).

A Paul Mitchell project climbed with 7 falls.

1984 Aug. 24	**Reverse Disco**	John Allen, Steve Bancroft.

1984 Sept. 4	**Business Lunch**	John Allen (solo).

1984	**Benign Lives**	Johnny Dawes (solo).

The technical ability of Dawes, to say nothing of his boldness, was beginning to show through. Top-roped first. Subsequently a pebble came away; first ascent without this was in 1986 by John Dunne.

1984	**The Famous Chris Ellis**	Paul Mitchell, Chris Ellis.

1984	**Fame at Last**	John Allen, Steve Bancroft.

1984	**Spine Chiller**	Steve Bancroft, John Allen.

Publication of the 1985 Derwent Gritstone guidebook.

1985 Spring	**Mastermind**	Paul Pepperday, Dave Candlin.

1985 June 19	**Greedy Pig**	Keith Sharples (unseconded).

1985	**Broken Heart, Performing Flea**	Matt Boyer (solo).

The latter route re-climbs the old line of Sickle Buttress Direct after a rock-fall.

1985	**Flake Climb**	Anon.

Also affected by the rock-fall.

1986 March	**Silver Lining**	Peter Beal.

Originally climbed with side-runners (and still is!).

1986 Spring	**Rambeau**	Mark Leach (solo).

1986 Aug 27	**Parallel Piped** Graham Hoey (on-sight solo). *Previously claimed by Colin Banton at HVS 4c.*

1986 Aug 27   **Parallel Piped**   Graham Hoey (on-sight solo).
Previously claimed by Colin Banton at HVS 4c.

1986 Oct. 3   **Ramp-art**   Martin Veale (solo)
Top-roped first.

1986 Nov.   **The Screaming Dream**   Mark Leach (unseconded).
*"If you've got what it takes, it will take all you've got!" ... Leach after his
successful ascent on day 26. Leach recalls that he did the crux on day 3
but kept falling off the top move after that. Britain's hardest
micro-route. Previously tried by every man and his dog.
Unrepeated until Spring of 1990 when Sean Myles made the second
ascent in just three days. Subsequently done later that year by Ben
Moon with one fall, and that was from the easy lower section getting up
to the crack!*

1986   **Neon Dust, Direct Start**   Ron Fawcett (solo).
Only possible on a winter's day!

1986   **Left-hand start to Long John's Slab**   Ron Fawcett (solo).

1986   **Toy Boy**   Ron Fawcett (solo).
*Another desperate route from Ron; his last to date on the edge in fact.
Ron wore his stiffest pair of boots to do the starting moves.*

1987 March 30   **Polyp Piece**   Nick Dixon.

1987 May 3   **Third Burglar**   Nick Dixon (solo).
*The Editor had just returned from Eire and (intentionally) did not hear
the correct version of the route name.*

1988 May 17   **Vomer Direct**   Chris Wright (solo).

1988 May   **Slide Show**   Paul Mitchell (unseconded).
A runner in The Big Crack prevented a nasty pendulum.

1988 Dec. 7   **Slingshot**   Jerry Moffatt.
*Top-rope problem.
Having previously tried it with Johnny Dawes, Jerry's ascent came after
3 days of perfect winter conditions. Acclaimed as Britain's first real 7b
move done on a route.*

1988   **Cockchafer**   Paul Mitchell.

1988   **Roman Orgy**   John Allen (solo).

1989 May 4   **Backseat Nothing**   Simon Cundy, Tony Coutts.
Allegedly done before by Paul Mitchell but not claimed.

1990 March 11   **Sunset Boulder Problems**   John Allen (solo).

1990 May 14   **What's Up Doc?**   Graham (Doc) Hulley, Tony Boreham.
Top-roped first.

1990   **Nanoq Slab**   Tom Metcalf, Dave Key.

1990   **Mushroom Black and White**   Paul Mitchell.

CURBAR EDGE

O.S. ref. SK 252759 to 260748

by Steve Bancroft

> *'Even now there are still possibilities for new routes on this*
> *escarpment, particularly on Curbar Edge. It would seem,*
> *however, that any such routes will either be extremely*
> *severe in nature or some connoisseur's trifle tucked away on*
> *one of the shorter and less conspicuous buttresses with*
> *which this crag abounds.'*
>
> Eric Byne, The Sheffield Area Guidebook, 1951.

SITUATION and CHARACTER

Curbar Edge lies just south of, and is the natural continuation to
Froggatt Edge. It starts a mere rope-length from the end of
Froggatt. Within a few minutes of leaving Froggatt Edge the
climber can be in solitude, away from the bare sandy paths and
chalk-covered holds, and in amongst the flora and fauna with all
the pleasures of a bygone age. This inevitably has its drawbacks
as vegetation and lichen abound in the initial part of the edge.
For the first two kilometres, small paths thread below the edge,
which appears and disappears in a variety of guises. Short crags
reminiscent of Burbage, secluded bays and bold buttresses
alternate. There are many fine routes to be found in this region,
with several lines left for the diligent connoisseur.

The famous, or indeed infamous, side of Curbar lies at the
southern end, the once-named 'Cloggy of the Peak', where a
more continuous section culminates in the impressive Eliminates
Wall. Here the character of Froggatt is re-established – open,
clean, steep areas devoid of vegetation and walls split by superb
crack-lines. Curbar is therefore an edge of contrast, although
most of the climbs do have one thing in common, they are all
steep, leaving little for the aficionados of the off-vertical.

APPROACHES and ACCESS

For climbs on the northern part of the edge, the easiest approach
is, as for Froggatt, starting up the footpath slightly south of the
Chequers Inn (O.S. ref. SK 247761). A small number of cars can

---

Graham Hoey on Cool Moon, Curbar Edge.
Photo: Ian Smith.

be accommodated just off the bend 75m down the road from the start of the footpath. The first buttress, Beech Buttress, is situated about 100m south of the last big buttress on Froggatt Edge, Chequers Buttress. Alternatively one can walk along the top of Froggatt Edge from the white gate. The Trent bus, No. 244, stops at the 'White Gate' and at the Chequers Inn. The Chequers Inn can also be reached in fifteen minutes by walking from Calver which is served by many buses.

For climbs at the southern end of the edge, car parking is available in small lay-bys below the Eliminates Wall and in the Peak District National Park car park at Curbar Gap (O.S. ref. SK 262747), where a small voluntary payment is requested. The path to the edge starts some 50m down the road towards the west. The Eliminate area is about 500m north of the car-park. For those using public transport, the Curbar Gap can be reached in 20 minutes from Calver (SYT No. 240).

The edge is owned by the Peak Park Joint Planning Board and there are currently no restrictions to access.

HISTORY by Keith Sharples (after Graham Hoey)

James W. Puttrell and his friends of the Kyndwr Club are the first climbers on record to have climbed on Curbar Edge. Their choice of ascent was a little ambitious, the line taken by P.M.C. 1, and after making little headway they retired to gentler rocks.

The edge was seldom visited for the next forty years. In 1932 Patrick Monkhouse stated in his book 'On Foot in the Peak' that 'The Curbar and Froggatt Edges are much broken up and little climbed'. Not the sort of comment likely to inspire a wave of exploration.

Curbar's climbing history really started in 1948 when Bob Thomsett and Len Chapman of the Polaris Mountaineering Club finished off what Puttrell had begun, so producing the fine *P.M.C. 1*. At the instigation of these climbers, the Valkyrie Club was introduced to the edge and, with Joe Brown's subsequent membership of that club, all hell was let loose. Many of the crag's classic routes were ascended including: *Owl's Arête*, *Keeper's Crack*, *Bel Ami*, *Argosy Crack* and *The Brain*. Things calmed down for a while as Brown did his National Service but on

Neil Foster on the first ascent of Ulysses or Bust, Curbar Edge.
Photo: Al Rouse.

his return the onslaught continued. In 1950 *Birthday Crack* and *Birthday Groove*, *Avalanche Wall* and *Elder Crack* (only VS!) were climbed and in the following year the *Left* and *Right Eliminates* and *The Peapod* all succumbed to Brown.

The formation of the Rock and Ice and the appearance of Don Whillans maintained the momentum and during the next four years many hard routes were developed on the crag earning it the nickname of 'The Cloggy of the Peak'. The *Deadbay* routes belong to Whillans and we have Brown to thank for *Tree Wall*, *Overtaker's Buttress*, *L'Horla* and *Green Crack*.

The next nine years were quiet, save for a brief appearance in 1958 by Hugh Banner who led *Insanity*. In 1963 John Gosling made the first of several appearances to produce *Mad Hatter*, a route with a horrendous mantelshelf finish. He returned in 1966 to do *Black, Tan, The Big Rocker, Vixen* and *Grooved Arête* and in 1967 and 1968, as on Stanage, he demonstrated his willingness to force some of the best remaining lines with aid: *Scroach, Usurper* and *Apollo* all fell to this approach.

The edge again lay dormant until the Seventies when a local team led by John Allen and Steve Bancroft began their new route campaign. Allen had already added a few minor routes to the edge; *Thin* and *The Line* in 1972, which were climbed with Neil Stokes and *Fidget* in 1973, but these were to pale in comparison to his subsequent ascents.

In 1974 Steve Bancroft led *Lamebrain* and went on to follow Allen on the superb *Moon Crack* but not on *Profit of Doom* in 1975. Allen did the latter route on his second attempt; a feat rarely repeated save for the well-informed climber. He even did it without using the left arête – even rarer.

Others were awakened however and Ed Drummond, who two years previously had desecrated the wall right of Right Eliminate to produce an aided ascent of *Linden*, cleaned up his act and free-climbed *Scroach*. In 1976 Allen continued the action with *Moon Walk*, another excellent route, *Incestuous, Vain, Cardinal's Backbone II* and a free ascent of *Predator*. *Smoke ont' Watter* however, was the work of Nicky Stokes .

Mick Fowler, a southern sandstone expert, made a free ascent of *Linden*. Accusations and counter-accusations flew about the presence of more chipped holds: but to no avail. Fowler returned a year later to link Scroach and Linden with the

underrated *Hurricane*. In the same year Nick Stokes freed
Usurper and Bancroft added the excellent *Saddy*. The next two
years were fairly quiet, although *Diet of Worms* was climbed by
Paul Mitchell in 1978 with pre-placed runners, and the terrifying
Don't Slip Now was soloed by Phil Burke a year later.

Then in 1980 Curbar was again subjected to an intense wave of
activity. Ron Fawcett, turning his eyes back to gritstone,
produced *Rigid Digit* up the groove left of Elder Crack. Burke,
using a side- runner, led *The Shape of Things to Come*. This was
later soloed by Fawcett who had used a side-runner to protect
One Step Beyond. The sinuous crack-line left of Maupassant was
climbed by Yorkshire raider, Tim Leech, to produce the
desperate *Moonshine*.

After a brief winter break, the action continued, but it was a new
band of climbers who entered the fray. The wall left of Moon
Walk was climbed by Daniel and Dominic Lee to give *Cool
Moon*. Unfortunately they used side-runners, in Moon Walk, to
protect their ascent. Nobody has yet managed to dispense with
these. Also Dominic soloed the extremely technical *Tin Drum*
(traditionally called Toylet). About the same time, Fawcett added
Dark Entries.

In 1983 there were no important additions apart from Fawcett's
desperate direct start to *One Step Beyond*. Fawcett unfortunately
tainted his 'solo' ascent by using a pre-placed nut and clipped
into the wire before making the difficult moves. In 1984 a brief
flurry of intense activity left a number of technical test-pieces
including: *Ulysses or Bust* by Neil Foster; *King of the Swingers* by
Fawcett; *By George* by Keith Sharples; *Tube of Foster's* by Paul
Mitchell; and *White Water*, and *Committed* by Johnny Dawes.
That year even saw the return of a team comprising Les Brown,
Claude Davies and Joe Brown, to fill in a direct version of Big
Rocker, 36 years after Joe's first visit to the crag. However,
probably the best route to appear was climbed by John Allen on
his return to England. *Forbidden Planet* is a route of the same
excellent quality as his earlier classics. Another Dawes'
desperate, *White Lines* just made the guidebook addendum.

Although a guidebook was published, 1985 proved to be a quiet
year. The only routes of note were from John Allen who ventured
across the wall right of Elder Crack to produce *Appointment with
Fear*. Impressive as it was, it failed to take *the* line. Allen also
added *El Vino Collapso* that year.

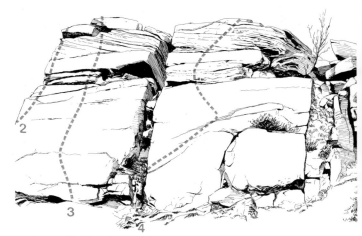

Beech Buttress

1986 saw the addition of some far more impressive routes. Johnny Dawes started with a direct ascent of the groove just right of Elder Crack to produce *Janus*. This effectively made Rigid Digit redundant. However Janus was to pale into insignificance when compared to his next two new routes, *Slab and Crack* and *The End of the Affair*. The former was a complete ascent of the direct start and finish to Fawcett's One Step Beyond. The End of the Affair had been attracting the attention of many climbers but typically it was Dawes who pushed out the boat to give one of the most serious routes on gritstone.

In spring of the following year, 1987, John Hart used side-runners to ensure that he remained a *Happy Hart*. John Allen was drawn back to Curbar Edge to attack the wall left of Profit of Doom, and although *The Fall* is undoubtedly hard, it is a wandering line and as such it is unlikely to become popular. Ron Fawcett, in what seems to have been his final fling of gritstone new-routing, did the outrageously serious *Moon Madness*. 1988 started with a bang (or rather a 'tap') when Andy Pollitt, having spent some

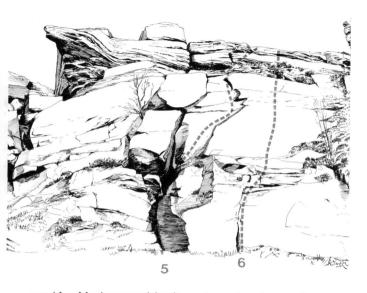

5   6

considerable time practising it, went one step closer to the impossible to record *Knockin' on Heaven's Door*. The name says it all; totally serious climbing. Fawcett was, impressively, straight in for the second ascent within a matter of days and although he down-graded it, the route remains one of the boldest routes on gritstone today and is a fitting conclusion to the Eighties. One wonders just what the Nineties will bring.

The CLIMBS are described from LEFT to RIGHT starting just south of the Froggatt – Curbar gap.

The first buttress, **BEECH BUTTRESS**, has a slabby appearance.

1 Angular Crack 8m HS (1948)

The slanting crack on the left wall of the first buttress.

2 Beech Buttress 12m VS 4c (1948)

From the base of Angular Crack move round the corner then climb the slabby arête, finishing slightly to the right . Delicate. An exciting alternative, the **Direct Start**, E1 5a, (1980), is to pull

directly over the arête, on good holds. Beware though of loose
footholds.

3 Don't Slip Now 12m E5 6a   (1978)
The centre of the slab is climbed by a precarious sequence of
delicate moves trending slightly leftwards to better holds.
Probably harder than Froggatt's Great Slab routes and the
landing is worse!

The grotty gully is **Beech Gully**, M, (1934-1951). The left arête is
Thought Cactus, E1 5b, (1981). The right arête is **Sunday**, HVS
5a, (1983).

4 Amethyst 8m VS 4c   (1978)
Pleasantly follow a glacis rightwards from the base of the gully. A
quick pull gains jugs and the top.

15m right is a short steep wall with a slab above.

5 Campion Groove 12m HS 4a   (1948)
The awkward corner crack on the left of the wall leads on to a
contrasting ramp above and right.

* **6 Campion Wall** 11m VS 4c   (1948)
Another varied route taking the prominent thin crack then the
delicate slab right of Campion Groove. A good direct start takes
the wall two metres right at 5c.

▶ **7 Campion Overhang** 9m VS 4b   (1951)
The evil-looking grass cornice in the angle. Rather you than me.

8 Power Failure 6m E1 5c   (1980)
The overhanging blocks on the right via huge buckets and a
monster reach.

*Round to the right is a problem slab. Just right is a buttress with a
projecting capstone.*

9 Groans 9m HVS 5a   (1978)
Starts from a flat rock. Climb up to a ledge. A steep layaway
move (avoidable on the right at VS) leads to a finish on the right
edge of the overhang.

10 Smiling Jenny 9m VS 4c   (1986)
Climb the wall on the right past a sapling and a small tree.

11 Dive 6m VS 4b   (1978)
Climb the corner to the right again, and the bulge above.

* **12 Port Wine** 8m HVS 5a   (1978)
Climb the steep wall until a thin flake allows a tricky move to be made to reach the top.

* **13 Pillar Slab** 8m D   (1965-1978)
The obvious and very pleasant slab.

25m right is the obvious **SHORT BUTTRESS** *which has a recess to its left.*

* **14 Happy House** 6m HVS 5c   (1986)
The rounded rib eight metres left of the recess gives a dainty little problem.

15 Short Buttress 8m VS 4c   (1934-1951)
Follow the big flake left from the recess, then make an awkward manoeuvre to gain the slanting crack. A direct start is slightly harder, but is more natural. Very dirty at present.

16 Short Chimney 6m S   (1934-1951)
The left-hand corner of the recess is awkward.

17 Short Crack 6m S   (1934-1951)
The right-hand of the two is just as heinous and grim for the grade. Mind you, they both used to be VD.

* **18 Blue Hawaii** 6m E3 6b   (1986)
The undercut left arête of Short Slab gives a good test of agility. Stiff-legged stick insects need not bother. Worth a star for *the* move.

* **19 Green Acres** 6m E1 5b   (1980)
Take the slab just left of centre. Delightful.

* **20 Short Slab** 6m HVS 5a   (1950)
The right-hand route on the slab is equally enjoyable and much easier.

21 Short Measure 6m D   (1965-1978)
The vegetated crack just to the right.

Six metres right is:

22 The Arête 5m VD   (1934-1951)
Pleasant and with good holds after a steep start.

* **23 Beech Layback** 6m VS 4c   (1953)
The prominent corner beyond a brushed wall gives a tough climb.

24 Hanging Crack 7m VS 4b   (1934-1951)
The steep fissure two metres right sports some hollow flakes.

25 Boa Crack 7m VD   (1950)
The next crack leads pleasantly past a tree to give a good but
slightly dirty climb.

26 Black Eye Bach 7m E1 5c   (1978-1985)
The overhung slab right of Boa Crack.

27 Reynard's Crack 7m HVD   (1950)
Right again is another curving crack with awkward moves at
half-height.

28 The Welcome 7m E1 5b   (1979)
A scary problem on the steep wall just right, using a large
pocket. Some welcome!

29 Heron Wall 7m D   (1950)
Take the corner crack direct.

*Round to the right is a steep wall with thin parallel cracks. Left of
these is:*

† **30 Nervosa** 7m E4 6a   (1986)
The centre of the mucky wall with a side-runner in the next route.

31 Thin 7m VS 4c   (1971)
Good moves and runners in the twin cracks.

* **32 Slack Crack** 6m VD   (1950)
The cracked arête right of Thin on good holds.

The edge now recedes to a grassy corner.
This gives **Oak Tree Groove**, VD, (1934-1951). On its left wall is:

* **33 The Line** 8m HVS 5a   (1971)
Follow the striking line of discontinuous cracks by reachy moves
between good holds.

34 C.B. Variant 12m VD   (1957-1965)
Right of Oak Tree Groove is a large flake which is
hand-traversed leftwards to finish as for that route.

Love of Life, E2 5c, (1981), and **The Egotist**, E3 5c, (1981), are
the two obvious lines above the C.B. Variant traverse. Both are
very dirty at present.

35 Demolition Chimney 6m HVD (1950)
Right of the flake, this steep shallow chimney has some creaking flakes.

45m right is a small jungly bay with a larger bay on its right.

Noon Wall, S, (1965-1978), is the vegetated left wall of the bay.

* **36 Twilight Crack** 7m VS 4c (1949)
The twisting crack on the back wall gives excellent jams to a tricky finish.

37 Shooting the Breeze 7m E2 5c (1984)
The thin crack just to the right.

38 Artists Only 7m HVS 5c (1984)
Right again is an open groove.

39 Crepuscular 7m - HS 4a (1965-1978)
The steep blocky crack in the strange tower.

The larger, though somewhat sunken, bay on the right is the
DEADBAY AREA, infamous for its steep walls and often being midge infested.

40 Deadbay Corner 11m S (1951-1957)
The left-hand bounding corner, then a flake and wall to finish.

** **41 Deadbay Groove Direct** 11m E3 6a (1976)
On the back wall is a twisting groove which is climbed past the odd fern to the capping roof. Swing out left to a good hold (runner) and a steep finish.

* **42 Deadbay Groove** 12m E1 5b (1954)
Whillans' original way. Swing right from the roof to finish up the next route.

* **43 Deadbay Crack** 11m E1 5b (1952)
The clean-cut central crack leads butchly, in the best Curbar traditions, to a precarious entry into the easy finishing chimney. Unfortunately rather overgrown at present.

44 Homicide 9m E3 5c (1979)
The very steep line to the right is about as humorous as the name suggests.

45 Deadbay Climb 13m HVS 5a (1951)
Another of Whillans's routes gaining the finish of Deadbay Crack from the corner on the right.

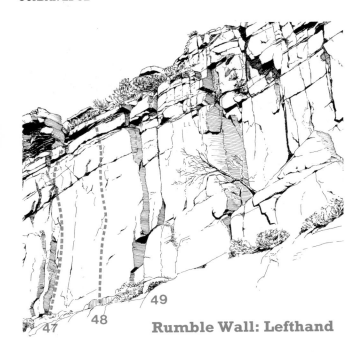

49

47 48 **Rumble Wall: Lefthand**

The next climbs are 200m right on the steep, quarried **RUMBLE WALL**.

46 Crumble 7m HVS 4c (1985)
Climb the thin crack and wall left of Sed's Crack.

47 Sed's Crack 7m VS 4b (1957-1965)
The first crack on the left.

* **48 Three Point Turn** 6m HVS 5a (1979)
To the right a steep wall has ample holds, giving nice climbing.

49 Rumble Wall 6m VS 4c (1958-1959)
Twin cracks right of the previous route.

Rumble Wall: Righthand

50 Rollerball 9m E3 5c (1982)
The wall on the right is taken at its highest point. Start in a
shallow corner and climb this and the steep crack above to a
sandy break. Finish up the short wall above. Better than it looks –
but then it looks pretty bad!

51 Death on a Stick 7m HVS 4a (1978-1985)
The horribly loose cracked wall two metres right of Rollerball.

A few metres right is **THE CIOCH**.

† **King of Crookrise**, E3 6a, (1991), climbs the arête five metres
left of Cioch Left Hand on its left side past a reachy move to a
standing position in the break. A very balancy move leads to an
awkward landing on the ledge.

* **52 Cioch Left Hand** 12m HVS 4c (1950)
Follow the left-hand of two cracks to a ledge. Step right and go
up until an exposed step left gains the final chimney.

53 Flea Circus 11m E2 5c (1975)
Take the right-hand crack then step left to finish up the obvious
thin layback flake.

* **54 Cioch Crack** 11m VS 4b (1950)
The crack near the right edge leads to a mantelshelf. Follow the
wider crack above, then step left to finish through what the 1965
guidebook called 'the paps', and more recent editions, 'the
cleavage'.

* **55 The Bear Hunter** 11m E1 5b (1981)
Climb the rust-coloured wall on the right-hand side of the
buttress with a hard move to gain a shallow crack and the top.

* **56 Cioch Wall** 12m VD (1950)
Step left from the start of the previous route then climb the
left-hand side of the wall until forced left to Cioch Crack for a
move, then step right and go up to finish.

To the right is a steep cracked wall.

57 Duggie's Dilemma 9m VS 4c (1954)
Climb, if you must, the tree-filled groove on the left-hand side of
the wall.

† **58 Lithuania** 10m E2 5c (1990)
Left of Tree Wall a thin crack peters out three metres or so from
the ground. Starting two metres left of the crack, gain a
horizontal slot and then the crack itself. Follow this to the top.

* **59 Tree Wall** 11m HVS 5a (1954)
The next line of cracks trends rightwards past a crucial layback
to gain a break and easier groove above.

60 Heather Wall 10m VS 4c (1950)
The third crack.

61 Wall End 8m VS 4c (1965-1978)
The fourth, and final crack gives a tricky exercise in jamming.

*120m right is the impressive **MOON BUTTRESS**. It is flanked on its
left by a steep tapered wall. On the left of this wall is a short steep
corner.*

* **62 Black Nix Wall** 7m E1 5c (1976)
From the base of the corner move daintily rightwards to climb
the centre of the wall past a couple of layaways.

* **63 Mastiff Wall** 7m VS 4c (1964)
Just right are thin parallel cracks with an awkward start and a
steep finish.

† **64 Camel Ticks** 10m E3 6a (1987)
The wall left of Rat Scabies.

* **65 Rat Scabies** 11m E3 6b (1975-1978)
An unusual route (fortunately) which assaults the prominent
overlap and wall above by means of a violent mantel followed by
easier moves to finish. An unfortunately positioned block adds
food for thought.

66 Bulldog Crack 11m HVD (1950)
The next feature is a corner/crack. *'The crack can be ascended
direct but, except for the purist, there is no compensation for the
large amount of extra work involved.' – 1956.*

67 John's Arête 11m HVS 5b (1975)
Climb the small protruding arête on its left to the halfway ledge.
Finish direct.

68 Derwent Groove 10m S 4a (1950)
Right of the arête is a steep green groove. An easier variation,
VD, escapes left up a slanting scoop.

** **69 Cool Moon** 12m E6 6c (1981)
Starting from the block on the left, the smooth wall on the right of
the groove is climbed with difficulty to gain then finish up a short
S-shaped crack. Friends are pre-placed and pre-clipped in the
wide horizontal break of the next route.

*** **70 Moon Walk** 12m E4 6a (1976)
After an awkward start the superb flaky arête leads fairly easily
to an intricate and exciting finish.

*** **71 Moon Crack** 14m E5 6b (1975)
On the front of the buttress is a thin bulging crack which leads
rather strenuously to a flared break whence a move right gains
the more amenable final groove.

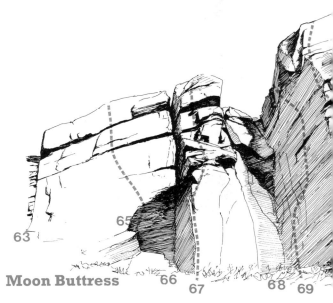

63   65   Moon Buttress   66   67   68   69

† **72 Moon Madness** 12m E8 6c   (1987)
The gruesome bulging wall right of Moon Crack. Well-named as
there is no protection and the landing has to be seen to be
believed!

* **73 Sorrell's Sorrow** 12m HVS 4c   (1950)
The impressive central crack of the buttress provides a good
traditional gritstone fight which is sustained, but thankfully can
be well-protected. *'The entrance to the crack is awkward and
difficult, but the angle eases above and it is possible to continue
more easily on arm and leg jams.'* – 1957.

74 Mister Softee 16m E1 6a (1973)
Hard moves (except for giants) lead up the wall on the right to a
break. Traverse left past Sorrell's Sorrow to attain the final
groove of Moon Crack. It is also possible to go up a much easier
corner to the right of the buttress and move left on to the front
face to join the usual route, 5c.

Moon Buttress: Righthand

* **75 The End of the Affair** 13m E8 6c   (1986)
The imposing right arête of Moon Buttress, for many years a last
great problem, has finally been climbed. Definitely Yorkshire
P4. Has yet to be led on-sight. Said to be death from the top floor,
though a fast and nimble belayer may be of some help.

Right: Dave Bates on Two Pitch Route, Curbar Edge.
Photo: Ian Smith.
Overleaf: Nigel Prestidge on Finger Distance, Curbar Edge.
Photo: Ian Smith.

81

82

78

77

Ulysses or Bust Area

** **76 Amphitheatre Crack** 8m D (1950)
The final route on the buttress follows the wide slanting crack on
the right. It yields pleasantly to elementary layback moves and
the odd back-and-foot move.

*Behind and right is a tapering buttress with several (rather high)
problems. Starting up the right edge is:*

77 Gladiator Buttress 8m HS 4b (1934-1951)
Climb the arête to a ledge. The crack above leads to a rounded
finish, or, better, step left to a thin crack.

78 Hidden Pleasures 7m E3 6a (1984)
Climb the narrow southern face of Gladiator Buttress. Interesting
and sustained climbing which can be protected by small wires.

79 Twin Crack 6m HVD (1950)
The left-hand of two recessed cracks.

Norman Elliot on The Brain, Curbar Edge.
Photo: Ian Smith.

80 Straight Crack 6m VD (1950)
The right-hand crack using a crack on the right wall which can be followed as a harder variation, (S).

* **81 Ulysses or Bust** 7m E5 6b (1984)
The right arête of the recess is climbed on the right-hand side with sustained and increasing difficulty until crux moves gain a good hold on its left-hand side up which the route finishes. It is possible, if a little harder, to follow the right-hand side of the arête throughout. The landing isn't anything to write home about but it has been tested, albeit when it was packed with rucksacks and attendant 'spotters'.

* **82 The Unreachable Star** 7m E2 6a (1980)
The tenuous crack to the right has a rounded finish. It gives a satisfying solo.

83 Dog-Leg Crack 5m VD (1978-1985)
Climb the dog-leg crack. The last line on the wall is a 6a layaway problem.

Across the gully on the right is the imposing **APOLLO BUTTRESS**. The boulder in between has **Andy Pollitt's Jacket**, E3 5c, (1984), with a long reach past the flake on its southern face.

Left of the big buttress are three wide cracks.

84 Buckle's Sister 6m HVD (1950)
The first crack.

85 Buckle's Brother 6m HVS 4c (1950)
The second crack requires good old fashioned wedging techniques and is consequently no place for wimps or anorexic little weirdos.

86 Buckle's Crack 6m HVS 4c (1950)
The third crack is even worse. Climbed by wedging or layback, it is grim either way. It was Severe in the previous guidebook and before that it was VD!

On the right is a fine buttress which has a crack in its left-hand wall.

* **87 Soyuz** 10m E2 5c (1972)
Climb the fine, short crack past a hard move to a break. Then move rightwards along the rounded break to a short finishing flake. The direct finish above the crack is slightly harder; try it!

Apollo Buttress

* **88 Dark Entries** 10m E4 6a (1980)

Two metres right of Soyuz is a short thin crack, which is gained via the bulge on the right. Hard, reachy moves right lead, an uncomfortable distance above your first runner, to slightly better holds and the top. Not a route to go on when your star-signs aren't at their best!

*** **89 Forbidden Planet** 12m E4 6b (1984)

An imposing route up the left side of the tower front. Starting around to the right of the previous route pull over the overhang to a horizontal break then a hard move up allows a standing

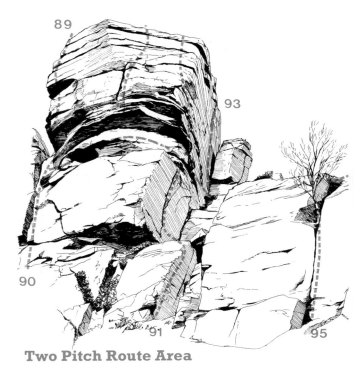

Two Pitch Route Area

position below the prominent roof to be gained (Friend 3½). Pull over the second roof and finish straight up with plenty of conviction.

* **90 Apollo** 17m E2 5c (1967/1967-1978)
Climb the scrappy cracks on the lower tier to belay on a flaky pillar at the start of the previous route, or, better still don't bother. Move right along the ledge and pull over the roof to a short hand-crack in a superb position. Another hard move leads to easier ground.

* **91 The Beer Hunter** (Hic) 15m E3 6a   (1979)
Start on the right-hand side of the lower tier. Climb the thin crack
to the ledge. Continue to the break above the roof then make
hard moves round to a hidden pocket on the left of the upper
arête. Move up, then go right along a slanting break to a steep
finish.

† **92 Zoot Route** 8m E2 6a   (1985-1991)
Climb the wall between The Beer Hunter and the upper crack of
Two Pitch Route, with a runner in the latter, and finish as for the
former.

* **93 Two Pitch Route** 13m VS 4c   (1950)
At the left-hand foot of the buttress is a wide crack. Follow this
and the crack above to a large ledge. Traverse right round the
corner past The Beer Hunter to a belay. The upper crack gives
impeccable jamming to a finish on monster jugs.

The three-tiered buttress on the right has several routes.

94 Art of Japan 5m E1 6b   (1986)
The small wall on the Froggatt-facing elevation.

95 Big Rocker 20m VS 4c   (1966)
A thin crack in the lower wall leads to a good ledge. The rib
above has a dirty groove in its front face; gain this from the left
and, from its top, traverse a ledge rightwards to a blunt arête.
Climb this moving leftwards to finish over a rocking block.

96 Combat Les Pellicules 6m HVS 5c   (1985)
Climb the short arête left of the first crack of Big Rocker, starting
on the left and finishing on the right.

97 Two Reach Route 6m HVS 5c   (1985-1991)
Takes the top wall direct towards the left-hand side of the face.

98 Body Torque 6m E3 5c   (1981)
A line on the upper wall of the buttress. Start on a ledge at the
top of the rib of Big Rocker. Step rightwards on to the wall and
make a series of difficult moves to reach the break. Finish direct.

*To the right, and at a much lower level, is a tower-like buttress with
a slabby lower section.*

* **99 The Brain** 18m VS 4c   (1948-1949)
Climb the slab on very delicate holds by a rising rightwards
traverse to gain the ledge at the base of the corner on the right
side of the tower (possible belay). Climb the corner.
A pleasant alternative is to step left from the corner at half-height
to the exposed arête. Another finish goes right from the corner to
a chimney.

100 Brain Variations 14m E2 5c (1983)
From the start of The Brain take a direct-ish line to the ledge
below the left arête of the tower. Follow this until it gets too hard
then climb off right to finish up the first of The Brain's variations.

101 Oblongata 7m S (1934-1951)
The shallow chimney of The Brain's slab.

102 Amphitheatre Chimney 7m S (1934-1951)
The fissure to the right of The Brain's top pitch. Awkward.

103 Postman's Slap 7m E5 6a (1988)
The peculiar rib left of Birthday Crack containing a letter-box has
serious moves using the right arête at the top.

* **104 Birthday Crack** 7m VS 4c (1950)
The crack on the right has a bulging start and isn't a very
accommodating width.

*Above and right is a steep and tapering wall with a prominent
arête which is taken by* Diet of Worms.

105 Walls have Ears 6m E3 6c (1986)
Climb the wall, several metres left of the arête, past a small loose
'ear'. Scuttle off left to finish. Poor.

† **106 King of the Swingers** 7m E5 6c (1984)
The wall left of the arête with a desperate stretch left as the crux.

* **107 Diet of Worms** 9m E4 5c (1978)
Climb rightwards to a rounded break on the arête (large Friend
de rigueur). Swing round right then move back left to finish. All
the way on the left is better and harder (6a).

* **108 Birthday Groove** 8m E1 5c (1950)
The elegant groove right of the arête. *'Very strenuous pulls on
small layback holds enable the groove to be entered. Move up the
now vertical groove to a good hold below the overhang, where a
running belay can be constructed. Swing round on to the right
corner when a mantelshelf on the vertical wall leads to a good
finishing hold.' – 1957.*

109 Afterbirth 6m E1 5c (1984)
Climb the wall on the right via an intriguing manoeuvre on a
hollow flake to a finish in common with Birthday Groove.

110 Flake Crack 6m HS 4b (1934-1951)
Ten metres right is a crack which widens awkwardly at 3m.

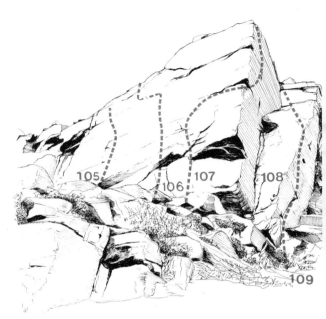

111 Not One of Us 6m E3 5c   (1984)
The balancy wall immediately right.

112 Humdrum 6m HVS 5a   (1984)
The enjoyable right arête of the wall.

20m right is a square block:

113 Foaming Jug 5m HVS 5b   (1984)
The central crack system has a rounded exit.

300m right is the fine **OVERTAKER'S BUTTRESS** *with its long capping overhang. The wall left of Overtaker's Buttress has twin cracks.*

110

Birthday Groove Area

† **114 Pot** 8m HVS 5b (1983)
Take the boulder problem wall left of the next route to the
horizontal break then the continuation crack above.

115 Black 6m HVS 5c (1966)
The left-hand crack with a thin move to reach the break.

116 Tan 6m HVS 5b (1966)
The right-hand crack is similar but easier.

* **117 Overtaker's Buttress** 18m HVS 4c,5b (1954)
1. 10m. From blocks on the left side of the buttress move right
and go up to a small ledge. Traverse right to a belay in the gully.
2. 8m. Swing up left on to the nose for an entertaining and
exposed finish.

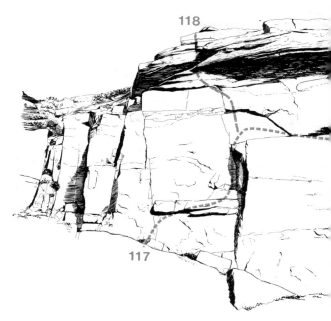

118 Overtaker's Direct 9m E3 5c   (1970-1978)
From the initial groove of Overtaker's Buttress, go straight up to
tackle the bulge on creaking holds.

* **119 White Lines** 13m E6 6c   (1984)
Climb the desperate wall below the traverse of Overtaker's
Buttress by an obvious mantel. Take the top overhangs direct via
a poor circular pocket.

Illiostomy, 10m, grade unknown, (1986), reportedly follows the
small slab right of Overtaker's Buttress.

Above and right of Overtaker's Buttress are two gullies.

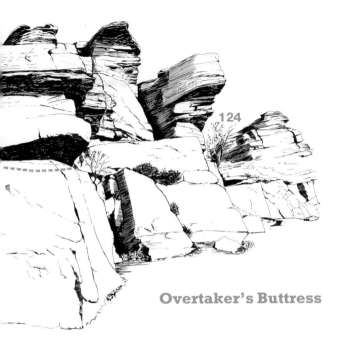

Overtaker's Buttress

120 Right Triplet Gully 7m VD   (1934-1951)
The right-hand fissure gives a good exercise in
back-and-footing. Once successful, head straight off to Wales for
more practice.

121 Soul Searching 7m E1 5c   (1986)
Take the left arête of the previous route, leaving all doubts
behind.

† **122 Lifeseeker** 7m E4 6b   (1973)
A total enigma which somehow gains the flake on the right wall
of Right Triplet Gully. E1 6b, if started from the gully.

Potter's Wall Area

123 Instant Karma 8m E4 6b (1983)
Starting as for the next route, climb the severely overhanging valley-facing blocky arête up its front.

* **124 Fidget** 6m E1 6a (1973)
Follow a short arête to a break. A long reach allows the final flake/crack to be gained. A miniature classic.

Rise of the Robots, HVS 5b, (1979), is a good problem just right again.

125 Mad Hatter 13m E1 5b (1966)
Start up the groove on the left (or the wall just right, harder). Trend rightwards till moves left lead to a grisly finishing mantel over the capstone.

* **126 Potter's Wall** 10m HS 4a (1934-1951)
The obvious direct line up the right side of the face gives a fine climb. Steep and not over-protected but with good holds.

127 Circus of Dinosaurs 9m HVS 5a (1989)
Climb the arête right of Potter's Wall.

140

Baron's Wall 142

143

128 Grooved Arête 9m VS 4c (1966)
Climb the groove in the right-hand sidewall of the buttress.

100m right again and at a higher level is a series of short buttresses.

The first buttress is split by two cracks which give two
ankle-breaking problems, 5b (left) and 4c (right). In between is
a brilliant problem with a desperate sitting down start, (6b) and
bounding the buttress on its right is a VD, which takes the
obvious V-shaped groove.

129 Short Circuit 7m VS 4b (1989)
Follow the crack and scoop in the right side wall of the V-shaped
groove left of Diddlum Wall.

130 Diddlum Wall 7m VS 5a (1958-1959)
Gains the right arête of the V-shaped groove by means of a
tricky short crack on the front face. The **Diddlum Wall Direct**,
E1 5a, (1985-1991), finishes just right of the bottom crack.

131 Honest John 7m HVS 5a (1965-1978)
Swing left out of the overhung recess and continue slightly right
on rounded holds (the original finish to Diddlum Wall). **Knacker
Man**, HVS 5a, (1978-1985), goes right from the recess to finish up
a hollow flake.

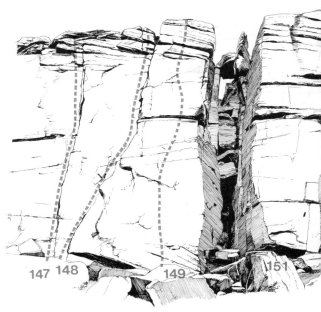

147 148 149 151

Right again is a long broken wall.

132 Vixen 9m HVS 5b (1965-1878)
A poor route based on the thin crack through the overlap in the centre of the face.

133 Little Layback 9m VD (1057-1965)
This pleasant corner bounds the face on its right.

† **134 Husk** 9m E3 6b (1985-1991)
Climb the right arête of the previous route, with a side-runner.

135 Mirror Image 9m HVS 5a (1978-1985)
An easy corner on the right of the prominent buttress leads to a tricky crack on the left wall.

To the right is an obvious shallow scoop.

153

152

154
Calver Wall

136 The Scoop 8m E2 5b   (1966)
The scoop is gained via a good ledge at two metres and climbed
precariously. **Scoop Crack**, HVS 5a, (1966), is the vegetated
crack just right. **Allen's Crack**, D, (1978-1985), the fissure just
right of Scoop Crack.

Three metres right is a thin crack.

* **137 Lamebrain** 9m E1 5b   (1974)
Finger-jam the crack to rounded breaks, which fortunately take
Friends.

* **138 Suspect Intellect** 9m HVS 5a   (1978)
The rounded arête right of Lamebrain is attained via the
prominent scoop round the corner.

139 Allen's Climb 9m D   (1966)
The twin cracks right again.

*36m right is the steep continuous **BARON'S WALL**.*

140 Tube of Foster's 9m E4 6b (1984)
Climb a slight rib on the left-hand side of the wall, then move left to gain the short finishing crack. Cries out for a direct start.

141 Squint Start 9m HVS 5a (1957-1965)
From a groove just left of Tube of Foster's' starting rib, hand-traverse right to the finishing crack of Baron's Wall.

* **142 Smoke ont' Watter** 9m E1 6a (1976)
The attractive central finger crack is gained by the hard lower wall. The right-hand start is 6a.

* **143 Baron's Wall** 9m HVS 5b (1958-1959)
A problem start just left of the arête gains a break and the easier right-hand crack. † **Biz**, E1 5b, (1985-1991), is a poorer variation finish up the scruffy right arête, runner in Baron's Wall)

Ten metres right is a similar cracked wall.

† **144 Amnesia Arête** 9m Quite Hard (1985-1990)
Details forgotten.

145 Blockhead 9m VS 4c (1978)
Right of the arête is a prominent niche which is gained awkwardly using twin cracks.

146 Sweet Gene Vincent 10m HVS 5b (1979)
Two metres right is a nasty start up a short wall. Move left to climb the thin crack just right of the previous route.

* **147 Saddy** 9m E2 5b (1977)
The thin crack in the centre of the face gives an enjoyable climb with an exciting finish past a moving block.

* **148 Wall Climb** 9m VS 5a (1950)
Just right is a steep shallow groove with a tricky entry.

149 Top Secret 9m E1 5c (1981)
Climb the right arête past a break and hard move to an easier finish.

150 Calver Chimney 8m M (1934-1951)
The chimney is convenient for descent as well as ascent.

Dougie Hall on Moonshine, Curbar Edge.
Photo: Neil Foster.

151 Colossus 9m E2 5b   (1981)
A rather artificial climb which takes the right arête of the
chimney, mainly on the left-hand side, to a nasty finish.

152 Calver Wall 8m VS 5a   (1934-1951)
Easily up the wall on the right to gain the left-hand of several
cracks, which gives a testing but well-protected finish. Finishing
up the wall farther left is **Vaguely Great**, HVS 5b, (1979).

153 Brindle Crack 10m HS 4b   (1934-1951)
From the base of the crack of Calver Wall, step right to climb the
next crack.

* **154 Polar Crack** 9m S   (1934-1951)
Down and right of the previous route, a wider fissure leads to a
steep finish up the third crack.

* **155 Arctic Nose** 8m S   (1965-1978)
Blocks round to the right lead to the right-hand crack.

20m right is a smooth left-facing corner.

156 The Corner 9m HVS 5b   (1955)
A nice bridging sequence leads to an easy finish. The wall on the
left gives two rather scary problems: 5c (right-hand), 6a
(left-hand).

157 Eyes Bigger Than T'ledges 12m E2 5c   (1985)
Follow the scars up the right wall of the corner.

* **158 Flying Buttress** 12m S   (1934-1951)
Climb the front of the buttress by the corner on the left of the rib.
Finish up the left-hand crack above the ledge.

159 Flying Buttress Right 10m S   (1965-1978)
A mirror image up the right side of the rib and buttress.

160 U.F.O. 7m VS 4a   (1965-1978)
The wall and disintegrating arête on the right of the tower.

The next feature is **QUARRY FACE** *which has a deep crack in its
centre.*

* **161 By George** 8m E3 6b   (1984)
The very thin crack on the left wall with the crux, where it should
be, at the top.

Alison Hargreaves on Insanity, Curbar Edge.
Photo: Ian Smith.

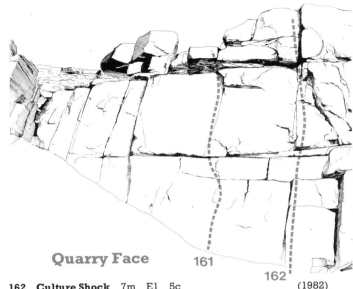

Quarry Face

161

162

162 Culture Shock 7m E1 5c   (1982)
Three metres right is another hairline crack with appropriately
thin moves.

163 Confidence Trick 7m E2 5c   (1985)
Climb the wall right again. Side-runners protect.

164 Litreage 9m HS 4b   (1979)
Climb the slanting crack left of the central crack.

165 Ling Crack 9m S   (1949)
The deep central crack.

† **166 Buzz** 9m E2 5c   (1985-1991)
The scrappy wall left of the upper section of Ling Crack with a
runner on the chockstone of that route.

167 Incestuous 10m E2 6a   (1976)
The obvious thin crack has hard, well-protected moves and a
steep finish. No pulling on heather (whether she likes it or not).

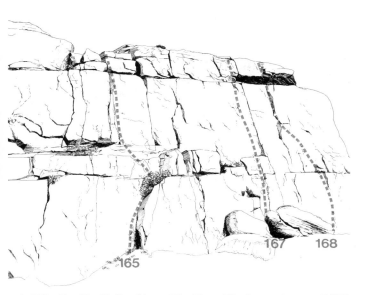

* **168 Cardinal's Backbone II**   12m E3 5c   (1976)
Climb the centre of the wall on the right then move left on a thin
break to gain the obvious wonky flake. A direct start is † **Loads a
Wee Beasties**, E3 6a, (1988).

The wall right of the flake has been cleaned... any takers?

* **169 Vain**   13m E3 5b   (1976)
The right arête of the wall is climbed at first on the left then on
the right. Falling off on either side is not to be recommended.

70m right is a VD *corner with a* Diff *up flakes on the left wall. On
the right wall are two cracks.*

170 Inch Crack   6m VS 4b   (1934-1951)
The first crack leans to the left and is an awkward width.

171 Little Innominate   6m VS 4c   (1950)
The right-hand crack is altogether a more butch proposition. A
bona fide Curbar VS!

172 Lepton 6m E2 6b   (1978)
The arête on the right is harder than it looks. Move right to finish
or try the direct at E3.

173 Amy 6m HS 4a   (1989)
Start at the arête on the right and follow a delicate ramp leading
leftwards to a crack which is followed to the top.

35m right are three slabs. The left-hand one is 4b.

* **174 Kayak** 9m E2 5c   (1964)
Climb the left-hand side of the central slab past a long-long
stretch and a move rightwards to gear and the finish.

* **175 Finger Distance** 9m E3 6b   (1980)
An excellent direct start up the middle of the slab. Not one for a
hot day. Getting longer as the landing wears away.

176 El Vino Collapso 8m E5 6b   (1985)
Climb up the right edge of the slab until a peculiar move gives
access to flutings and the top.

177 Canoe 6m E2 6a   (1970-1978)
Climb the left-hand side of the third slab, using rounded pockets
and a sloping break. Tricky.

178 Stopper 7m E5 6b   (1987)
The slab immediately right of Canoe with the crux at the top.

* **179 White Water** 7m E6 6c   (1984)
Just right again. A desperate start gives access to an even harder
finish. Tough. The landing is very hard, but the fall from the last
move has been tested. It remains a long way nevertheless!

180 Done Years Ago 6m E3 6b   (1984)
The next line right, trending right to finish up the arête.

Round to the right of the slab is Curbar Corner, a popular 5b
problem. The left arête is a neat 5c, whilst the right arête is a
little stiffer at good 6a.

Right, and behind this, is the large and impressive **AVALANCHE
WALL**.

However, before describing this area, a huge boulder can be
seen down below the edge. **Pockets and Pebbles**, E2 6b,
(1986), follows the wall right of the south-west arête to finish up
the arête above a notch.

Returning to the edge proper an obvious crack system (which is taken by Avalanche Wall) *splits the wall.*

181 Portrait of a Legend 9m E4 6b   (1987)
On the left side of the wall a thin crack can be seen in the upper half. This is the substance of the route. Not as hard as appearances first suggest but it is no stroll either.

** **182 Avalanche Wall** 12m HVS 5a   (1950)
'The route is well-named, for a careless leader could quite easily build a permanent cairn on the top of an unfortunate second man.' – 1957. The prominent twin cracks are taken to an awkward entry into the upper section which, despite appearances, is best climbed by staying on the 'outside'.

** **183 One Step Beyond** 20m E6 6b   (1980)
A serious and very sustained route which breaks out rightwards from three metres up Avalanche Wall past a difficult leftwards rockover, then right to a slot (good small wires). Continue in the same line to easy ground above Owl's Arête.

** **184 Slab and Crack** 15m E7 6c   (1986)
Combines the direct start and finish of One Step Beyond to create a technical and serious masterpiece. Starting at an obvious layaway, climb boldly up the wall direct to the slot then finish with difficulty up the hairline crack (poor RPs).

* **185 Owl's Arête** 15m VS 4c   (1949)
The obvious clean-cut grooved arête is followed past a tricky move to easy ledges.

186 Owl's Crack 13m VS 4c   (1934-1951)
The obviously inhabited corner on the right is perhaps best avoided. If the pigeons are not in situ, a lot of muck and the steep finish will be!

† **187 Little Chef** 12m E5 6b   (1987)
Takes the obvious thin flake/crack-line up the left-hand side of the back wall.

* **188 Predator** 13m E2 5c   (1957/1976)
'To the left of Argosy Crack, a thin crack splits the back face of the bay. It has not been climbed and may only yield with considerable artifical aid.' – 1951. The crack is now climbed on good holds except for the crux bulge at 8m. No bridging out to the right as the B.M.C. has had the next route electrified!

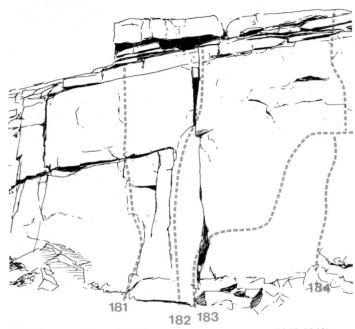

189 Argosy 14m VS 4b   (1948-1949)
The right-hand corner of the recess gives an awkward and
usually dirty struggle.

* **190 P.M.C. 1** 15m HS 4a   (1948)
*'It is a fine open climb, and if difficulty is not taken as a criterion,
the finest on Curbar.' – 1951.* Just right, twin cracks lead to a good
ledge. Step right and follow flakes rightwards up the exposed
wall. Good climbing and protection. Please respect the flakes.

Avalanche Wall Area

† **191 The Fall**   16m E6 6b   (1987)
The big wall on the right by a very roundabout, and wandering
route. Start just left of centre and climb straight up until forced
rightwards to a resting place on the arête of 'Profit' – scary.
Climb the left-hand side of the arête to a hard and terrifying last
move.... even scarier.

*** **192 Profit of Doom**   16m E4 6b   (1975)
The tantalising hanging groove in the arête on the right. Climb
rightwards up the wall on good holds to a ledge on the arête.

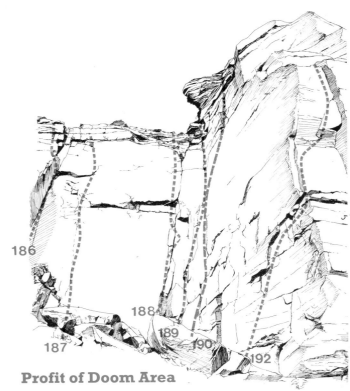

Profit of Doom Area

Move up right (wire high in the corner) and attack the sustained and strenuous groove with gusto. Once one of the hardest routes in Britain! (Unfortunately the key runner placement has become somewhat worn and most climbers place the runner from an abseil rope.)

* **193 Rigid Digit** 18m E5 6b   (1980)
On the front of the buttress is a right-facing groove which forms a natural direct start to 'Profit'. Climb the groove to a resting place

193   194   195   197   199

on that route. Place the runner in the corner, then starting at the obvious flake on the right arête move right and make superb moves up the tower until a hard move gains the right-hand groove. Struggle up this to finish.

* **194 Janus** 17m E6 6b (1986)
The groove which forms the finish of Rigid Digit is climbed
directly from a ledge left of Elder Crack. The runners are good
but hard to place and the climbing is pretty hard and sustained.

* **195 Elder Crack** 18m E2 5b (1950)
A grand old Curbar classic but fortunately not as hard as some of
the Severes! Take the impressive crack which splits the buttress,
the bulge at ten metres supplying the fun. A long stick enables a
runner to be placed (irretrievably?) in the back of the crack.
Bring your own swear box.

*Right of Elder Crack is an imposing wall, for many years a last
great problem.*

† **196 Appointment with Fear** 20m E5 6a (1985)
Climb the scoop and small arête in the lower wall. Once over the
bulge, traverse scarily leftwards into Elder Crack. (On the first
ascent a side-runner was pre-placed in Elder Crack, plus one in
Keeper's Crack placed whilst leading.) Avoids the main
challenge of the wall and is perhaps destined to be forgotten.

* **197 Knockin' on Heaven's Door** 18m E9 6c (1988)
Total death, probably Yorkshire P4 plus a bit! Follow
Appointment with Fear (presumably without the side-runner)
until a hand-placed peg complete with a long sling (placed by
abseil) can be clipped. Step back right and climb the
horrendous wall past shot-holes to finish. Now say hello to the
nice men in white coats.

198 Keeper's Crack 15m HS 4b (1949)
Bounding the big wall on the right is an awkward wide crack.
The continuation corner is a little easier.

199 Bill 7m E4 6b (1984)
The difficult arête to the right of Keeper's Crack. **Ben**, E2 5c,
(1984), is the continuation on the left above the ledge.

Six metres right, past a descent, is a polished slab.

200 Peter Rabbit 9m VS 4c (1988)
Climb the wall left of Slab Route via an obvious ledge.
Alternatively, **The Toddler**, E1 5b, (1988), moves left from the
ledge to finish near the arête.

201 Slab Route 9m HVD (1948)
Follow worn holds rightwards past a runner slot to a steeper exit.

202 Pretty Friend 18m HVS 5a (1984)
Climb the shallow groove right of Slab Route then, artificially, ascend the wall left of Bel Ami.

** **203 Bel Ami** 18m VS 4b (1948-1949)
A good varied route which takes the steep jamming crack in the angle right of Slab Route, then the brittle and exposed arête above.

*** **204 Green Crack** 11m HVS 5b (1957)
From the bottom of Bel Ami's corner, climb the big layback flake on the right wall to the roof then undercut right to good finishing holds. Alternatively, **Nesh**, HVS 5a, (1984), finishes over the roof.

† **205 Phone the Hallamshire** 12m E5 6a/c (1987)
Start down and right from Green Crack and climb the left side of the arête with a desperate move or a huge reach, 6a, to start. From the jug at five metres, swing right to join the next route.

*** **206 Usurper** 12m E4 6a (1967/1977)
On the right of the arête is a line of discontinuous cracks. These lead, with increasing difficulty and excellent protection, over a bulge to the finish of Green Crack. A modern classic.

† **207 Lardmaster** 17m E3 5c (1988)
An eccentric mini-girdle. Start up Usurper to the bulge, then follow the break round to Maupassant. Go up a couple of moves then swing wildly right across the overhanging wall to the photogenic position of L'Horla which provides the finish.

** **208 Moonshine** 13m E6 6b (1980)
Start as for Maupassant then swing left to thin cracks in the bulging headwall. Follow these leftwards with determination. Very strenuous but well-protected with a Friend 1½ proving useful as well as small wires.

** **209 Maupassant** 10m HVS 5b (1955)
On the right side of the buttress are three cracks. This is the first one with a dramatic layback at the top.

*** **210 L'Horla** 9m E1 5b (1957)
Awkward moves up the centre crack to the roof, then either swing heroically up the groove direct or climb left and crank up to the top.

* **211 Insanity** 8m E2 5c (1958)
The third crack is safe as houses with modern gear but the
layback is as hard as ever. Weeds with thin hands may prefer to
jam.

* **212 Committed** 7m E6 6b (1984)
The wall right of Insanity is climbed diagonally leftwards past an
obvious rockover to a nightmarish finish.

Insanity Area

In the angle is a greasy descent chimney with a cracked wall on its right.

213 Tin Drum 6m E4 6b   (1981)
The first crack is gained by a hard rockover and followed with difficulty. Traditionally known as Toylet. Desperate and rarely climbed.

214 Be Bop Deluxe 7m E4 6b   (1984)
Start as Tin Drum, but avoid the crack by the wall on the right. Sees very few ascents.

224   225   226   227

Eliminates Area

* **215 The Toy** 6m E1 5c   (1965-1978)
The prominent thin crack with the crux move at about half-height.

216 Plaything 6m E2 5c   (1983)
The face on the right, with a bold final section, is climbed using
the right arête near the top.

Right of an easy chimney is a steep crack.

217 Pretty Face 7m HVS 5b   (1975)
An artificial line just left of the crack.

218 October Crack 7m HS 4a   (1949)
The steep crack.

219 Shallow Chimney 7m VD   (1934-1951)
The pleasant chimney right again.

220 Grey Face 7m VS 5a (1964)
The benign-looking crack right of Shallow Chimney is deceptive.
Fortunately a jug on the right comes to the rescue.

221 Thirst for Glory 7m HVS 5b (1978-1985)
The centre of the wall on the right is climbed direct.

222 Pale Complexion 6m VS 4c (1965-1978)
The trivial right arête of the wall.

Below the edge at this point is another large boulder/block. The
NW arête gives **Veale Thing**, E1 5c, (1986), and the SW one is
Fab Arête, HVS 5b, (1985-1991). The overhanging face of the
adjacent boulder is **Gorilla Warfare**, 6b, (1986).

Next is the very impressive **ELIMINATES WALL**.

*'It is one of the largest buttresses on Curbar Edge and is split by
three fierce cracks, each of which has attracted considerable
attention over the years.'*

*'For generations passing climbers had paused to admire these
cracks, then, after scrutiny, raised their hats in acknowledgement
of the impossible. Brown, however, has never been prepared to
acknowledge the impossible until he has tried getting to grips with
it, and it must be confessed that he has logic on his side. Three of
these cracks stand together in a high, smooth, overleaning face and
were then known as "the little crack on the left", the Peapod, and
"the Great Crack". The first and last of these have now been
re-named the Left and the Right Eliminate. All of them, through
most of their length, are of that awkward kind which is too wide to
jam easily and too narrow to chimney – except for the central part
of the Peapod where, however, the chimneying gets more trying as
the overhanging walls converge. The Left Eliminate is perhaps the
hardest of the three technically, but it was first to fall. Next came
the Peapod, named from the shape of the overhanging scoop at
mid-height, which is more imposing but relatively less difficult; and
finally the "Great Crack" itself, steadily leaning and peculiarly
holdless, demanding a good deal of confidence and muscular
output. All three were green and mossy, and all three were led
on-sight, though not at the first attempt.' – Eric Byne, High Peak.*

Right: John Codling on Brightside, Froggatt Edge.
Photo: Graham Hoey.
Overleaf: Trevor Peck, belayed by Peter Biven, on Great Slab, Froggatt Edge.
Photo: K Leech.

** **223** **Tantalus** 18m S   (1934-1951)
The first route on the buttress is an exciting but rarely done
traverse above the big wall. From the top of the left-hand corner
of the buttress descend an easy crack to a large ledge. Step
down then move right to a friable crack which is followed, past a
block, to a horizontal break. Traverse back left round a bulge
then go up to the top.

* **224** **Left Eliminate** 12m E1 5c   (1951)
A Curbar special. The left-hand crack is wide and demands a
variety of techniques (or otherwise) for its ascent.

*** **225** **The Peapod** 18m HVS 5b   (1951)
A fine classic line though once *'a genuine tour de force.'* – 1957.
Remember – Whillans fell off this route. Having decided which
way to face (try left), the crux is quitting the pod to gain a ledge
and the still tiring upper section.

** **226** **The Shape of Things to Come** 18m E5 6a   (1980)
A serious proposition up the wall right of The Peapod. Climb the
centre of the wall, with only a low runner, aiming for the obvious
blind flake/groove.

*** **227** **Right Eliminate** 11m E3 5c   (1951)
                (Please feel free to re-grade this route!)   (1951)
*'It is serious and exposed, ranking as the hardest climb on Curbar
Edge.'* – 1957. The pride of Curbar, 40 years old and still striking
terror into the hearts of stick insects everywhere. *'The crack is
wide, awkward and unrelenting, the passage of the small overhang
at mid-height being particular troublesome.'* – 1957. Yorkshire E6
for sure.

*** **228** **Linden** 23m E6 6b   (1973/1976)
*"This is the most serious route I have ever done on gritstone, and
possibly my most serious lead anywhere (excepting perhaps The
Moon on Anglesey). This is free-climbing with skyhooks which is
not at all the same as genuine aid-climbing."* – Drummond, 1973.
Start on a flake leaning against the wall. Hard and barely
protectable moves off the flake lead to small flakes. Move left
onto a tiny slab, then more hard moves, with very little real
protection, lead to easier ground and eventually a ledge. A

Previous Page: Wilfred White leading Birthday Crack, Curbar Edge.
Photo: M. T. 'Slim' Sorrell.
Left: Eric Weightman on Flake Crack, Baslow.
Photo: Michael Howe collection.

second pitch (5a) exists moving rightwards up the upper wall to finish at a jammed flake. A serious route with the start unfortunately chipped.

† **229 Happy Hart** 18m E7 6c   (1987)
The wall is bounded on its right by a shallow corner and crack (Scroach). Start two metres left of this and climb the blind crack-line directly using side-runners in Scroach.

* **230 Scroach** 21m E2 5c,5a   (1967/1975)
Leave the large block with difficulty and follow the crack to a good ledge. Either finish here or traverse left to a groove, then climb this and continue diagonally left to finish.

* **231 Hurricane** 21m E4 6a   (1977)
Climb the crux of Scroach then move left to gain a delicate and exposed ramp which leads to a finish in common with Linden.

232 Hercules 10m E1 5a   (1949)
'The route is extremely strenuous.' – 1951. The wide crack on the right of the Scroach block is laybacked by heroes and grovelled by mortals. Either way there's no gear. Originally graded Severe!

233 Alpha 10m HVD   (1949)
Pleasantly climb the shallow groove right of Hercules.

234 Pinhead Moonstomp 8m E1 5b   (1985)
Climb the right side-wall of the buttress, starting in the loose gully.

The next routes are 50m right in a dingy quarry.

235 Quad Crack 11m HVS 5a   (1952)
The steep and rather loose crack in the left corner of the bay.

† **236 Walk on By** 12m E3 6c   (1980)
Good advice! The depressingly blank wall right of the previous route leads, in theory at least, to a steep crack.

237 Quarry Climb 11m S   (1951-1957)
The next climb is a sandy chimney which is probably best left alone.

† **238 Old Codger** 7m E3 6a   (1987)
Take the clean wall right of Quarry Climb. Climb a flake-line until a hard move allows a good break to be reached. Traverse right to a large flake and finish up this.

20m past the quarry is a small tower.

239 Crack and Face 7m VD   (1951-1957)
Climb the crack to the ledge then climb the face on the right.

30m right past small quarried walls, which give some problems, is the final buttress with two cracks on the right-hand side.

240 Roadover 7m VD   (1957-1965)
The left-hand crack.

241 Little Rocker 7m HVD   (1957-1965)
The other crack, with an awkward start and a rocking block.

242 Thomas the Tanked-up Engine 6m E3 5c   (1990)
Climb the right wall of the buttress, starting at the left arête.

CURBAR EDGE LIST OF FIRST ASCENTS

The first recorded climbing on Curbar was by James W Puttrell who tried but failed on what is now P.M.C.1.
Ironically, the first route was:

1948	**P.M.C.1** Bob Tomsett, Len Chapman. *Members of the Polaris Mountaineering Club.*
1948	**Angular Crack** Joe Brown, Merrick (Slim) Sorrell.
1948	**Beech Buttress** Wilfred (Wilf) White, Tony Hyde.
1948	**Campion Groove** Don Chapman, J R (Nat) Allen.
1948	**Campion Wall** Nat Allen, Don Chapman.
1948	**Slab Route** C A (Chuck) Cook, Ray Handley.
1949	**Twilight Crack** K Brindley, Wilf White.
1949	**Owl's Arête, Ling Crack** Slim Sorrell, Nat Allen.
1949	**Hercules** Chuck Cook, Nat Allen.
1949	**Alpha** Chuck Cook.
1949	**October Crack** Wilf White, Slim Sorrell.
1949	**Keeper's Crack** Slim Sorrell, Wilf White. *Nat Allen recalls that the 'keepering' of the edges at that time was so absolute that the keeper shot at them from the lodge!*
1948-1949	**Bel Ami** Wilf White, Chuck Cook.
1948-1949	**Argosy** (*née* Argosy Crack) Slim Sorrell, Chuck Cook.
1948-1949	**The Brain** Slim Sorrell, Nat Allen, Wilf White.
1950	**Boa Crack, Reynard's Crack, Heron Wall, Slack Crack** Nat Allen, Wilf White.
1950	**Demolition Chimney, Twin Crack, Heather Wall, Straight Crack** Slim Sorrell, Nat Allen.
1950	**Cioch Crack, Cioch Wall** Nat Allen, Sandy Alton.

1950	**Buckle's Sister, Buckle's Brother, Buckle's Crack** Nat Allen, Sandy Alton, Bob Kerry.
1950	**Bulldog Crack** K Brindley, Wilf White.
1950	**Derwent Groove** Nat Allen, E Burton.
1950	**Sorrell's Sorrow** Joe Brown, Slim Sorrell.
1950	**Little Innominate, Wall Climb, Birthday Groove, Birthday Crack, Amphitheatre Crack, Cioch Left Hand** Valkyrie Mountaineering Club.
1950	**Two Pitch Route, Short Slab, Avalanche Wall, Elder Crack** Joe Brown.
1951 Mar. 25	**The Left Eliminate** Joe Brown, Slim Sorrell.
1951	**Campion Overhang** A J Allen.
1951	**Deadbay Climb** Don Whillans, Nat Allen.
1951	**The Peapod, The Right Eliminate** Joe Brown, Slim Sorrell.
1952 Mar. 23	**Quad Crack** Don Whillans, Joe Brown, Nat Allen, Don Chapman.
1952	**Deadbay Crack** Don Whillans.
1953 June 18	**Beech Layback** R A (Dick) Brown, E MacConnell.
1953 June 19	**The Little Red Monkey** Dick Brown, E MacConnell.
1954	**Deadbay Groove** Don Whillans.
1954	**Tree Wall** Joe Brown.
1954	**Overtaker's Buttress** Don Chapman, Nat Allen. *Omitted from the 1957 guidebook by accident.* *It was considered to be unjustifiable because of its looseness. It was re-ascended in the late Fifties by several Rock and Ice climbers as well as by Don Morrison. It was finally cleaned up to a safe condition by Mike Simpkins.*
1954	**Duggie's Dilemma** Doug Belshaw, Nat Allen.
1955	**The Corner** Joe Brown, Joe (Morty) Smith.
1955	**Maupassant** Don Whillans, Joe Brown.
	Publication of the 1956 Sheffield Area guidebook. *Other routes whose first ascent details are unknown include:* **Beech Gully, Short Buttress, Short Chimney, Short Crack, The Arête, Hanging Crack, Oak Tree Groove, Gladiator Buttress, Oblongata, Flake Crack, Right Triplet Gully, Potter's Wall, Calver Chimney, Calver Wall, Brindle Crack, Polar Crack, Flying Buttress, Inch Crack, Owl's Crack, Shallow Chimney, Tantalus, Amphitheatre Chimney.**
	Publication of the 1957 Further Developments guidebook. *This included* **Green Crack** *and* **Insanity***, although these routes were not climbed until later.* *Other routes whose first ascent details are unknown include:* **Deadbay Corner, Quarry Climb, Crack and Face.**
1957	**Predator** (some aid) Joe Brown, Ron Moseley. *First free ascent in 1976.*

1957	**L'Horla** (some aid), **Green Crack** (some aid) Joe Brown, Morty Smith.	

1957 **L'Horla** (some aid), **Green Crack** (some aid)   Joe Brown, Morty Smith.
First free ascents anon.

1958 **Insanity**   Hugh Banner.
An impressive ascent from a climber who is still active today.
However, there is an unconfirmed report of Don Whillans making an ascent in 1955.

1958-1959 **Diddlum Wall**   Don Hadley, Dennis Gray.

1958-1959 **Baron's Wall**   Joe Brown, Nat Allen.

1958-1959 **Rumble Wall**   Derek Burgess, Nat Allen.

1964 **Mastiff Wall**   Nat Allen, Derek Burgess.

1964 **Kayak**   Colin Mortlock (solo).

1964 **Grey Face**   Dennis Gray, Nat Allen, Des Hadlum.

Publication of the 1965 Sheffield Area guidebook.
Other routes included whose first ascent details are unknown include:
Roadover, C.B. Variant, Little Rocker, Sed's Crack, Little Layback, Squint Start.

1966 Oct. **Black, Tan, The Big Rocker, Allen's Climb, Mad Hatter**   John Gosling.

1966 Oct. **Grooved Arête**   Mike Simpkins, Bill Birch, Arthur Robinson.

1966 **The Scoop, Scoop Crack**   John Gosling.

1967 June 25 **Scroach** (1pt)   John Gosling, M Emery.
Climbed with 1 sling for aid and 1 old peg for protection.
First free ascent in 1975.

1967 **Usurper** (2pts)   John Gosling, Dave Little.
First free ascent in 1977.

1969 July **Apollo** (some tension)   John Gosling, Mike Simpkins, Arthur Robinson, Boyce Cardus.
First free ascent between 1969 and 1978.

1971 Nov. **Thin**   John Allen, Neil Stokes.
The first route on Curbar Edge from a rising star.

1971 Nov. **The Line**   Neil Stokes, John Allen.

1972 **Soyuz**   John Allen, Neil Stokes.
"I had been told that Brown had top-roped this and it was a big deal for me to lead it." – Allen.

1973 April 25 **Linden** (2pts)   Ed Drummond, Hamish Green-Armytage.
Drummond, being as controversial as ever, led this route after top-roped practice and using two skyhooks strapped to his wrists!
First free ascent 1976.

1973 Aug. 1 **Fidget**   John Allen (solo).

1973 **Mister Softee**   John Allen.
Named by Allen to reflect his 'cowardice' as he avoided the main challenge of the magnificent arête above. This later became The End of the Affair.
Top-roped first.

1973   **Lifeseeker**   John Allen, Neil Stokes.

1974 July 7   **Lamebrain**   Steve Bancroft, John Allen.

1975 April 6   **Moon Crack**   John Allen, Steve Bancroft.
Allen recalls that the first ascent was done on-sight with only one nut runner and it was a Peck-Cracker at that!
Gabe Regan soloed the second ascent of this route, having previously failed to lead it. This must have been the most audacious solo on grit at that time.

1975 July 26   **Profit of Doom**   John Allen.
Another stunning route from Allen which justifiably won the acclaim of the climbing press. The two latter routes represented another significant advance in standards. Profit was graded 6b in Recent Developments in 1977, probably because Bancroft failed to second it!

1975 July 26   **Flea Circus, John's Arête**   Steve Bancroft, John Allen, Con Carey.

1975   **Scroach**   Ed Drummond.
First free ascent.

1975   **Pretty Face**   Paul Mitchell.
Unrecorded until 1983.

1976 April 25   **Moon Walk**   John Allen, Nicky Stokes, Mark Stokes.
Gabe Regan soloed the second ascent of this route having already taken a thirty-foot fall whilst trying to lead it on an earlier attempt.

1976 Dec. 11   **Linden**   Mick Fowler, John Stevenson.
First free ascent.
Fowler, having recently moved north from London, was having a field day in the Peak District. However Fowler's critics were stunned by his claim about Linden, but they recovered enough to accuse him of hold chipping, amongst other things. Photographic evidence later repudiated the critics' claims and he emerged unscathed, just!

1976   **Incestuous**   John Allen, Nicky Stokes.
One wonders whether the name reflects the first ascensionists' possible feelings as they certainly dominated a great deal of the new route development at the time.

1976   **Vain**   John Allen (solo).
Both Vain and Incestuous were originally graded HVS.

1976   **Predator**   John Allen.
First free ascent.

1976   **Deadbay Groove Direct**   John Allen, Steve Bancroft.

1976   **Cardinal's Backbone II, Smoke ont' Watter**   Nicky Stokes, John Allen.

1976   **Black Nix Wall**   Steve Bancroft (solo).

1977 May 11   **Hurricane**   Mick Fowler, John Stevenson.

1977 June 19   **Usurper**   Nicky Stokes, Al Manson.
First free ascent.
Stokes eventually succeeded after much effort by other parties. Bancroft, assigning a grade for his 1977 guidebook questioned Nicky how hard it was... "not too bad really" was the reply; hence the 5b+ grade. Only later did the truth come out as Steve quizzed Nicky a

second time ... "yes, not too bad really, about the same as Strapadictomy".

| 1977 | **Saddy** Steve Bancroft, Nicky Stokes, Neil Stokes. |

1977 **Saddy** Steve Bancroft, Nicky Stokes, Neil Stokes.

1978 April 3 **Amethyst, Groans, Dive, Blockhead** Clive Jones, Dave Gregory.

1978 April 8 **Suspect Intellect** Clive Jones, Dave Gregory.

1978 April 22 **Lepton** Al Rouse, Nick Colton, Rab Carrington.
All soloed: later claimed by Ron Fawcett as Kaffleout.

1978 Nov. **Tendon Wall** Dave Pearce, S Tynell.
No longer described.

1978 Nov. **Don't Slip Now** Phil Burke (solo).
Attempted, on a top rope, by many of the Eldon Pothole Club. As Burke soloed it after his own top-roped ascent, Abbie Soles commented "for f...'s sake don't slip now".

1978 Dec. 17 **Port Wine** Mark Kemball (solo).

1978 **Diet of Worms** Paul Mitchell.
With pre-placed stacked hexes on the arête.

1970-1978 **Overtaker's Buttress Direct** Mike Simpkins, John Gosling.

1970-1978 **Canoe** Ed Drummond.

1975-1978 **Rat Scabies** Gabe Regan.

Publication of the 1978 Froggatt Area guidebook.
Other routes whose first ascent details are unknown include:
Pillar Slab, Short Measure, Noon Wall, Crepuscular, Wall End, Apollo (first free ascent), **Honest John, Vixen, Arctic Nose, Flying Buttress Right, U.F.O., The Toy, Pale Complexion.**

1979 April 22 **Litreage, Rise of the Robots** Gary Gibson (solo).

1979 June 3 **Sweet Jean Vincent** Gary Gibson (solo).

1979 June 10 **Three Point Turn** Bill McKee.

1979 July 1 **The Beer Hunter** Steve Bancroft, Tim Rhodes, Robin Thomson.
Surprisingly overlooked by earlier explorers.

1979 Aug. **Homicide** (*née* Deadbay Biz) Gabe Regan, Steve Webster.

1979 **Vaguely Great, The Welcome** Colin Banton.

1979 **Walk on By** Steve Foster.
Climbed using traditional 'combined tactics' for the initial wall. Rob Gawthorpe gave the shoulder the cold shoulder following an extensive bouldering session.
The upper section of this route bears more than a passing resemblance to Quadrangle, which was claimed on 27 October 1978 by Ian Kerr and P Schofield.

1980 March 2 **One Step Beyond** Ron Fawcett, Phil Burke, Chris Gibb.
Burke had previously top-roped most of the route, but had been unable to do the middle move on the crux traverse. He returned only to find Fawcett and Gibb ready for their attempt. A side-runner was used in Avalanche Wall, at the dog-leg, and a second rope held from under P.M.C.1. Upon seconding, Burke 'discovered' a chipped hold, the creator of which was never found, on the traverse.

1980 March 2	**Finger Distance** Gary Gibson (solo).	

Top-roped first.

1980 June 19   **Beech Buttress Direct, One Step Behind, Power Failure, Green Acres**   Gary Gibson (all solo).

1980 Sept.   **Moonshine**   Tim Leach, Graham Desroy.
Climbed during a raid by a party from 'up north'. During the protracted siege, several small wires were snapped. As each one went it was replaced from abseil.

1980   **Dark Entries**   Ron Fawcett, Gill Fawcett.

1980   **Rigid Digit**   Ron Fawcett (unseconded).

1980   **The Shape of Things to Come**   Phil Burke.
Originally climbed with a side-runner halfway up The Peapod to supplement those on the route itself, which were at the same height. The side-runner was eliminated on the second ascent by Ron Fawcett.

1980   **The Unreachable Star**   Mark Stokes (solo).
Later claimed by Andy Bailey in 1983 as 7 Metre Crack.

Undoubtedly a vintage year for Curbar Edge.

1981 April 12   **Top Secret**   Gary Gibson, Derek Beetlestone.

1981 April 12   **Colossus, Thought Cactus**   Gary Gibson (solo).

1981   **Love of Life**   Paul Mitchell (unseconded).

1981   **The Egotist, Body Torque**   Paul Mitchell, Mick Ward.

1981   **Cool Moon**   Daniel Lee, Dominic Lee.
Originally, and on all repeats so far, climbed with pre-placed and pre-clipped runners in Moon Walk. Ron Fawcett, during the second ascent, reputedly placed these runners whilst en-route. Much confusion arose as Fawcett was erroneously credited with a solo ascent. Under-rated, and under-graded at first, it still sees few repeats.

1981   **Tin Drum**   Dominic Lee (solo).
The repeats can be counted on the fingers of one hand!

1981   **The Bear Hunter**   Bob Bradley.

1982 June   **Rollerball**   Bob Bradley.

1982 Oct. 23   **Culture Shock**   Ian Riddington, Keith Sharples.

1983 Feb.   **Blue Sister**   Bill McKee.
No longer described.

1983 Mar. 7   **Brain Variations**   Andy Bailey (unseconded).

1983 April 5   **Pot**   Andy Swan.

1983 Dec. 4   **Sunday**   Doug Kerr, Jo Moffatt.

1983 Dec. 10   **One Step Beyond: Direct Start**   Ron Fawcett (solo).
Attempting to 'straighten out' his original line, Fawcett fell repeatedly from increasing heights until he eventually resorted to a pre-placed wire, with a long sling which could be clipped halfway through the crux move.
Ron later justified this pre-placed wire by saying; "Cos I was too gripped to do the move below without a runner to go for".

Incidentally, the wire was later eliminated by Dawes on the third ascent, but one must record that he made the second ascent with it! Finally (one hopes), Dawes made the fourth ascent on the first ascent of Slab and Crack.

1983	**Plaything** Gary Gibson (solo).

1983	**Instant Karma** Greg Lucas.

Publication of the 1983 Peak Supplement.

1984 Jan.	**Nesh** Nick Holliday.

1984 Mar. 25   **By George** Keith Sharples, Graham Hoey.
Climbed in the proverbial snowstorm....honest!

1984 April 3   **Ulysses or Bust** Neil Foster (solo).
Named retrospectively by Foster after his brush with Ulysses, the following day, when he severely fractured his ankle. The second ascent, also after top-roping, fell immediately to John Allen, but the first on-sight solo followed a few minutes later by Johnny 'bouncing' Dawes who fell from the crux at half-height into a strategically gathered morass of climbers and rucksacks. Gritstone aficionado, Graham Hoey, later commented after his own on-sight solo on an extremely windy evening "Only E4 really, but the wind probably kept me on"!

1984 April 3   **Hidden Pleasures** Andy Bailey, Al Rouse, Richard Haszko, Mark Stokes (top-roped).

1984 April 3   **Andy Pollitt's Jacket** Al Rouse (solo).
Top-roped first.
Named in praise of Andy's new 'freebie' jacket.

1984 April 3   **Forbidden Planet** John Allen, Mark Stokes.
Another classic from Allen equalling his earlier routes.
Stokes, some weeks prior to this ascent, talking to Keith Sharples in the 'cafe' and trying to get hold of a needed Friend ... "Psst have you got a 3½ Friend we could borrow" ... Sharples, helpful as ever but distinctly puzzled, "No I'm using mine"!
A memorable day's activity on such a small area of crag.

1984 April 15   **White Water**, **One-liner**, **Done Years Ago** Johnny Dawes (all solo).
Dawes repeatedly fell from the break near the top of the first route; Alf Bridge eat your heart out!

1984 April 21   **Afterbirth** Steve Bancroft, John Allen.

1984 April   **Tube of Foster's** Paul Mitchell.
Top-roped then climbed with a side-runner in Smoke ... Awaits a direct start. Named after the celebrated lager but it also refers to the climbing accident which put Neil Foster in a pot!

1984 June 9	**Pretty Friend** Alan James, S Gee.

1984 July	**Shooting the Breeze** Paul Pepperday, Dave Candlin.

1984 July	**Artists Only** Paul Pepperday, Dave Candlin (both solo).

1984 Oct.	**Not One of Us**, **Humorum**, **Foaming Jug** Paul Harrison (solo).

1984   **King of the Swingers** Ron Fawcett (solo).
A throw back to the Sixties? Not likely, it's desperate and reputedly

involved a crucifix move for the 6′ 2″ Fawcett. (The imperial Editor smiled at this one.)

1984	**Committed** Johnny Dawes (solo).	

First on-sight solo Simon Nadin 1985.

1984   **Be Bop Deluxe**   Ron Fawcett

1984   **White Lines**   Johnny Dawes.
Just made the addendum of the 1985 guidebook. A major line and at the time of writing it is un-repeated.

1984   **Bill**, **Ben**   Johnny Dawes, Alan Haynes.

1978-1985   **Black Eye Bach**   Paul Mitchell, Nick Colton.

1978-1985   **Death on a Stick**   Paul Mitchell.

Publication of the 1985 Derwent Gritstone guidebook.
Other routes whose first ascent details are unknown include:
Dog-Leg Crack, **Mirror Image**, **Thirst for Glory**, **Knacker Man**, **Allen's Crack**.

1985 Jan. 9   **Pinhead Moonstomp**   Mark Pretty (solo).

1985 March 6   **Appointment with Fear**   John Allen, Mark Stokes, Nicky Stokes.
Climbed on-sight with a pre-placed side-runner in Elder Crack and a side-runner, placed whilst climbing, in Keeper's Crack. The obvious challenge of this wall however still lived on....

1985 March   **Combat Les Pellicules**   Bill McKee (solo).

1985 June 19   **Crumble**   Doug Kerr (solo).

1985 Aug. 17   **Confidence Trick**   John Russell, Doug Kerr.
Climbed with side-runners after top-roping.

1985 Oct. 27   **Eyes Bigger Than T' Ledges**   Andy Barker (unseconded).

1985   **El Vino Collapso**   John Allen (solo).
Top-roped first.

1986 May 16   **Homeward Bound**   Peter Beal (unseconded).
Five metres of new climbing which starts some ten metres above the ground. Climbed after top-rope practice and with pre-placed runners. Now the finish to Slab and Crack.

1986 May 18   **Smiling Jenny**   Jacek Juszczyck, Chris (Boris) Gilbert.

1986 May 28   **Happy House**, **Blue Hawaii**   John Allen (solo).

1986 July 17   **Veale Thing**, **Fab Arête**, **Gorilla Warfare**   Martin Veale (solo).

1986 July 17   **Pockets and Pebbles**, **Walls have Ears**   John Allen (solo).

1986 July 27   **Janus**   Johnny Dawes (unseconded).
Finishing what Fawcett's Rigid Digit avoided. Originally graded E7 7a because Johnny thought the grooves looked like 7's.
Janus is the ancient Roman two-faced god of doors.

1986 Sept. 4   **Slab and Crack**   Johnny Dawes (unseconded).
The first complete ascent of two previously unlinked 'problems': i.e. Fawcett's direct start to One Step Beyond and Beal's Homeward Bound. Top-roped first.
Unrepeated at present.

1986 Sept. 7   **The End of the Affair**   Johnny Dawes, Nick Dixon.
Top-roped and attempted on a number of occasions before the successful ascent. A real 'giant step' for Dawes. Repeated within the month by Dixon (leading, that is!).
A brilliant series of first ascents from Dawes as he polished off three of the best 'last great problems'.

1986 Oct. 12   **Soul Searching, Art of Japan**   John Allen (solo).

1986 Oct. 12   **Iliostomy**   Nicky Stokes.

1986   **Nervosa**   Paul Mitchell, Matt Boyer.
Top-roped, then led with low side-runners.

1987 March 21   **Happy Hart**   John Hart (unseconded).
Climbed after top-roping and with a low side-runner in Scroach. A fall low down resulted in a nasty crash into the pillar of Scroach and a realisation that a fall from higher up would be really serious.

1987 April 17   **The Fall**   John Allen, Dave Fearnley.
"A sudden attack of new route paranoia whilst driving to The Roaches compelled me to turn around, head for Curbar and pluck up the courage for this line I'd inspected some 12 years ago! I was convinced Fawcett was going to do it at any moment" – Allen.

1987 April 18   **Old Codger**   Pete Oxley (solo).

1987 April 24   **Portrait of a Legend**   John Allen, Johnny Dawes.

1987 May   **Phone the Hallamshire**   Ron Fawcett (solo).

1987 Oct. 24   **Camel Ticks**   Mike Hammill (solo).

1987   **Little Chef**   Chris Plant, Stuart Campbell.
Previously climbed with a peg runner as Happy Eater by Mark Pretty on 30 January 1987.
The peg was then removed by a member of the Sheffield climbing community. Exactly who it was is known only to a select few; Pretty himself is not supposed to know... but he does! Plant re-established the route and re-named it some months later.
A better name would have been Pretty Larceny.

1987   **Stopper**   Ron Fawcett (solo).

1987   **Moon Madness**   Ron Fawcett (solo).
"I could only get it one go in fifteen on a rope. I thought that adrenaline would get me up; so I soloed it." Quote, Ron Fawcett.

1988 Feb. 15   **Lardmaster**   John Allen, Steve Bancroft, Paul Mitchell

1988 March 2   **Knockin' on Heaven's Door**   Andy Pollitt.
Top-roped first. A hand-placed peg was used, but later it was established that a 'hand-held hammer' was also needed!
A major route snatched from the 'jaws of Dawes'. Repeated in double-quick time by Fawcett, who was also 'aware' of the possibility.

1988 April   **The Toddler, Peter Rabbit**   Al Evans, Andrea Evans.

1988 June 16   **Loads a Wee Beasties**   Neil Travers (solo).

1988 July 15   **Postman's Slap**   Pete Oxley (solo).

1989 March 11   **Amy**   Graham Iles (solo).

1989 Sept. 17	**Circus of Dinosaurs** Roy Bennett, Dave Simmonite.
1989 Sept. 17	**Short Circuit** Dave Simmonite, Roy Bennett.
1990 April 29	**Lithuania** Falko Rech, Pete Brayshaw.
1990 Summer	**Thomas the Tanked-up Engine** Steve Bancroft, Marie Fisher.
1985-1990	**Amnesia Arête** Ron Fawcett
	This line was referred to as Ron's Route for a while and it appears that he was climbing routes so fast and furiously that he hadn't time to stop and record this one.
1991 Aug. 8	**King of Crookrise** Andy Barker, Martin Veale, Chris Ellis.

Other routes included whose first ascent details are unknown include: **Zoot Route**, **Two Reach Route**, **Diddlum Wall Direct**, **Husk**, **Biz**, **Buzz**.

BASLOW EDGE

O.S. ref SK 260746 to 261737

by Hilary Lawrenson

'Alison 70 feet Difficult
The final face presents a problem. It has been led by a tall
man, who jumped for the high handhold. The leader who is
not so tall can bring up his second and have the benefit of
his shoulder. But if the leader or last man cannot do the
direct face unaided it is still possible to ascend the left
corner and swing round to the face for a finish.'

Geoff Sutton and Eric Byne,
Sheffield Area Guidebook, 1951.

SITUATION and CHARACTER

Baslow Edge runs southwards from Curbar Gap, dwindling to its
end near Wellington's Monument above the A621 Sheffield to
Baslow road. One of the smaller gritstone crags in the area,
Baslow Edge enjoys pleasant views westwards over the Derwent
Valley and a solitude not found on its more popular neighbours.
The climbing tends to be in the lower grades, although there are
some last great problems yet to be solved. It is an ideal venue
for the solo climber to spend a few peaceful hours. The edge
consists of small, isolated buttresses, best linked along the top,
since scrub and boulders below the crag make walking difficult.
The rock varies from compact to friable, some of it quarried, and
a green coat adorns some of the shadier parts.

APPROACHES and ACCESS

The SYT bus No. 213 and the X23 pass close by on the A621,
Sheffield to Baslow road. Alight at Bar Brook crossroads and walk
1 mile westwards to Curbar Gap. Buses 170 (Chesterfield –
Matlock) and X66/67 (Manchester – Mansfield) pass through
Baslow village. Footpaths lead up to the edge from the villages of
Curbar and Baslow. Vehicles can be parked in the car park at
Curbar Gap or in the laybys on the road below the edge. The
edge is less than a minute's walk from the gate on the south side
of the road.

The edge is owned by the Peak Park Joint Planning Board and as
such there are no access difficulties.

Flying Crag

HISTORY

Back in pre-history, before even James W. Puttrell touched rock, the Eagle Stone behind Baslow Edge was reputedly an attraction for local young men who were, or so the story goes, keen to prove themselves ready for marriage by reaching its top. Even so, the indefatigable Puttrell claimed the first formal ascent in 1900, in the company of Ernest A. Baker and other members of the Kyndwr Club. He also wriggled his way up *Gun Chimney* and *Capstone Chimney*. Then, as now, the charms of Froggatt and Curbar Edges proved stronger and there was a lull in activity until Eric Byne and Clifford Moyer (prompted by Puttrell) came to the edge in 1933 to explore. Byne began recording routes and in 1940 with his wife Ivy put up one of Baslow's best routes, *Index Climb*. The first guidebook, Climbs on Gritstone Volume 2, appeared in 1951, with *Flying Crag Groove*, a notable inclusion.

The leisurely approach to this crag's development continued; the next spate of new-routing was in the mid-Sixties, when work on a new guide by Nat Allen brought Derrick Burgess, Dennis Gray,

Des Hadlum and others to the edge to expand the repertoire. Two Dons made their mark with a couple of tricky routes; Don Whillans did *Pensioner's Bulge*, and Don Morrison, *Don's Mantel*. Les Gillot also crowned Byne's Index Climb with a fine direct finish.

The Seventies saw some more worthy routes, including *Renaissance* by Clive Jones and *Jam and Blast It*, which is a gritstoner's delight. During the Eighties there were ventures on to the looser and more vegetated areas with Paul Pepperday and Dave Candlin climbing the worthwhile lines, *Gary's Little Joke Book* and *Hidden Sect* respectively. Some energetic gardening by messrs Warwick, Judson and Sanderson temporarily exposed *The Bend*, *Delsey* and *Klingon* respectively.

There are many short lines which remain unnamed, most of which have probably had dozens of 'first ascents'; the fun of Baslow is to climb where you fancy and feel like a pioneer. However, the walls of Flying Crag and the Cave await determined leaders keen to get their name in print or their limbs in pots.

The CLIMBS are described from LEFT to RIGHT, ignoring the intention of the pedestrian pioneers who named the first buttress and last route. Approaching the edge from Curbar Gap a path leads to a 'belvedere' which has been built above Bacchus Buttress.

At the left-hand end the ironically-named, **FINAL BUTTRESS**, overlooks the Curbar Gap road.

1   Corner Route   8m   D   (1934-1951)
Follow the left rib from below where the barbed wire fence meets the rock.

2   Curbar Cracks   8m   M   (1934-1951)
Just right is a short dirty corner and a crack above.

45m right is the more substantial **BACCHUS BUTTRESS**.

3   Rum and Pep   11m   VD   (1934-1951)
Climb the chimney on the left of the buttress, finishing up the steep corner above. Other possibilities abound.

4   Mauvais Pas   11m   VD   (1934-1951)
Follow the gully two metres right to a ledge, move right with interest and finish up the left wall.

5   Bitter   9m   HS   4a   (1965)
The obvious overhanging crack is less difficult than it looks.

6   Shandy   9m   M   (1934-1951)
Take the easiest line up the arête, wall and corner just right.

7   Polar Climb   8m   VD   (1934-1951)
Climb the left side of the short wall three metres right direct.

To the right is a stile in a stone wall, then 45m right again is:

Jerry Moffatt on Toy, Curbar Edge.
Photo: Ian Smith.

8 Left-hand Flake Crack 6m VD   (1934-1951)
The obvious flake and crack on the left of the buttress.

* **9 Central Crack** 6m VS 5a   (1934-1951)
Climb the slanting crack and overhang with unexpected
difficulty.

10 Flake Crack 6m D   (1934-1951)
The well-cracked flake just to the right.

70m right is a stepped buttress with a steeper wall above.

11 Alison 20m HS 4b   (1934-1951)
Follow the various steps to the final wall, which is climbed on the
left with difficulty.

12 Death to Khomeini 8m S   (1978-1985)
Ascend the wall just right of the final part of the last route,
passing a friable flake.

13 Niched Wall 8m S   (1951-1957)
The short crack right again is taken direct over the bulge.

90m right is an isolated buttress beyond a wide dry gully.

† **14 Has Shaun Got False Teeth?** 6m E3 6b   (1988)
The concave wall on the left of the buttress.

15 Dick's Dilemma 11m HS 4b   (1951)
This indeterminate route starts at the right arête of the buttress
and moves up and right to finish up the cracked wall.

*55m right again is the **FLYING CRAG** with its impressive
unclimbed side wall. Left of its centre is an obvious corner.*

16 Wasted Youth 6m VS 4b   (1981)
The left arête of the corner is climbed on the left.

* **17 Flying Crag Groove** 8m VS 4c   (1951)
The undercut corner is most difficult at the start.

* **18 Don's Mantel** 9m E1 5b   (1965)
Climb the face rightwards past a sloping shelf, to finish direct.

19 Flying Crag Crack 11m HVS 5a   (1934-1951)
*'This is the hardest route on the edge and it has not been led.
Rubbers advised.....An ascent on a rope before attempting to lead*

Peapod, Curbar Edge.
Photo: Dave Wilkinson.

this climb is strongly emphasised.' – 1951. The flaky crack-line just right is climbed from a dismal pit.

20 The Flying Crag 14m VS 4b   (1940)
The front of the crag is climbed, starting up the crack on the right and moving left to finish on some highly dangerous rock. There are two variation starts. A short 4b crack on the side face to the horizontal break, traversing right to the original route. Alternatively, a 5b problem follows the corner crack directly below the finish.

20m right is a short slab taken by the next route.

* **21 Laicifitra 1** 8m VS 4c   (1965)
Climb the left-hand side by an awkward mantelshelf. Don't touch the arête!

22 Laicifitra 2 8m S   (1965)
The crack on the right is a simpler proposition.

20m right is a small quarried bay.

23 Batu Motel 8m E1 6c   (1985)
The left-most part of the wall; for the tall.

24 Second Hand Goods 6m HS 4a   (1989)
Climb thin cracks five metres left of the next route.

25 Quarry Wall 8m HS 4c   (1965)
On the left wall of the corner, an often greasy slab leads to a thin crack through the bulge on good holds.

26 Quarry Crack 8m VD   (1940)
Ascend the corner crack.

27 Hot Ziggerty 8m E2 6b   (1982)
The steep quarried wall with some friable rock right of the corner. The disappearance of a crucial hold has made this rather scary and possibly somewhat harder.

28 Whatisit 8m HVS 5b   (1976)
The narrow front face of the projecting block.

20m right is a short pock-marked wall – **GULLIES WALL**.

29 Route 1 6m D   (1977)
Climb direct one metre right of the left arête.

30 Route 2 6m VD   (1977)
Ascend the wall two metres right again.

* 31 Renaissance 6m HVS 5b (1977)
The steeper pocketed wall right of an easy crack.

32 Left Hand Gully 6m M (1934-1951)

33 Gully Wall 6m D (1977)
The blocky rib and cracked final wall.

34 Gully Wall Variation 6m D (1977)
More steeply up the large holds to the same finish.

35 Right Hand Gully 6m M (1934-1951)

36 Shallow Rib 6m M (1957-1965)
The shallow slab leads to a steeper finish.

37 Broken Buttress 20m D (1934-1951)
Begin far below and climb a series of boulders, crossing the path
to finish.

18m right is a low bay with rock on either side.

The grooved rib on the left edge of the bay is D and the shallow
groove just right a loose VD.

38 Shake 8m VS 4b (1965)
Follow the shallow groove/ramp five metres right to a surprising
finish over an overhang.

39 Green Crack 6m VD (1957-1965)
The awkward flared crack in the back wall.

40 Black Crack 6m D (1934-1951)
The short flake crack just to the right.

Right again is a short slab which gives a few good problems.

41 The Crack 7m D (1965)
The obvious crack in the right rib.

42 The Rib 7m VD (1965)
From the first moves of the previous route move left on to the
arête. The direct start is much harder, 5b.

*Below the edge in this area are various boulders, including the
Matterhorn Block and the Peanut. Both have well-scratched
problems. 45m right is a steep slab.*

The crack and wall to the left are VD.

* **43 Rough Wall Climb** 6m VS 4c   (1934-1951)
Climb the steep slab following the line of a crack.

44 Jolly Green Dwarf 6m VS 5a   (1982)
The shallower slab to the right is climbed leftwards to the arête.

Just right is a steeper buttress topped by a prominent block.

45 Pensioner's Bulge 6m VS 4c   (1965)
From behind the oak tree, follow a thin crack leftwards over a
bulge.

46 Gun Chimney 6m S   (1900)
The chimney leads easily to an awkward but well-protected
finish leftwards.

Santa Claus Retreats, HVS 5a, (1980's), is a direct finish to Gun
Chimney following the crack-line over the capping block.

47 Hair Conditioned Nightmare 6m HVS 5b (1978-1985)
The narrow face right of the chimney. Gaining it from the
chimney avoids the crux.

To the right a wall runs up to the edge.

48 Wall Groove 12m S   (1965)
From the wall dirty rock leads to a finishing crack.

Gun Chimney Area

The next two routes on **LARCENY WALL** *have rather more than their share of friable rock.*

49 Larceny 12m HVS 5a (1765-1976)
Climb the crumbling wall four metres right to a ledge and take a steeper cracked wall to finish.

50 Gary's Little Joke Book 12m E2 6a (1982)
Follow the corner right of Larceny and a groove above with the crux at the top.

51 Problem Wall 6m HVS 5b (1976)
The wall just left of Fingers Crack.

52 Fingers Crack 6m VS 4b (1964)
Climb the delightful thin crack in the lower wall to the right with leftward moves to finish when fingers no longer fit.
Cracked Fingers, 5b, (1985), climbs the lower wall of Fingers Crack to the ledge then takes the thin crack direct.

53 Work The Wall 6m HVS 6a (1985)
Climb straight up the wall just to the right of Fingers Crack.

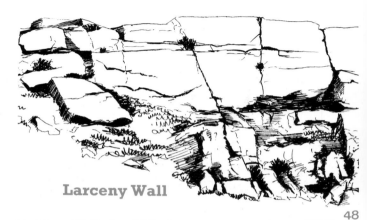

Larceny Wall

48

54 Finger Wall 6m HVS 5c   (1985)
Two metres right of the crack follow a rightwards trending ramp
and the wall above, avoiding the temptations of the arête.

*90m right is a hidden quarried bay with a small oak tree at its
entrance. Best approached along the top of the edge.*

Religious Gathering, HVD, (1977), follows the left-hand corner
crack and loose wall.

To the right are two diagonal cracks:

55 Cliff College 9m E1 5b   (1985)
The lower left-hand crack.

56 Hidden Sect 11m E1 5c   (1982)
The higher, fingery crack to the right.

57 Angle Climb 9m D   (1957-1965)
The dirty right-hand corner.

58 Dusty Crack 9m S   (1965)
The crack one metre right.

59 Depression 8m D   (1934-1951)
The short crack near the right arête is hard to start.

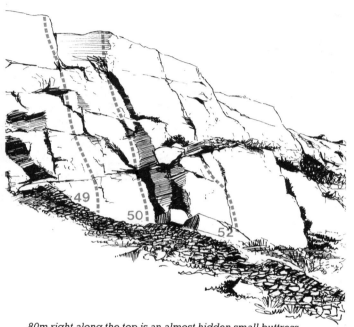

80m right along the top is an almost hidden small buttress.

60 Wigible Chimney 6m M   (1934-1951)
The chimney which splits the buttress.

61 Wigible Arête 12m D   (1965)
The arête on the right and the wall above.

20m right again, just past a large solitary boulder, is a fine clean buttress with an undercut base and large flattened tree.

Juddo, D, (1977), takes the wide left-hand crack and friable slab above. The dirty groove on the right of the slab is VD.

69

* **62 Index Climb** 12m S (1940)

From the foot of the left arête of the main buttress, move up and right into a groove. Follow this to the overhang, then move right and back left to an airy finish. Variation Finish, D; instead of stepping back left near the top, continue up the easy groove, as for the next route. The **Direct Finish**, VS, 4c, (1964), takes the overhang direct on satisfying holds.

The crack four metres right is the direct start (S) to:

63 Heather Climb 12m D (1934-1951)

The wide crack two metres right again leads to jungle so move left quickly.

70 71 **The Cave Area**

Six metres right is a small buttress with a corner rising from a pit.

* **64 Sewer Plumb** 11m VS 4c (1957-1965)
Ascend the interesting corner-crack. Beware loose rock.

65 The Bend 11m VS 4c (1982)
Follow the arête right of Sewer Plumb for a few feet, then move right across the face to finish over a block.

66 Delsey 10m VS 4c (1982)
The arête right of The Bend.

Klingon, VD, (1982), which follows the wall just right, has been reclaimed by the tree.

35m right is a larger buttress with a sloping, slabby top and a large side face split on its left by a through cave. This is **THE CAVE AREA**.

* **67 Above and Beyond the Callisthenic Barrier** 9m S (1977)
From one metre right of the cave, climb via a series of ledges with a long reach to finish.

68 Left-hand Gully Buttress 9m S   (1934-1951)
From the right arête move left on to a ledge and go back right to an exciting exposed finish.

69 The Cave Gully 8m VD   (1934-1951)
Five metres right, past the impressive overhanging front face of the buttress, is an undercut chimney/crack which provides the substance of the route.

70 Cave Climb Indirect 9m VS 4c   (1934-1951)
Climb the wall on the right to a thin crack, finishing left or right at the top block.

71 Cave Climb Direct 9m VS 4c   (1934-1951)
Go easily into a circular cave then energetically follow twin cracks past a roof.

Left Break, HS, (1965), and **Right-hand Break**, VD, (pre-1978), take the dirty cracks in the wall to the right.

72 Block Chimney 8m M   (1934-1951)
The chimney behind the block.

73 Leaning Block 10m D   (1934-1951)
The left-hand arête and face of the block.

74 Broken Crack 9m M   (pre-1956)
The crack two metres right.

Right again are some rather more attractive cracks in a corner.

* **75 Jam and Blast It** 9m HVS 5a   (1977)
The overhanging left-hand crack.

76 Corner Crack 9m VS 4c   (1934-1951)
The corner crack direct with an awkward wide finish. A more natural combination of the previous two routes gives a good VS 4c.

77 Not Now John   12m   E1   5b   (1984)
The blunt arête, on the right and slightly lower, gives a hard start
up to a ledge. Using the arête and a thin flake, climb the upper
slab, crux.

78 Heather Wall   11m   D   (1934-1951)
From the corner move up and round the arête and climb a crack.
May be started direct with considerably more effort and
difficulty.

79 Capstone Chimney   11m   D   (1900)
The obvious chimney right of the previous route.

80 Capstone Chimney Crack   11m   S   (1934-1951)
The undercut crack just right requires an energetic start.

81 Lost Fortune   10m   E2   5c   (1985)
The wall right again is climbed directly then move diagonally
right via shallow holes and step on to the ledge of Twin Cracks.

82 Twin Cracks   9m   M   (1934-1951)
The pleasant cracks to the right have an undercut start.

83 Slapdash   9m   E1   6a   (1985)
The very thin crack to the right.

The arête right of the last route gives an easy climb.

30 m right of Twin Cracks is **Pothole Wall***, D, (1934- 1951). 60m
right again is a short buttress with a tower-like top, this gives:*

84 Introductory Crack   9m   VD   (1934-1951)
A short crack leads to a ledge. The face above gives a tricky
problem if taken direct.

85 The Last Post   6m   VS   4b   (1985)
Climb the obvious arête on the tower right of the previous route.
Belay on the post.

Behind the edge on the moor is the Eagle Stone, a typical
gritstone tor. There are two normal lines of ascent: follow the
polish and the children, although the girdle traverse proves
more interesting. There is also a classic 6a problem on the back
wall and a 6b mantelshelf on the front face.

BASLOW EDGE LIST OF FIRST ASCENTS

Pre-1900	*History records ascents of the Eagle Stone by local 'young' men.*
1990	**Gun Chimney** James W Puttrell.
1900 Jan.	**Capstone Chimney** James W Puttrell.
1900	**Eagle Stone** James W Puttrell, E A Baker and Kyndwr Club members.
	In 1933 Eric Byne and Clifford Moyer roamed along the edge and completed many of the easier routes.
1940	**Index Buttress, The Flying Crag, Quarry Crack** Eric Byne, Ivy Byne.
	Also at this time the Bynes prepared a manuscript of the recorded routes. However the first published script was in the 1951 Climbs on Gritstone guidebook. In preparation for this publication the Oread Mountaineering Club used the Bynes' manuscript as a basis to work from. During this period George Sutton, Harry Pretty, David Penlington, Keith Axon, and Eric Byne all recorded new routes. Before it appeared new routes were again added, viz:
1951 Feb.	**Flying Crag Groove** Wilfred (Wilf) White, J R (Nat) Allen.
1951 June 2	**Niche Crack, Dick's Dilemma** R A (Dick) Brown, D E W White.
Pre-1957	**Niched Wall** Wilf White, Nat Allen.
	Publication of the 1957 Further Developments guidebook. Other routes whose first ascent details are unknown include: **The Flying Crag Crack**.
1964 June	**Index Buttress Direct** Don Morrison, Les Gillott.
1964 Sept.	**Fingers Crack** Des Hadlum.
1965	**The Crack, The Rib, Wigible Arête, Wall Groove** Derrick Burgess, Nat Allen.
1965	**Laicifitra, Quarry Wall, Left Break** Dennis Gray.
1965	**Shake, Dusty Crack** Des Hadlum.
1965	**Bitter** David Boore.
1965	**Pensioner's Bulge** Don Whillans.
1965	**Don's Mantel** Don Morrison, Les Gillott.
	Publication of 1965 Froggatt Area guidebook.
Pre-1976	**Larceny** Nat Allen, Derrick Carnell.
1976 July	**Problem Wall** Graham Hoey (solo).
1976 July	**Whatisit** Sam Sansom (solo).
1977 Oct. 7	**Above and Beyond the Callisthenic Barrier** Clive Jones, Dave Gregory.
1977 Oct. 8	**Route 1, Route 2, Gully Wall** (and variation), **Religious Gathering** Dave Gregory, Charles Darley (solo). *Climbed during guidebook work.*

1977 Oct.	**Renaissance** Clive Jones.	
1977 Oct.	**Jam and Blast It** Charles Darley, Dave Gregory.	
1978	**Shallow Rib, Broken Buttress, Right-Hand Break** Charles Darley, Dave Gregory.	
1978	**Juddo** J. Judson et al.	
	Publication of the 1978 Froggatt Area guidebook.	
1981	**Wasted Youth** A (Boris) Hannon (solo).	
1982	**Hot Ziggerty** Dominic Lee (solo).	
1982	**Gary's Little Joke Book, Hidden Sect** Paul Pepperday, D Candlin.	
1982	**Jolly Green Dwarf** Pete Robertson (solo).	
1982	**The Bend** T Warwick, J Judson, M Sanderson.	
1982	**Delsey** J Judson, T Warwick, M Sanderson.	
1982	**Klingon** M Sanderson, T Warwick, J Judson.	
	Publication of 1985 Derwent Gritstone guidebook. Other routes whose first ascent details are unknown include: **Death to Khomeini, Hair Conditioned Nightmare, Finger Wall, Cliff College, Lost Fortune.**	
1984 Oct. 7	**Not Now John** Malcolm Taylor, Alan Taylor.	
1985 March 12	**Slapdash** Doug Kerr, Paul Harrison.	
1985	**Batu Motel, Work The Wall** Paul Pepperday (solo).	
1985	**Santa Claus Retreats** Paul Mitchell, John Kirk and party.	
1988 June 23	**Has Shaun Got False Teeth?** Neil Travers (solo).	

GRADED LIST (of starred routes)

Graded lists are controversial at the best of times and this is no
exception. During the blaze of indifference when there was an
'anti graded list lobby', a few climbers argued strongly against
the inclusion of such a list. In the event those enthusiasts who
wanted a list had little input, leaving the job to be done by those
who didn't want one in the first place. The following list is
therefore exclusively to put the case against having graded lists.

E9
Parthian Shot (7a)
Knockin' on Heaven's Door (6c)

E8
Captain Invincible (6c)
Moon Madness (6c)
The End of the Affair (6c)

E7
Living in Oxford (6c)
Slab and Crack (6c)
Monopoly (6b)
The Screaming Dream (7a)
The Braille Trail (6c)
The Master's Edge (6b)
Scritto's Republic (6b)
Masters of the Universe (6c)
Happy Hart (6c)

E6
One Step Beyond (6b)
Messiah (6c)
Benign Lives (6b)
Linden (6b)
Narcissus (6b)
Committed (6b)
White Water (6c)
Mean Streak (6b)
Beau Geste (6c)
Clock People (7a)
White Lines (6c)
Jugged Hare (6a)
Hairy Heart (6a)
Lost World (6c)

E6 (cont.)
Janus (6b)
Nosferatu (6b)
Adam Smith's Invisible Hand (6b)
Cool Moon (6c)
Moonshine (6b)
Winter's Grip (6b)

E5
The Shape of Things to Come (6a)
Science Friction (6a)
Edge Lane (5c)
Hairless Heart (5c)
Heartless Hare (6a)
Artless (6b)
Ulysses or Bust (6b)
Green Death (6b)
Frank Sinatra Bows Out (6b)
Blind Date (7a)
Pulsar (6c)
Great Arête (5c)
Jermyn Street (6a)
Pebble Mill (6b)
Meeze Brugger (6b)
Offspring (6b)
Ai No Corrida (6b)
Adios Amigo (6b)
London Wall (6a)
Rigid Digit (6b)
Wall Street Crash (6b)
Big Bad Wolf (6b)
Greedy Pig (6b)
Quality Street (6b,6a)
Bat out of Hell (6a)
Crème de la Crème (6b)

E5 (cont.)
Goliath (6a)
London Pride (6b,5c)
The Simpering Savage (6b,5a)
White Wall (6b)
The Hunter House Road Toad (6b)
The Snivelling (6a)
Moon Crack (6b)
Strapadictomy (6a)
The Rack (6a)
Coventry Street (6b)
The Knock (6a)

E4
Above and Beyond the
    Kinaesthetic Barrier (6b)
Home Cooking (6c)
Hot Knives (6b)
Forbidden Planet (6b)
Profit of Doom (6b)
Downhill Racer (6a)
Pool Wall (6b)
The Sander (6b)
Usurper (6a)
Moon Walk (6a)
Tea for Two (6a)
Hurricane (6a)
Flute of Hope (6a)
Jealous Pensioner (5c)
Dark Entries (6a)
Block Wall (6b)
Remergence (6b)
High Plains' Drifter (6a)
High Street (6a)
Silent Spring (5c,5c)
Diet Of Worms (5c)
Blind Bat (5c)
Boulevard (6a)
Oedipus! Ring Your Mother (6b)

E3
Rat Scabies (6b)
Oxford Street (5a,6b)
By George (6b)
Rock Around The Block
    (5a,6a,5c,4c)
Saville Street (6a)
The Beer Hunter (6a)

E3 (cont.)
Cave Wall (5c)
The Great Slab (5b)
Watling Street (5b)
Right Eliminate (5c)
The Rasp Direct (6a)
Finger Distance (6b)
Cardinal's Backbone II (5c)
Twikker (5c)
Xanadu (5c,5b)
Vain (5b)
Scoop Connection (5b)
Deadbay Groove Direct (6a)
Time for Tea (5c)
The Mighty Atom (5c)
Gates of Mordor (5c)
Pretzel Logic (6a)
Dextrous Hare (5c)
Long John's Slab (5c)
The Gully Joke (5c)
Indoor Fisherman (5c)
High Flyer (5b)
Blue Hawaii (6b)

E2
The Gully Joke (5c)
Insanity (5c)
The Rasp (5b)
Elder Crack (5b)
Knightsbridge (5b,5c)
Apollo (5c)
Billy Whiz (5c)
Brightside (5c)
Predator (5c)
Regent Street (5c)
Piccadilly Circus (5b,5c)
Zeus (5b)
Keyhole Cops (5a,5c)
Scroach (5c)
The Boggart (6b)
The Verdict (6a)
Stone Dri (6a)
Under Doctor's Orders (5c)
Erb (5c)
Cave Crack (5c)
Coldest Crack (5c)
Pinstone Street (5c)
The Big Crack (5b)

E2 (cont.)
Great West Road (5b,5b)
Synopsis (5c)
Suspense (5c)
Soyuz (5c)
Sorb (5c)
Embankment 1 (4c,5c)
Stiff Cheese (5c)
Esau (5c)
The Sentinel (5b)
L'Horla (5b)
Brown's Eliminate (5b)
The Unreachable Star (6a)
Kayak (5c)
Windrête (5b)
Great Peter (5b)
Saddy (5b)
March Hare (5b)

E1
Deadbay Groove (5b)
Left Eliminate (5c)
Nicotine Stain (6b)
The Toy (5c)
Lotto (5c)
The Knack (5c)
The Screamer (5c)
Frustration (5c)
The Fin (5b)
All Quiet on the Eastern Front (6a)
Birthday Groove (5c)
The Dover and Ellis Chimney (5b)
Smoke ont' Watter (6a)
Embankment 4 (5b)
Embankment 3 (5b)
Now or Never (5b)
The Bear Hunter (5b)
Millwheel Wall (5b)
Deadbay Crack (5b)
Don's Mantel (5b)
Lamebrain (5b)
Brimstone (5b)
Small Arctic Mammal (6a)
Fidget (6a)
Banana Finger (6a)
Black Nix Wall (5c)
Dork Child (5c)
Chalked Up (5a)

E1 (cont.)
Three Pebble Slab (5b)
Strapiombante (5b)
Strapiombo (5b)
Captain Sensible (5b)
Long Tall Sally (5b)
Only Just (5b)

Hard Very Severe
Xanadu Original (4c,5b)
Overtaker's Buttress (4c,5b)
Delectable Direct (5b)
Myolympus (4c,5b)
Burssola (5b)
Charlie's Crack (5b)
Chequers Crack (5b)
Delectable Direct (5b)
Supra Direct (5b)
The Whore (5b)
The Grogan (5b)
Surform (5b)
Limmock (5b)
Chequers Buttress (5b)
Tody's Wall (5a)
Wednesday Climb (5b)
Dexterity (Direct) (5b)
Baron's Wall (5b)
Bacteria Cafeteria (5b)
Great Portland Street (5b)
Green Crack (5b)
The Peapod (5b)
Hades (5b
Soho Sally (5b)
Stormfactor (5b)
Diamond Groove (5b)
Billingsgate (5b)
Maupassant (5b)
Renaissance (5b)
Zapple (5b)
Dexterity (Left Hand) (5b)
Brooks' Crack (5a)
Great North Road (5a)
Plexity (5a)
Quiddity (5a)
Shaftesbury Avenue (5a)
Sorrell's Sorrow (4c)
Cioch Left Hand (4c)
No Zag (4c)

Hard Very Severe (cont.)
Gimbals (5b)
Tree Wall (5a)
Estremo (5a)
Lyon's Corner House (5a)
Pedestal Crack (5a)
Knight's Move (5a)
Whitehall (5a)
Tower Crack (5a)
Avalanche Wall (5a)
The Riffler (5a)
Mayday (5a)
Bond Street (5a)
Wuthering Crack (5a)
David (4c)
Gable Route (4c)
Great Harry (4c)
Right Fin (5a)
Jam and Blast It (4c)
April Arete (4c)
Sunset Slab (4b)
Gingerbread (4b)
Embankment 2 (4c,4b)

Very Severe
Spider Crack (5b)
Downes' Crack (4c)
Crew Cut (4c)
Birthday Crack (4c)
Stomach Traverse (4c)
Austin's Variation (4c)
Excalibur (4c)
Keep Crack (5a)
Great Crack (5a)
Dunkley's Eliminate (4c)
The Mall (4c)
The Grazer (4c)
Yourolympus (4c)
Once Pegged Wall (5a)
Two Pitch Route (4c)
The File (4c)
Cioch Crack (4c)
The Brain (4c)
Tiptoe (4c)

Very Severe (cont.)
Wall Climb (5a)
Chequers Climb (4c)
Obscenity (4c)
Owl's Arete (4c)
Chapman's Crack (4c)
Sulu (4c)
Broken Crack (4c)
S.T.P. (4c)
Fall Pipe (4c)
Roof Route (4c)
Sewer Plumb (4c)
Knight's Move Alternative (4c)
Holly Groove (4c)
Hawk's Nest Crack (4c)
Twin Cracks (4c)
Campion Wall (4c)
Rough Wall Climb (4c)
Trapeze Direct (4c)
Bel Ami (4b)
Flying Crag Groove (4c)
Covent Garden (4b,4c)
Reginald (4b)
Mutiny Crack (4b)
Hollyash Crack (4b)
Limpopo Groove (4b)
Byne's Crack (4b)
Neb Crack (4b)
Terrace Crack (4b)
Pulcherrime (4b)
Greeny Crack (4b)
Jankers Groove (4c)
Cardinal's Crack (4b)
Delectable Variation (4c)
Sunset Crack (4b)
Fingers (4c)
Latecomer (4b)
Fox House Flake (4b)
Lambeth Chimney (4b)
Brooks' Layback (4b)
Black Slab (4b)
Rainy Day (4b)
Day Dream (4b)
Rose Flake (4b)

PREVIOUS EDITIONS & SUPPLEMENTS

1923 Recent Developments on Gritstone. Edited by Fergus Graham.

1934 Mountaineering Journal. Vol. 2 No. 4. A Guide to Burbage by The Sheffield Climbing Club including: E. Byne, B. Connelly, I. Critchley, M. Grainger and A. Roberts.

1935 Mountaineering Journal. Vol. 3 No. 2. Some Lesser-known Gritstone Climbs by Eric Byne.

1951 The Sheffield Area. (Climbs on Gritstone. Vol. 2). Edited by Eric Byne and other writers included: R. Townsend, W. White, G. Sutton and H. Pretty.

1956 The Sheffield Area. (Climbs on Gritstone. Vol. 2) Edited and revised by Eric Byne.

1957 Further Developments in the Peak District. (Climbs on Gritstone. Vol. 4). Edited by Eric Byne and Wilfred White. Writers included R. Townsend, J.R.N. Allen, Peter B. Marks, R. Pillinger, A. Shutt, G.A. Leaver, Peter Biven and M.T. Sorrell.

1965 The Sheffield-Froggatt Area (Rock Climbs in the Peak. Vol. 3) Edited by Eric Byne. Writers included: David Gregory, George H. Kitchin, John A. Loy, Alan Clarke, D. Morrison, P.B. Marks, Len Millsom and J.R.N. (Nat) Allen.

1977 Recent Developments (Rock Climbs in the Peak) by Steve Bancroft. Edited by D. Gregory.

1978 The Froggatt Area (Rock Climbs in the Peak. Vol. 3) Edited by Dave Gregory. Writers included: Clive Jones, Chris Addy, Jim Reading, John Stevenson, J.A. Loy, Giles Barker, Geoff Milburn, Brian Benton, Adrian Hubbard, Steve Bancroft, Gabriel Regan and Nat Allen.

1981 Peak District New Routes 1980-1981 by Gary Gibson

1983 Peak Supplement (Peak District Climbs. Fourth Series) Compiled by Gary Gibson. Edited by Geoff Milburn.

1983 Stanage Millstone (Peak District Climbs. Fourth Series) Edited by Geoff Milburn. Writers included: Steve Bancroft, Paul Mitchell, Andy Barker, Chris Jackson, Simon Horrox, Adey Hubbard, Dave Gregory and Dave Farrant.

1985 Derwent Gritstone (Peak District Climbs. Fourth Series) Edited by Geoff Milburn. Writers included Chris Calow, Bill McKee, Graham Hoey, Bob Bradley and Dave Farrant.

1986 New Climbs 1986 (Second Series Vol. 1) Compiled by Gary Gibson.

1987 New Climbs 1987 (Second Series Vol. 2) Compiled by Gary Gibson.

1988 New Climbs 1988 (Second Series Vol. 3) Compiled by Gary Gibson.

THE PEAK DISTRICT GUIDEBOOK PATTERN

First Series – Climbs on Gritstone.
Volume 1 – Laddow Area (1948)
Volume 2 – The Sheffield Area (1951)
Volume 3 – Kinder, Roches and Northern Area (1951)
Volume 4 – Further Developments in the Peak District (1957)
Volume 5 – West Yorkshire Area (1957)

Second Series – Rock Climbs in the Peak.
Volume 1 – The Sheffield–Stanage Area (1963)
Volume 2 – The Saddleworth–Chew Valley Area (1965)
Volume 3 – The Sheffield–Froggatt Area (1965)
Volume 4 – Chatsworth Gritstone (1970)
Volume 5 – The Northern Limestone Area (1969)
Volume 6 – The Bleaklow Area (1971)
Volume 7 – The Kinder Area (1974)
Volume 8 – The Southern Limestone Area (1970)
Volume 9 – The Staffordshire Gritstone Area (1973)

Third Series – Rock Climbs in the Peak.
Volume 1 – Stanage Area (1976)
Volume 2 – Chew Valley (1976)
Volume 3 – Froggatt Area (1978)
Volume 4 – Northern Limestone (1980)
Volume 5 – Derwent Valley (1981)
Volume 6 – Staffordshire Area (1981)

Fourth Series – Peak District Climbs.
Volume 1 – Stanage–Millstone (1983)
Volume 2 – Derwent Gritstone (1985)
Volume 3 – Peak Limestone–Stoney (1987)
Volume 4 – Peak Limestone–Chee Dale (1987)
Volume 5 – Peak Limestone–South (1987)
Volume 6 – Moorland Gritstone–Chew Valley (1988)
Volume 7 – Staffordshire Gritstone (1989)

Fifth Series – Peak Rock Climbs.
Volume 1 – Stanage (1989)
Volume 2 – Moorland Gritstone–Kinder and Bleaklow (1990)
Volume 3 – Froggatt (1991)

INDEX

INDEX

INDEX